TRANSCENDING STEREOTYPES

Discovering Japanese Culture and Education

Edited by

BARBARA FINKELSTEIN

ANNE E. IMAMURA

JOSEPH J. TOBIN

A Publication of the International Center for the Study of Education Policy and Human Values
University of Maryland, College Park, Maryland

INTERCULTURAL PRESS, INC.
Yarmouth, Maine

For information, contact:
Intercultural Press, Inc.
P.O. Box 700
Yarmouth, Maine 04096, USA

Cover design by LetterSpace.
Book design by Jacques Chazaud.
Printed in the United States of America.

96   95   94   93   92   91   1   2   3   4   5   6

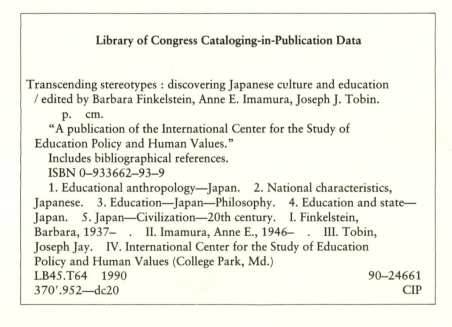

Library of Congress Cataloging-in-Publication Data

Transcending stereotypes : discovering Japanese culture and education
/ edited by Barbara Finkelstein, Anne E. Imamura, Joseph J. Tobin.
    p.   cm.
    "A publication of the International Center for the Study of
Education Policy and Human Values."
    Includes bibliographical references.
    ISBN 0–933662–93–9
    1. Educational anthropology—Japan.   2. National characteristics,
Japanese.   3. Education—Japan—Philosophy.   4. Education and state—
Japan.   5. Japan—Civilization—20th century.   I. Finkelstein,
Barbara, 1937–   .   II. Imamura, Anne E., 1946–   .   III. Tobin,
Joseph Jay.   IV. International Center for the Study of Education
Policy and Human Values (College Park, Md.)
LB45.T64   1990   90–24661
370'.952—dc20   CIP

The following articles are republished here with the permission of the author and/or the original publisher.

Doi, Takeo. *The Anatomy of Dependence: The Individual Versus Society.* Tokyo: Kodansha International Ltd., 1974.

———. *The Anatomy of Self: The Individual Versus Society.* Tokyo: Kodansha International Ltd., 1985.

Fujita, Hidenori. "A Crisis of Legitimacy in Japanese Education: Meritocracy and Cohesiveness." *Bulletin of Research* (Nagoya University) 32 (1985): 117–33.

Fukue, Hitoshi. "The Persistence of Ie in the Light of Japan's Modernization." In *Toward Multiculturalism: A Reader in Multicultural Education,* edited by Jaime S. Wurzel, 123–31. Yarmouth, Maine: Intercultural Press, Inc., 1988.

Hirasawa, Yasumasa. "Japan." *Integrated Education* (now published as *Equity and Excellence*) 120 (November-December 1983): 18–22.

Horio, Teruhisa. "Education Policy and Human Rights: A Case Study in Failure." In *Educational Thought and Ideology in Modern Japan: State Authority and Intellectual Freedom,* edited and translated by Steven Platzer. Tokyo: University of Tokyo Press, 1988.

Imamura, Anne E. "New Lifestyles for Housewives." *Japan Echo* 7, special issue (1980).

Kennedy, Rick, and Mikie Yaginuma. "Life Is So Simple When You Know Your Place." *PHP Intersect Magazine* 6 (May 1986): 35–39.

Kitamura, Kazuyuki. "Japan's Dual Educational Structure." In *Educational Policies in Crisis: Japanese and American Perspectives,* edited by William E. Cummings, Edward R. Beauchamp, Shogo Ichikawa, Victor N. Kobayashi, and Mirikazu Ushiogi, 135–69. New York, Westport, CT, London: Praeger, 1986.

Kobayashi, Yasuhiro. "Japanese Schools Can't Cope with Cosmopolitan Kids." *Asahi Shimbun,* translated by the Asia Foundation Translation Service Center, 1987.

Lewis, Catherine. "Cooperation and Control in a Japanese Nursery School." *Comparative Education Review* 28 (February 1984): 69–84.

Mannari, Hiroshi, and Harumi Befu. "Internationalization of Japan and *Nihon bunkaron*" (Japanese Culture). In *The Challenge of Japan's Internationalization,* edited by Hiroshi Mannari and Harumi Befu. Kyoto: Kwansei Gakuin University and New York: Kodansha International Ltd., 1983.

Murakami, Yoshio. "Bullies in the Classroom." *Japan Quarterly* 32 (October-December 1985): 407–11.

Peak, Lois. "Training Learning Skills and Attitudes in Japanese Early Education Settings." In *Early Experience and the Development of Competence: New Directions for Child Development* 32, edited by W. Fowler. San Francisco: Jossey-Bass, 1986.

Rohlen, Thomas P. *For Harmony and Strength: Japanese White-Collar Organization in Anthropological Perspective.* Berkeley: University of California Press, 1974.

Shimahara, Nobuo. "The College Entrance Examination System and Policy Issues in Japan." *Journal of Qualitative Studies in Education* 1 (1988): 39–49.

Simons, Carol. "They Get By with a Lot of Help from Their *Kyôiku Mamas.*" *Smithsonian Magazine* (March 1987).

Singleton, John. "*Gambaru:* A Japanese Cultural Theory of Learning." In *Japanese Schooling: Patterns of Socialization, Equality, and Political Control,* edited by J. J. Shields. University Park and London: The Pennsylvania State University Press, 1989.

Tobin, Joseph J., David Y. H. Wu, and Dana H. Davidson. "Class Size and Student/Teacher Ratios in the Japanese Preschool." *Comparative Education Review* 31 (1987): 533–49.

Tsuneyoshi, Ryoko Kato. "Meanings of Equality: Lessons from Japanese Debate." *Educational Forum* 54 (Winter 1990): 185–95.

U.S. Department of Education. *Japanese Education Today: Report from the U.S. Study of Education in Japan.* Washington, DC: U.S. Government Printing Office, 1987.

CONTENTS

PART II: FAMILY AND SOCIETY

PART III: EDUCATION AND CULTURAL TRANSMISSION

PART IV: EDUCATION POLICY AND THE DILEMMAS OF REFORM

PART V: INTERGROUP TENSIONS IN JAPANESE SCHOOL AND SOCIETY

Acknowledgments

We are deeply indebted to many people who, over the last five years, have helped us develop the orientation of this book. First, there is the array of participants in the Mid-Atlantic Region Japan-in-the Schools (MARJiS) regional leader program who critiqued the manuscript in its earlier forms in a manner that, we believe, has made this book uncommonly helpful to educators. Second, there are our good friends and colleagues, Thomas Rimer, Eleanor Jorden, and Masano Hidaka, who have supported and contributed substantively in ways they are not even aware of. Third, there are our authors who have been uncommonly tolerant of the need to edit for a broad audience of educators. Finally, there is the extraordinary staff of the International Center: Linda Wojtan, Associate Director of MARJiS, who has edited with characteristic intelligence and skill; Midori Matsuyama Brameld, Associate Director of the National Intercultural Education Leadership Institute, who translated and clarified numerous Japanese citations; Geraldine McCarthy, Executive Secretary, who has overseen several production phases, and Susan Dorsey, who prepared this manuscript for publication with such care and precision.

Finally, we want to acknowledge the sustaining support of the United States-Japan Foundation, the Japanese Commerce Association, the Maryland State Department of Education, and the District of Columbia Public Schools during the formative years of this effort.

Beyond Appearances

Barbara Finkelstein

This book has many dimensions. It is a cultural primer—a book of readings and interpretive introductions aimed at providing educators, and others who wish to understand the essence of Japan, with a capacity to observe and interpret Japanese culture and education. Additionally, it is an intercultural text designed to transcend simple stereotypes and call attention to the complexities of culture and the follies of overgeneralization.

We hope that while exploring Japanese educational patterns, readers will be able to both interpret Japanese behavior and penetrate Japanese culture unencumbered by Western mindsets and rigid commitments to rational rather than intuitive ways of knowing. Our intention is to encourage readers to view the world through Japanese eyes and to mute the tendency to (1) oversimplify in an attempt to make another culture more understandable, (2) overgeneralize to reduce feelings of ambiguity, and (3) become judgmental when encounters with different cultural perspectives cause discomfort.

As people grow up in a culture, they learn "common sense" and then mistake it for what is natural and normal for all human beings. In the United States, we shake hands or hug as we greet, wean our babies as early as possible, and put them (if we can afford it) in their own bedrooms. We send our children off to school when they are five or six, encourage them to choose their own clothes, friends, activities, dates, and, eventually, their mates.

As adults, we believe in making independent decisions about marriage, careers, and where to live. We encourage mobility, we buy our own burial sites, and too often, we live and die alone in nursing homes.

The American love of independence, freedom, and individual expression, of mobility, choice, and change are all learned behaviors—habits of association—what Robert Bellah has called "habits of the heart" in his book of that title. They are what historians call mentalities or mindsets, what anthropologists call culture, what sociologists call society, and what we will be calling the habits of everyday life.

The Japanese people, like the people of the United States, are similarly laden with such habits. This book provides an introduction to the structure and meaning of Japanese daily life as it is revealed through the thoughts, perceptions, and images of sensitive cultural observers who, as they try to make sense of Japan, also document the power, diversity, and complexity of Japanese culture as the Japanese understand it. We will study Japanese culture by examining its educational system—the processes of teaching and learning which nurture character, identity, and group loyalty and which recreate culture from one generation to the next. In doing so we will attempt to see Japanese education as it really is, with all its strengths and weaknesses, and stir in the reader an understanding and respect for the culture of Japan which they will want to pass on to the younger generation.

PART I

JAPANESE CULTURE

In this section of the book, we attempt to destabilize an array of exaggerated stereotypes that have characterized Western thinking about Japan and discouraged generations of Westerners from penetrating beyond surface appearances to a deeper understanding of Japanese cultural forms and daily habits. The papers included in this section suggest that the Japanese are neither as "strange" nor as "inscrutable" as has been commonly assumed nor as unrelentingly hierarchical, formal, group-dependent, or inexpressive. In attempting to understand Japanese culture as revealed by the Japanese, we have an opportunity to learn not only something about Japan but something about our own cultural habits as well—and in so doing, to begin a process of mental stretching that will enrich our collective imaginations and our own cultural consciousness as well as our knowledge of the Japanese people.

INTRODUCTION

Images of Japan and the Japanese

JOSEPH J. TOBIN

For Westerners, Japan has long been an important "other," the antipodes, an object for conquest and commerce and also for fantasy. In part, Columbus sailed West in search of the fabulous Xipangu (Japan) described by Marco Polo. In 1552 the Jesuit missionary Francis Xavier reported to his superiors on his return from his visit to Japan: "These are the best people so far discovered, and it seems to me that among unbelievers no people can be found to excel them."

American involvement with Japan began in earnest in 1853 with the arrival of Commodore Perry's black ships. Perry described the Japanese as "the most polite people on earth," and yet he also found them evasive and hypocritical. American images of Japan from Perry forward have been deeply ambivalent. During the period of Meiji modernization (1868–1912), Americans viewed traditionally garbed Japanese as primitive but exotically elegant and Western-dressed Japanese as ridiculous yet somehow endearing in their awkward attempts to copy our styles and customs. Following Japan's defeat of Russia in 1905, Americans began to respect if not yet fear the Japanese. In the 1930s, after Japan conquered Manchuria, the spectre of the "Yellow Peril" emerged, and with Pearl Harbor the Japanese became not just the people of a feared, aggressive nation but an enemy. Hateful wartime images of the Japanese were complemented by Ruth Benedict's *The Chrysanthemum and the Sword*, which portrayed an image of Japan as profoundly enigmatic, a land of opposites, of cultural antipodes.

During the Occupation and on into the 1960s, Western cultural lenses once again transformed the Japanese, this time into eager protégés and democratic aspirants trying to emulate American democracy, industry, and popular culture. But by the end of the 1970s, as Japan began to best the United States economically, images of the Yellow Peril returned.

Today, Americans are unlikely to see Japanese as the Madame Butterflies and Mr. Motos of the prewar era or as the sadistic prison guards of wartime movies. Our images of Japan have altered. On the negative side, we tend to see Japan as a nation of unscrupulous, ruthless trading partners, soulless and uncreative competitors. We see Japanese workers as a disciplined army of self-sacrificing, diligent conformists who are employed for life. On the positive side, we view the Japanese as unvaryingly high-achieving, productive, energetic, hardworking, and service-oriented.

We want to destabilize these simple stereotypes. It is too easy to view the Japanese people as unrelievedly formal and unfeeling, group-dominated, and hierarchical or, alternatively, as perfectly disciplined, harmonious, self-sacrificing, and obedient.

The Japanese are formal, but there is leeway for the expression of feeling and spontaneity. As Takeo Doi explains in his second article below, without formality there can be no feeling, without structure there can be no spontaneity. For example, the Noh theatre mask, in severely limiting the range of facial expression, increases rather than reduces the possibility for communicating human feeling. The Noh dancer, in following the stylized, shuffling footsteps of the dancers who have come before him, has the possibility, with the slightest nuance of timing or posture, to suggest breathtaking creativity. It is true that the Japanese value dependence, but they also value individual initiative, perseverance, and a spiritual creativity that, Doi suggests, is fostered rather than compromised by interdependence with family, friends, and coworkers. It is true, as Thomas Rohlen's study of bank employees shows, that the Japanese enjoy group affiliation, yet within these groups they pursue complex individual strategies. The Japanese are sensitive to subtleties of hierarchy, and yet, in important ways they are more egalitarian than we are.

The papers in this section suggest not that the Japanese are strange or inscrutable but rather that the strangeness or inscrutability we see in Japanese cultural patterning lies in the observer's ethnocentrism or lack of imagination, not in Japanese culture.

In his best-selling book, *The Anatomy of Dependence* (1974), the Japanese psychoanalyst, Takeo Doi, defines *amae** as "presuming on the benevolence of others." Doi suggests that amae is a natural behavior, found in every human being in every culture. He also suggests that the Japanese are more comfortable with the dependence embodied in amae than are Americans and that Japanese culture values and supports amae while American culture disparages and discourages it.

Amae is often translated into English as "dependence," consistent with the notion that the U.S. values independence and Japan, dependence. Americans have seen in Japanese "groupism," childraising, consumerism, management techniques, sleeping arrangements, and gift giving examples of the essential dependence of Japanese character and culture. But while scholars from both sides of the Pacific might agree that numerous issues are patterned differently in Japan from the United States, many would object to applying the pejorative label *dependent* to the people and culture of Japan. Some scholars have recommended using the term *interdependent* to suggest the reciprocal nature of amae. Doi takes this line of thought a step further, arguing that giving is a kind of receiving and receiving a kind of giving. In this charming excerpt from *The Anatomy of Dependence,* Doi recounts how he personally encountered these different perceptions of dependence and independence.

Giving and Receiving

TAKEO DOI

First, I should say something of how I originally became preoccupied with the concept of *amae*. It is related to my experience of what is generally referred to as "culture shock." In 1950 I went to America on a scholarship to study psychiatry. It was still not long after the end of the war, yet I was dazzled by the material affluence of the United States and impressed by the cheerful, uninhibited behavior of its people.

Nevertheless, from time to time I began to feel an awkwardness

---

*Definitions for all Japanese terms can be found in the glossary.

arising from the difference between my ways of thinking and feeling and those of my hosts. For example, not long after my arrival in America I visited the house of someone to whom I had been introduced by a Japanese acquaintance. While we were talking, he asked me, "Are you hungry? We have some ice cream if you'd like it." As I remember, I was rather hungry, but finding myself asked point-blank if I was hungry by someone whom I was visiting for the first time, I could not bring myself to admit it and ended by refusing the offer. I probably cherished a mild hope that he would press me again; but my host, disappointingly, said "I see" with no further ado, leaving me regretting that I had not replied more honestly. And I found myself thinking that a Japanese would almost never ask a stranger unceremoniously if he was hungry but would produce something to give him without asking.

Another thing that made me nervous was the custom whereby an American host will ask a guest, before the meal, whether he would prefer a strong or a soft drink. Then, if the guest asks for liquor, he will ask him whether, for example, he prefers scotch or bourbon. When the guest has made this decision, he next has to give instructions as to how much he wishes to drink and how he wants it served. With the main meal, fortunately, one has only to eat what one is served, but once it is over, one has to choose whether to take coffee or tea, and—in even greater detail— whether one wants it with sugar and milk and so on. I soon realized that this was only the American's way of showing politeness to his guest, but in my own mind I had a strong feeling that I could care less. What a lot of trivial choices they were obliging me to make—almost as though they were doing it to reassure themselves of their own freedom. My perplexity, of course, undoubtedly came from my unfamiliarity with American social customs, and I would perhaps have done better to accept it as it stood, as an American custom.

Nor is it true that the Japanese never ask a guest his preference. Nevertheless, a Japanese has to be very intimate with a guest before he will ask him whether he wants something that has been offered to him. The custom, rather, in serving a guest who is not such a close friend is to produce something with a deprecatory "It may not suit your taste but...." An American hostess, on the other hand, will sometimes proudly describe how she made the main dish, which she produces without offering any alternative even though she gives her guests freedom of choice concerning the drinks that precede or follow it. This struck me as very odd indeed.

In this connection, the "Please help yourself" that Americans use so often had a rather unpleasant ring to my ears before I became used to English conversation. The meaning, of course, is simply "Please take what you want without hesitation," but literally translated it has somehow a flavor of "Nobody else will help you," and I could not see how it came to be an expression of goodwill. Japanese decorum would demand that, in entertaining, a host should show sensitivity in detecting what was required and should himself "help" his guests. To leave a guest unfamiliar with the house to "help himself" would seem excessively lacking in consideration. This increased still further my feeling that Americans were a people who did not show the same consideration and sensitivity towards others as the Japanese. As a result, my early days in America, which would have been lonely at any rate so far from home, were made lonelier still.

This excerpt is taken from Takeo Doi, *The Anatomy of Dependence: The Individual Versus Society* (Tokyo: Kodansha International Ltd., 1974), 11–12.

Takeo Doi, in his writings, discusses the paired terms *omote* (front) and *ura* (back) and the related terms *tatemae* (formal appearance) and *honne* (inner feeling). Family and backdoor guests are treated with much more spontaneity than formality while the ratio is reversed for frontdoor callers. The relative formality and restraint of employee/boss relationships during the business day dissolve into openness and frivolity as soon as worker and boss enter the bar after work. In this paper, Doi introduces and explains the terms *tatemae* and *honne.*

Formal Appearance and Inner Feeling: *Tatemae* and *Honne*

TAKEO DOI

—

First, consider the etymology of the word *tatemae*. Beyond a doubt, the *tatemae* in *tatemae-honne* originates from the word *tatemae* in Japanese architecture, which means "raising the ridgepole." This work was considered to be so important that the owner of the building under construction would treat the master builder and his helpers to a lavish banquet after it was completed. *Tatemae* is also the word used in the tea ceremony for the formal movements of the host in presenting utensils and serving the tea (Kyogoku 1983). In both architecture and the tea ceremony, the tatemae is essential; without it, the building could not be built, the tea ceremony could not be performed.

In fact, dictionary definitions of *tatemae* define it as principles or rules that have been established as natural and proper. For example, the use of *tatemae* in Kabuki refers to the fact that play scripts were composed according to established conventions.

We can also approach this problem by looking at modern usages of *tatemae*. Here are some examples: "The system requiring all students to live in dormitories is the tatemae of this school." "We uphold the tatemae of equality between the sexes." "It has been decided that, as the tatemae, Japan will not maintain war capabilities."

These examples also suggest that *tatemae* refers to conventions created by people on the basis of consensus. Seen in this light, it is even more clear that the *tatemae* under discussion here originally had the same meaning as *tatemae* in architecture or the tea ceremony. In short, *tatemae* always implies assent.

In contrast to this, *honne* refers to the fact that the individuals who belong to the group, even while they consent to the tatemae, have their own motives and opinions which are distinct from it and which they maintain within themselves. In fact, these individual, personal ways of viewing the tatemae can themselves be said to be honne.

As a concrete example, consider the case of a news media campaign to stir up popular opinion. These campaigns are permitted because freedom of speech is guaranteed by the constitution. In this sense, freedom of speech is the tatemae of mass communication. But when a given news organization launches a media campaign on a given issue, it may be because the company secretly wants to manipulate popular opinion in ways that will prove profitable to itself or because the reporter or editor in charge wants a promotion. In this case, the Japanese would refer to these hidden motives by saying that they are the honne of the situation.

To avoid any misunderstanding, I should point out here that I do not mean to suggest by the above example that tatemae is morally good and honne morally evil. Nor do I want to say that honne is the truth and tatemae mere pretense. Rather, I am attempting to demonstrate that tatemae and honne are mutually constitutive; one does not exist without the other. Speaking in terms of the previous example, freedom of speech is predicated upon the expectation that individuals will actually say whatever they like, and it guarantees their right to do so within the political tatemae of freedom of speech. Anyone may indeed speak on the basis of his or her own honne.

However, it is essential to note here that the individual is not always self-consciously aware of the distinction between tatemae and honne. Take the case of a male teacher who is especially earnest in teaching one of his female students. Since it is his job to teach, we may interpret his actions as those of a teacher faithfully observing the tatemae of his profession. But a careful investigation of his speech and behavior might reveal that, in fact, he secretly has deeper feelings for the student. If he is clearly aware of these feelings, then they are his honne. But it is also conceivable that he will insist that he is only doing his job and has no honne at all in this situation.

The same thing may be said of a housewife who is unusually enthusiastic about volunteer work. On the one hand, of course, she is enthusiastic because her consciousness has been raised and she wants to make a contribution to society. But her enthusiasm might also be the result of trouble at home; or perhaps she just wants to get out of the house and away from the everyday tasks of housework and taking care of her family. In some cases she will be clearly conscious of these motives as her own honne; in others she will be unable to recognize them.

Similarly, when a person who is normally shy and retiring suddenly begins denouncing others in the name of justice, it is almost certain that he or she is conscious only of the tatemae (in this case "justice") and believes that there is no honne. Whenever something is done in the name of justice—whether it is launching a world war or merely a media campaign—it is no exaggeration to say that the people involved are almost never aware of their own honne.

I want to emphasize once again that in citing these concrete cases I do not mean to suggest that tatemae is good and honne evil. It is simply the nature of things that tatemae is revealed to the outside and honne is concealed within; there is nothing inherently wrong with this relationship.

It is quite a different matter when a person does not recognize his or her own honne for what it is and actually goes so far as to deny its existence. When this happens, the person loses control of honne and, as a result, it can run rampant. As I suggested above, tatemae legitimizes honne. But, in this case, difficulties arise because that legitimization is emphasized so strongly that the person loses sight of the very existence of honne.

This condition corresponds to what is called rationalization in psychoanalysis, a condition in which instinctual impulses are justified not as impulses that thrust up from below but as something rational. In more general terms, it is the mentality of those who say that "the end justifies the means." Once this mentality is established, once it is decided that as long as the end is good, the means no longer matters, we arrive at the worst possible scenario, in which evil is committed in the name of good.

The characteristic feature of the relationship between tatemae and honne is that tatemae conceals honne even as it represents honne. The English words *public* and *private,* which correspond to ōyake and *watakushi* in Japanese, signify realms that are strictly distinguished. As such, they never overlap. In contrast to this, tatemae and honne coexist as two contiguous principles. It is interesting to note Allessandro Valignano's observations in his *Historia del Príncipo y Progresso de la Compañía de Jesús en las Indias Orientales, 1542–1546,* concerning the Japanese near the end of the sixteenth century, in which he listed the following as one of the defects of the Japanese:

> As they do not know the difference between the prudence of the flesh . . . and genuine prudence, they fall into this error, attributing to prudence the state of being misleading, and showing themselves in the exterior in such a way that it is impossible to understand what they have in their hearts. If only they would modify this characteristic in accordance with genuine prudence, it would be praiseworthy indeed, for in this respect, they deal more thoughtfully than we do in many matters. They know how to keep quiet and dissemble when the occasion calls for it, and from this, many benefits would follow if only, as I have said, this prudence would not exceed the boundaries of reason. But because the Japanese cannot restrain this habit, prudence becomes a vice; they become so deceptive that they can be understood only with the greatest difficulty, and it is quite impossible to know by their words and outward signs what they are feeling and thinking in their hearts (Valignano, 40).

This statement is all the more interesting because Valignano also praised the Japanese for their highly developed sense of ethics. A contemporary of Valignano was probably referring to the same phenomenon when he wrote that the Japanese are fond of ambiguous language, and complained of their "false smiles."

The phenomenon of tatemae and honne was recognized much earlier in Kenkō's *Tsurezuregusa,* which is thought to have been compiled in the first half of the fourteenth century (Kenkó 1977). Kenkó describes a scene in which an Easterner criticizes the people of Kyoto for making excellent promises they have no intention of fulfilling:

> Gyóren Shónin, abbot of the temple of Hidenin, whose secular name was Miura something or other, was an unrivaled warrior. A person from his native place came to visit him and, in the course of his stories about home, said, "It is people from the East whose words can be trusted. As for the people of the capital, only their promises are good, but there is no truth to them." The holy man clarified the principles of the matter thus: "You no doubt believe this to be true, but I have lived in the capital for a long time and have become well acquainted with the people, and I do not believe their hearts to be inferior. It is because in general their hearts are gentle and they have human sympathy that they find it difficult to say no to what another has said, that they cannot speak out about everything they are thinking, and that they meekly make promises. They do not mean to deceive, but since they are poor and in straitened circumstances, there are doubtless many things in which they cannot carry through their own true intentions [honne]. The people of the East are my own compatriots, but, in truth, their hearts are not

kind, and because they are a blunt and unaffable people, they do not hesitate to say no from the very beginning. It is because of their prosperity and wealth that they are trusted by others" (Keene 1967, 127–8).

In modern terms, the abbot's defense amounts to this: Kyoto people speak in this way only because they are expressing tatemae. It is mistaken to believe that this is hypocrisy. Instead, one should see in their attempts to construct a tatemae evidence of their real sincerity.

To a certain extent, these observations concerning the people of Kyoto would apply to a comparison of the

Japanese people as a whole, who deal with everything in terms of tatemae and honne, to foreigners.

This is excerpted from Takeo Doi, *The Anatomy of Self: The Individual Versus Society* (Tokyo, New York, San Francisco: Kodansha International Ltd, 1985).

REFERENCES

Keene, Donald. *Essays in Idleness.* New York: Columbia University Press, 1967.

Kenkó, Yoshida. "*Tsurezuregusa,* Episode 141." In *Shincho nihon koten shusei* 10 (Shincho Compendium of the Japanese Classics). Tokyo: Shin Cho-sha, 1977.

Kyogoku, Junichi. *Nihon no seiji* (Japanese politics). Tokyo: Tokyo University Press, 1983.

Valignano, Allessandro. *Historia del Príncipo y Progresso de la Compañía de Jesús en las Indias Orientales, 1542–1546.* Translated by Michael Cooper (personal correspondence).

In *The Anatomy of Dependence* (1974) Takeo Doi suggests that in infancy the Japanese develop a dyadic, interdependent dimension of self, which Doi discusses in terms of the Japanese concept of *amae*. This first level of self, learned largely through repeated dyadic interactions between mother and child, includes the sense of being lovable and being able both to give and to receive pleasure in intimate, interpersonal relationships.

In *The Anatomy of Self* (1985), Doi explains that the paired terms *omote* and *ura*, which mean, literally, front and rear, are used in common phrases to distinguish that which is presented to the outside world from that which is hidden from public view. (For example, *omote-ji* is the outer fabric, *ura-ji,* the lining of a kimono.) Following a line of thought he introduced in a 1972 paper on " . . . the Japanese Two-Fold Structure of Consciousness," Doi suggests that the Japanese self is two-tiered, with omote and ura dimensions. Omote is the front side of the self, the side one shows in public; ura is the private side of the self, the side one shows only to family and friends.

In the reading which follows, Joseph J. Tobin applies these and other concepts to child socialization, suggesting that it is crucial to teach young children to know the difference between omote and ura and to be able to move easily back and forth between formal and informal modes of speech and action.

Front and Rear
(*Omote* and *Ura*)

JOSEPH J. TOBIN

Putting Doi's theories into a developmental context would suggest that the Japanese child's first two years of life are focused on learning *amae* while the years from three to six are focused on learning *kejime*—the ability to make distinctions (Lebra 1986; Hendry 1986), for example, distinctions between *omote* and *ura* (front and rear), *tatemae* and *honne* (formal appearances and inner feelings), and *uchi* and *soto* (private and public). Japanese children begin to learn these distinctions at home as infants. Under their parents' and siblings' tutelage they learn to bow, to use polite language, and to be polite with, but a little leery of, outsiders. In developing the second dimension of self more fully, however, children need to move outside the boundaries of mother and home and become members of more complex social groups.

During the second stage of the development of the self, Japanese children are asked not to renounce their dependency, not to reject their desire to practice amae—as, for instance, infantile—but instead to learn to seek satisfaction of their dependency drives in relationships beyond the boundaries of the family and to cultivate a sense of self not only as a son or daughter in a family but also as a group member and as a person in society. During this second stage of development Japanese children, already competent in the informal, spontaneous give-and-take of family life, develop a more outward-facing sense of self that will allow them to interact comfortably with non-kin and strangers. The ability to shift levels of intimacy and restraint, which the child learned in the inner circle of family relations as a toddler, is expanded during the preschool years to the larger circles of peers, teachers, and neighbors.

Is any of this uniquely Japanese? Westerners, like Japanese, also ideally have two-tiered selves, selves able to adjust to different people and different situations. Western children also learn the difference between indoor and outdoor voices, learn the need to be circumspect and polite in formal contexts, learn to control the display of their emotions and to channel the gratification of their impulses.

The difference thus may be less one of psychology than of ethnopsychology, less a difference between Japanese and Western psyches than a variance in the way the dimensions of the self are portrayed and evaluated in Japan and the West. In Japan, unlike in the U.S., circumspection, circumlocution, formality, ceremony, ritual, and manners are viewed as vehicles for expressing as well as masking pleasure and for realizing rather than for binding the self. Less likely than Americans to view social conformity as a sign of weakness of character, joining the group as a betrayal of individuality, or ritualized public discourse as hypocrisy, the Japanese value the omote, the formal dimension of the self, as much as the ura, the more spontaneous dimension.

On the road to adulthood Japanese children must learn lessons more complex than simply distinguishing inside from outside, front from back, public from private, and family from strangers. To have a proper, two-tiered Japanese sense of self one must learn to make much more fluid and subtle distinctions, learn to step back and forth across the gap dividing omote from ura in the course of a conversation, or indeed, even in the midst of a single phrase. A slight wink of an eye or a change in the level of politeness of a verb ending suddenly signals a slight but crucial warming up or cooling down of relations. As Doi suggests, omote and ura are complementary rather than opposing. There is omote, inevitably, in ura and ura in omote. In even the most formal, public interactions (tatemae) there is the potential for experiencing real human feeling (honne). In even the closest of relationships there is always a hint of omote, an unspoken awareness of the chasm that separates all human beings and that makes a degree of restraint necessary even among family members. As the Japanese saying puts it, "Strangers begin with siblings."

This essay is excerpted from a longer unpublished article by Joseph J. Tobin titled "Japanese Preschools and the Pedagogy of Self."

REFERENCES

Doi, Takeo. *The Anatomy of Dependence: The Individual Versus Society.* Tokyo: Kodansha International Ltd., 1974.

———. *The Anatomy of Self: The Individual Versus Society.* Tokyo: Kodansha International Ltd., 1985.

Hendry, Joy. *Becoming Japanese.* Honolulu: University of Hawaii Press, 1986.

Lebra, Takie Sugiyama, and William P. Lebra, eds. *Japanese Culture and Behavior.* Honolulu: University of Hawaii Press, 1986.

In Japanese culture it is crucial to know early who is senior and who is junior in every interaction. In talking to one's senior one must use a proper tone of voice, a proper level of formality in verb endings, and appropriate honorific particles, verbs, and nouns. The Japanese word for teacher—*sensei*—literally means "born before." Business relationships cannot begin until *meishi* (name cards) are exchanged because they contain critical clues to rank and status and thus make clear who is to defer to whom.

In the following excerpt, Thomas Rohlen describes *sempai/kōhai* (senior/junior) relationships in a Japanese bank, and suggests that it is crucial for a young worker to have "friends at court." The principles of verticality that Rohlen outlines in the business setting can be seen as well in school settings in relationships between students and teachers, younger and older students, boys and girls. (The focus of Rohlen's article is on male-male relations, thus the consistent use of the pronoun *he*.)

Up and Down

THOMAS P. ROHLEN

In Japan many valued relationships involve a difference in age (Norbeck and Befu 1958; Bennett and Ishima 1963; Kawashima 1963; Nakane 1970; Whitehill and Takezawa 1968; Cole 1971). Those between parents and children and between teachers and students are the most prominent, and they provide models for other relationships. Strong personal bonds between people of different ages have, for example, been noted among those working together in labor gangs, gangster outfits, village communities, and factories.

Intergenerational ties are visible in the relationships among people in banks as well. The most recent and prominent analysis of modern Japanese organization (Nakane 1970) gives a central place to the importance of what rather unfortunately must be termed senior-junior relations. It is Nakane's conclusion that this relationship is crucial to our understanding of the uniquely Japanese qualities of modern organization. Clearly this aspect of interpersonal relations at Uedagin (the name of the bank) deserves our close attention. And in fact, a detailed look at senior-junior relations will permit us to understand a great deal more about the daily reality from which the ideological image of hierarchy is taken. It will also help us understand leadership style, and it will illustrate the crucial role seniors often play in the process of the newcomer fully joining the company.

By way of introduction we should note that an awareness of relative age is a constant necessity in the proper use of the Japanese language (Niyekawa 1968). A person will converse with those older by using a more polite vocabulary and set of grammatical forms. This is quite the reverse of the American tendency to minimize age differences in a search for the intimacy of equal status, and it seems that an appreciation of the satisfactions of senior-junior ties is not one we come to easily. The Japanese, it will help to remember, have a generally positive attitude toward relations involving age differences, and, as in the work group, the hierarchy of age not only serves organizational purposes but can be a matter of intimacy and emotional involvement. This point will help us to grasp the underlying character of senior-junior relations at Uedagin.

General Description

Discussions among young men and women of personal affairs and reactions to working in the bank generally lead to the mention of a senior person who has offered help and advice. The term for senior, *sempai,* is a compound of two characters, the first meaning "before" or "ahead" and the second meaning "companion." Sempai may be understood to mean a person who proceeds or leads, with the implication that those that follow are his or her companions in the same pursuit, career, or institution. *Kōhai,* literally "companion that is behind," expresses the other half of the senior-junior relationship. The complete image created by the characters is one of companions, one leading and the other following, passing along the same road. Sempai-kōhai relations are present in the bank's informal organization at all levels, but it is during the first four or five years of work in the bank that they develop and are notably influential.

In the most general sense, all people in the company are sempai to those younger, and all people younger are kōhai to their seniors. Usually, the application of those designations is limited to persons of one's own sex. Women are sempai for women, and men are sempai for men. One never hears a young man refer to an older woman as his sempai, and when women use the word they mean an older woman. Among the reasons for this division along sex lines is the implied comradeship between senior and junior, a form of comradeship that does not exist across the boundaries of sex.

We will distinguish several different kinds of sempai-kōhai relationships in Uedagin Bank. All of them share the following basic characteristics:

1. The sempai is older than his kōhai, has worked longer for the bank, and is in a position of power relative to him. This power enables the sempai to assist the kōhai in one or more ways. It also means that the sempai is secure and established as compared to his kōhai.
2. The sempai is beneficially disposed toward the kōhai.
3. The kōhai accepts the benefits bestowed by the sempai.
4. These acts and related feelings are the basis of the relationship, though no explicit agreement is stated.
5. Ideally, the kōhai feels gratitude to the sempai for his beneficence, and this feeling is accompanied by a desire to return the favor along with a commitment to become, in turn, a good sempai for someone younger.

A chain of relationships of "good turns" is thus created. This is not, however, between equals, nor is the exchange balanced, in the narrow sense of the word. The senior is more powerful, and he gives more than he receives, but when the junior (who has received) occupies the position of senior (who gives), balance is introduced. In time, the kōhai may also have opportunities to repay his sempai through personal loyalty. The time may even come, as it does with parents and their children, when the power to assist and the need for assistance are reversed between the two. We have, therefore, an exchange relationship between unequals in which time is a factor of great significance in the establishment of a semblance of balance. However, developing as it does over time and involving numerous acts of unknown relative value, balance is impossible to compute. It is a vague ideal and an ultimate goal. No one is so naive as to be unaware of the many long-standing imbalances. Nor, however, are people encouraged to be cynical about commitment to this sort of relationship. Juniors may forget their obligation to be in turn good seniors. Seniors may demand too much of their juniors. Some kōhai are ungrateful. The system of interrelationship, however, continues to follow the form set by the ideal of unselfish sympathy and involvement. Mood, that is, feelings of attachment-disaffection and satisfaction-dissatisfaction, ultimately serves as a measure of the balance.

The similarities between this relationship and that of parent and child or older and younger sibling are more than coincidental. In fact, family relationships provide analogies, as in the statement, "Sempai are like older brothers." These analogies are instructive if we examine the ideology of the Japanese family. First, interdependency and continuity, rather than individual independence, are the family ideals. Second, the emphasis on continuity translates into a prescription of gratitude to past generations and obligations to assist future ones. Third, affection and hierarchy, rather than being contradictory, are understood as mutually reinforcing. Last, the dependency of the younger, weaker party is not only accepted, it is the focal point of the relationship. These are, one can say, basic ingredients of one major Japanese code of interpersonal relations. And this code can make seemingly dissimilar situations and involvements, such as a family and an office group, comparable. Because of this code, the patterns of Uedagin senior-junior interrelationships receive powerful reinforcement from comparable relations throughout the society since they all repeat essentially the same message.

Ideally, sempai will represent, advise, console, teach, and discipline their kōhai. Kōhai, in turn, will confide in, listen to, depend upon, follow, and respect their sempai. The sempai is older and therefore has more experience and knows his way around better. He has contacts in the age groups above him. Probably he can call on his own sempai for help. Thus, seniority, particularly as it stands for the relative length of time in the institution, is the major source of the senior's power to assist his kōhai.

While everyone who is older is, in a general sense, a sempai, the term usually connotes a specific older individual who is particularly close and protective. It is seldom advisable or necessary to have close relationships with more than one or two seniors, although there are a number of people in the bank who, as sempai, have more than a few kōhai.

As an Ideal of Leadership

The influence of the sempai-kōhai pattern on feelings about official superior-subordinate relationships is worth noting. The pattern of close involvement between an older and a younger man, between a more experienced and a less experienced man, between a more established and a less established man, describes an ideal working relationship—one that is secure, beneficial, reciprocal, and selfless (to a degree). This ideal is often applied to the relationship of superior and subordinate in the official system of organization roles. Company leaders are occasionally referred to as sempai, and there is an implication that leadership should be as sympathetic, protective, and unselfish as are good sempai. In other words, the relationship is to a significant degree the basis for the ideal of superior-subordinate relations, and while this ideal of course often goes unrealized, it does establish a set of expectations about proper leader and follower conduct.

The superior finds his authority strongly limited by the general expectation that he will look after the best interests of those who work below him, that he will be their guardian or patron. The subordinate, on the other hand, finds that he should be submissive because of inexperience and out of gratitude.

It would be erroneous to view Japanese superiors simply as pseudoparents or their followers simply as docile believers in the faith. These two extremes, neither totally contradictory nor totally allied, create between them a fluid context rich in ritual gestures, maneuver, and subtle intrigue; and here, daily reality is to be found.

Gratitude, loyalty, beneficence, and sympathy are but the most prominent and readily appreciated aspects of particular hierarchical situations. Other realities (promotions, personal animosities, business necessities, and the like) are interwoven with and often translated into this more elevated language of personal relationship. The sempai-kōhai code is, in effect, a sacred language for discussions of vertical relations in the bank.

As dissatisfactions with leaders or followers mount, the credibility of the conceptual scheme may come into doubt. Private skepticism is far from unknown. But gestures symbolic of the coherence and vitality of the sempai-kōhai model are almost inevitably forthcoming in times of trouble, and their acceptance reiterates the fundamental premises of this relationship. By such things as self-sacrifice, magnanimous gestures, and intimate contact, superiors (including management in general) can represent their commitment to the scheme, just as patience and self-sacrifice symbolize commitment on the part of subordinates. These gestures must of course be accepted and at some point reciprocated for the preservation of the total orientation, but it is virtually impossible in normal circumstances to withhold acceptance for too long. As gestures continue to be made, resistance is both a disregard for the other's humanity and an antisocial act for it threatens the existence of the group or the total organization. A rise of cynicism or a complete breach of relationships would lead necessarily to the establishment of a new order, one based on impersonal rules, power, and the assumption of conflict. That this has not happened at Uedagin is testimony to the powerful Japanese dislike of cynicism and to the power of symbolic redress provided by the sempai-kōhai ideal.

This piece is excerpted from Thomas P. Rohlen, *For Harmony and Strength: Japanese White-Collar Organization in Anthropological Perspective* (Berkeley, Los Angeles, London: University of California Press, 1974).

REFERENCES

Benedict, Ruth. *The Chrysanthemum and the Sword*. Boston: Houghton Mifflin, 1946.

Bennett, John W., and Iwao Ishima. *Paternalism in the Japanese Economy*. Minneapolis: University of Minnesota Press, 1963.

Cole, Robert E. *Japanese Blue-Collar Workers*. Berkley: University of California Press, 1971.

Drucker, Peter F. "What We Can Learn from Japanese Management." *Harvard Business Review* (March-April 1971): 110–22.

Folsom, Kenneth E. *Friends, Guests, and Colleagues: The Mu-Fu System in the Late Ch'ing Period*. Berkeley: University of California Press, 1968.

Hsu, Francis L. K. *Americans and Chinese: Purpose and Fulfillment in Great Civilizations*. Garden City: Natural History Press, 1970.

Kawashima, Takeyoshi. "Dispute Resolution in Contemporary Japan." In *Law in Japan: The Legal Order in a Changing Society*, edited by Arthur Taylor von Mehren. Cambridge: Harvard University Press, 1963.

Nakane, Chie. *Japanese Society*. Berkeley: University of California Press, 1970.

Niyekawa, Agnes M. "A Study of Second Language Learning." Project Report of the Bureau of Research. Office of Education, U.S. Department of Health, Education and Welfare, 1968.

Norbeck, Edward, and Harumi Befu. "Japanese Usages of Terms of Relationship." *Southwestern Journal of Anthropology* 14 (1958): 66–86.

Whitehill, Arthur M., and Shin-ichi Takezawa. *The Other Worker*. Honolulu: East-West Center Press, 1968.

Wolf, Erik. "Kinship, Friendship and Patron-Client Relations in Complex Societies." *The Social Anthropology of Complex Societies*. A.S.A. Monographs 4. London: Travistock; New York: Praeger, 1966.

To be mature in Japan is to know how to recognize contexts and to modulate one's behavior accordingly. Speaking to one's senior in age or status calls for a different language and demeanor than addressing a junior. Status in Japan is fluid and relative, dependent on the context: one's junior at work can become one's senior in a neighborhood organization. At a funeral a younger woman representing a stem family outranks her older male cousin from a branch family and will be seated accordingly. It is as inappropriate and even insulting to greet a front-door guest with informal speech as it is to greet a backdoor guest formally. In the following paper, Mikie Yaginuma and Rick Kennedy provide a crash course in Japanese manners, stressing that life is simple in Japan—when you know your place.

Up and Down Etiquette

RICK KENNEDY AND MIKIE YAGINUMA

No nation has a more carefully worked-out system of etiquette than Japan. Japanese etiquette prescribes, for example, just how one should move into a new neighborhood. No later than three days after moving in, you and your family should pay a visit to the houses on either side of your new home, the house directly across the street, and the houses on either side of that house, leaving a little gift at each. It must be the same little gift, perhaps a package of soba noodles, which are long and thus symbolic of one's hope that the new relationship will be long-lived.

When you send a wedding present, to give another example, you can expect to receive a reciprocal gift, the value of which will be about half that of your gift. The same is true if you attend a funeral and give the family a gift of money—except if it is the funeral of the family's breadwinner in which case the reciprocal gift will be about one-third the value of your gift. All Japanese know that in a limousine the most distinguished person will take the seat behind the driver, the next most distinguished will sit at his or her side, and the most junior person will sit up front with the driver—an understanding which has the advantage of eliminating curbside scuffle. And any young Japanese lady called on to serve tea to guests she has never met will know exactly where in the room the most distinguished guest will be seated—information that is essential, after all, if she is to be certain of giving this guest the optimally poured cup of tea.

It might seem that such an elaborate social code is an inevitable by-product of an ancient society that shook off the last traces of feudalism a little more than one hundred years ago. But it is more than that. In Japan, etiquette is not simply a prescription for the appropriate social response. Japanese etiquette offers a complete guide to how one should conduct oneself for maximally congenial social interaction with a minimum of strain and confusion as well as what amounts to a prescription for a life of fulfillment.

Manners Maketh the Smooth-Running Society

Americans and Europeans, on first discerning the bare outlines of what appears to them to be an almost ludicrously complex social code, are apt to remark on what they feel to be its rigidity. "How terribly confining it must be to live this way!" they will remark with a mixture of bewilderment and sympathy.

But from the Japanese point of view, Japanese etiquette is not confining at all. When a conflict arises between social form and someone's personal feelings, social form can give way with remarkable ease. We recall a young lady who had just begun work for a Japanese company as what is called an "office lady" or general factotum. She noted that her female colleagues regularly took turns serving cups of green tea to everyone in the office but that none of the men ever deigned to volunteer for the job. Thinking to strike a blow for female emancipation, she approached her boss and told him that since she hadn't been hired to serve tea, she would not do it. "That's perfectly all right," said her boss. "Please don't worry about it. I can't think why the other ladies do it, but it's very nice of them." What often seems in Japan to be a burdensome social obligation turns out, in fact, to be only one person's socially accepted gesture of goodwill toward another.

We live next to a golf course. Twice each year, on one of the days set aside in July and December for the giving of gifts to people to whom you feel you owe an obligation, the golf course owner brings around to our house a carton of good Japanese beer, presumably as thanks for enduring the inconvenience (the occasional stray shot, some gentle cursing in the distance) of living next to the course, though he has never actually said why he does it. As a result, we feel well disposed toward the course. This pleasant little semiannual encounter probably would not take place if there were no season for the giving of gifts.

Of course, to live in accordance with an intricate social code requires a certain dedication, an attention to detail. It is not possible to live an uncaring, unaware life in Japan without being in serious violation of social form, but the trade-off is that you always know exactly what your social obligations are, you always know what to expect from others, and your position in the scheme of things is reasonably well defined and relatively secure. There is no cause for despair, therefore, at failing to achieve a particular status, or cause for anxiety about the possibility of not having done the right thing.

The Little Things

It is in the little things that the workability of Japanese etiquette makes itself apparent. When receiving a wrapped gift, the recipient does not immediately open the package as one is obliged to do in the West, thus being forced into an awful charade of polite delight no matter how inappropriate the gift might be. Japanese etiquette prescribes that the gift be laid aside to be opened later and responded to when one has had time to reflect on a response that will be reassuring to the giver of the gift. When money is given, it is always presented in an envelope, and the amount is discreetly noted on the back of the envelope.

When guests leave your home, you do not immediately close the door after them. In this way they do not have the feeling they are being shut out of your house; and, if they should have to come back a few minutes later to retrieve an article or for any other reason, they will not have to ring your doorbell again. This spares you from having to go through the greeting ritual all over again.

In the Japanese view, the purpose of etiquette is to provide a time-tested framework within which to get on with the details of one's life with a minimum of stress and anxiety. Living without a well-worked-out social code looks to the Japanese too much like chaos, which is why traveling outside Japan still seems to many Japanese like going for a trek in the jungle. They are convinced of this when they happen upon their first cocktail party (for which there is no Japanese equivalent), an occasion in which as varied an assortment as possible of people who have never met before are brought together for no discernible reason. The Japanese wonder if this is not complicating life unnecessarily, rather like playing roulette with people instead of playing with a little ivory ball. It seems very reckless because the results are so unpredictable (and, of course, so eerily fascinating). Cocktail parties seem like a microcosm of

Western society: a very noisy forum for people to practice trumpeting their individuality.

Social Roles and Obligations

When two Japanese businessmen meet for the first time, they exchange business cards, which note their managerial rank—section manager, division manager, deputy president—with considerable precision. They then know how they should relate to each other—who should pay deference to whom. From a Western point of view, relating to another person based on how many people he or she happens to (theoretically) oversee at his or her place of business smacks of an almost comic artificiality, seeming to encourage pomposity on the one hand and servility on the other. The Japanese, however, having grown up in a society that fixes one's social role from the moment one is born—as either elder or younger brother or elder or younger sister—find such an arrangement completely natural and even convenient. The point Westerners are apt to miss is that, in Japan, one does not so much define oneself in terms of one's social role as that one's social role is simply a given. It is as if to fight a forest fire, you have been assigned the job of brushcutter on fire lane 2. It is a job, and you know that if you do it well, the fire will more probably be contained. No one pretends that it is the whole meaning of life.

All Japanese know that if they are the eldest son in a family, it is their responsibility to take care of their parents as they age (and that, as recompense, they can expect the family house to devolve to them). They know that a wife's role is to handle the family finances, oversee the children's education, and dutifully support her husband. They know that if they are a teacher, they can expect deference and respect from their pupils. They know that if they are a customer, they can expect service, for in Japan the customer isn't simply right, he or she is paramount. They know that if they are born into a family that professes one of the classical arts, they will be expected to carry on the line. They know that if they are a manager, they are responsible for the happiness and well-being of everyone working under them, to the extent of advising on family problems and of introducing young employees to potential marriage partners and acting as the official go-between at their wedding ceremony and banquet. All this has already been decided. No negotiations are necessary.

And so it is that, depending on one's social role, one acquires *giri*, or certain obligations. To ignore one's obligations, that is, to enjoy a position, to partake of a favor or benefit from a kindness (without redressing the balance by diligently performing one's social duties), would be unthinkable. One action deserves another, and once a relationship is established, it tends to be nurtured, if only by seasonal greetings and ritual gift exchanges, and so grows stronger as the years pass.

The Safety Valve

To Westerners inured to weeding faded friendships out of their address books, the enduring quality of Japanese relationships may smack of a cocoonlike confinement and obligations of oppressive weight. But dangerous pressure is relieved with a safety valve. It is understood that one can be excused from one's social obligations by *ninjō*, human feelings. One is obliged by social custom, for instance, to visit the family burial plot four times a year. The entire extended family gathers—sometimes four or even five generations—for a ritual visit to the family temple and, afterwards, a meal together. The occasion is an important social obligation and one reason for the strength of the Japanese family. But one could easily be excused from attending by ninjō (illness in the immediate family or when attendance would cause a hardship). Thus, ninjō turns what looks at first glance like a rigid structure into a system that is quite as flexible, quite as loose, as social arrangements in the West.

Belonging Is Everything

The Japanese think it is right and natural for people to form relationships among themselves, to form groups. A group is supportive, can get a complicated job done more efficiently, and enlarges the pool of life experiences its members can draw on. If one belongs to no group, one is bound to be isolated and lonely. As time goes by, the members of any group become increasingly conscious of their obligations to each other, and their group feelings grow stronger. Japanese etiquette, in ritualizing obligations and defining relationships with great clarity, may be the mechanism that makes Japanese group consciousness so powerful. Groups of people held together by a network of promises and obligations make for a stable society, which, in Japan, is the ultimate social good.

This group consciousness makes the drawing of a line between in and out, between us and them, between group and nongroup natural and, ultimately, even desirable. But while group consciousness in the West carries implications of snobbery and misanthropy, in Japan it does not. In Japan, the emphasis is on belonging, not exclusion. The practical effects of this thinking of oneself not as an individual but as a member of a group are to underline the obligations one has to the other members of the group and to relieve one of any obligation to anyone not a member of the group. (This is why you cannot expect an apology if you are trampled on during rush hour: in such an every-person-for-himself/herself battlefield, apologies are just not practical.) It is a practical fact that one cannot lavish one's polite concern on the world as a whole or it will become unfocused and diluted. But one can devote oneself to a circle of like-minded people and expect to have a useful impact.

Westerners, romantics at heart, seem to be at home with absolutes: one God, the Truth, Right and Wrong. The Japanese are not so sure, feeling that a group of people may find comfort sharing a value system because it is valid for them, but they should not expect others to espouse the same values.

The Social Graces

In a stable society where people are secure in their social roles, there is little utility in such frontier social values as rugged individualism and the ability to out-argue the fellow on the other side of the table. People who seek to impress their personalities on others only serve to disrupt social harmony.

In Japan, the prevailing social virtues are restraint, patience, modesty, and what can only be called thoughtfulness, which includes an extreme reluctance to cause anyone embarrassment. These are not simply maidenly virtues but are values that pervade the society and could just as well describe the character of a tough, self-made entrepreneur with offices in the Ginza.

The great value the Japanese put on modesty, restraint, and accommodation is in clear contrast to the Western values of self-confidence, decisiveness, and individuality. The one seeks to produce a harmonious society, with everyone living and working together without drama; the other seeks to produce a challenging, dynamic, striving society. It is entirely predictable that Westerners tend to think of Japanese society as dull, punctuated only by the drinking of endless cups of tea, while the Japanese view Western society as impossibly wearisome—exciting, but in the end too exciting, with too little chance of living to venerable and respected old age, which is, after all, the whole point of existence.

This piece is excerpted from Rick Kennedy and Mike Yaginuma, "Life Is So Simple When You Know Your Place," *PHP Intersect Magazine* 6 (May 1986): 35–39.

Japan is a culture which, linguistically, socially, and architecturally, pays great attention to the boundaries between "inside and outside." Every Japanese home has a *genkan,* a combination threshold and entrance hall, a space simultaneously inside and out, where slipper-clad household members meet visitors and salespeople wearing shoes. Entrances and exits from each level of the education system from nursery school through university are punctuated by rites of passage. People leaving on trips are sent off by groups of well-wishers at airports and train stations in ceremonies of *sayōnara* and *banzai.*

Group membership in Japan is communicated by looking and acting one's part unambiguously and unambivalently. Kindergarten children wear uniforms and caps that show their school and class names. Elevator operators wear distinctive uniforms of their department stores. Bankers dress (in dark suits) like bankers; artists dress (in berets and turtlenecks) like artists. Even foreigners in Japan belong to a group—*gaijin*—which means, literally, "outside people." As gaijin, they are expected to look and act like foreigners. If a foreigner manages to act Japanese in some way (such as speaking Japanese or enjoying sushi), he or she is called a *henna gaijin,* a strange foreigner.

In an increasingly cosmopolitan Japan, is this distinction between insiders and outsiders losing some of its salience? No, argues anthropologist Harumi Befu, who looks skeptically at Japan's internationalization. In the following paper, Befu argues that beneath contemporary interest in internationalization lies an enduring or even reviving sense of Japanese homogeneity and cultural uniqueness and superiority. Befu suggests that, despite a national policy of internationalization and increased contact with foreigners at home and abroad, the Japanese remain acutely aware of and interested in the difference between "we" (Japanese) and "they" (foreigners).

Inside and Outside

HIROSHI MANNARI AND HARUMI BEFU

Japan's position in the international scene has become increasingly visible and important in the last ten years. It is worthwhile to recall, however, that every aspect of Japanese life has been touched by pervasive and profound contact with the West.

The diffusion of Western culture into Japan has gone on for more than a century and continues to this day. With the defeat of Japan and the Occupation of the Allied powers, the impact of American culture in Japan has become ever more visible. Today, the process of Westernization is often called "internationalization."

Gaijin Syndrome

The *gaijin* syndrome is a poignant expression of the separateness which the Japanese are trying to assert. Among the several Japanese terms referring to foreigners, *gaijin* is probably the most frequently used in contemporary Japan. In its popular sense, *gaijin* refers specifically to Caucasians. (One does not see Japanese children pointing to Koreans saying, "Gaijin, gaijin!") Foreigners in Japan are foreigners no matter how many generations they have lived there, no matter how well they speak the language, and no matter how well they have adapted to Japanese culture. The term *gaijin* is a label forever attached to Caucasians and symbolizes permanent outside status. "Once a gaijin, always a gaijin" is the unalterable principle.

It is one thing, in the minds of the Japanese, to take on features of Western culture. It is another entirely to admit foreigners as categorical Japanese. The Japanese claim to racial identity, unity, and social group distinctiveness takes on a greater importance as their culture becomes inundated with foreign elements. By setting gaijin immutably apart, the Japanese can maintain a distinct identity and incorporate foreign cultural elements simultaneously.

We can illustrate the dialectic between outside influence and Japanese identity by exploring an average salaryman's daily routine. In the morning he is as likely to arise from a Western-style bed as from a futon. He removes his pajamas and dresses in a dark suit, possibly designed by Pierre Cardin, and may even have a breakfast of ham and eggs, bread and butter, and coffee. He reads the morning newspaper printed by a computer originally invented in the West and composed of printed words adopted originally from the Chinese. He then dashes out to catch the commuter train, unless he is driving his "my-car"—both originally imported. He arrives at his office in a ferroconcrete building and sits at his desk all day. If he works for a trading company, he may spend his day negotiating the import of grains from the United States or meat from Australia. After work, he is likely to stop by at a favorite bar with his coworkers for a shot or two of Western-style whiskey and discuss how the Tokyo Giants are doing in the baseball league. On the train home, he might read in the evening paper about the continuing growth of the Japanese auto industry and Japan's status as Number One in the world.

When he returns home, he is just as likely to have a ministeak dinner as rice and fish while he considers the cost of beef and listens to his favorite Beethoven piece on the radio or stereo set. Before retiring, he goes to the family altar to thank the deity imported from India via China and Korea that he is 100 percent Japanese.

What is it that makes him so sure that he is 100 percent Japanese and no less? It is indeed because the question of being Japanese excludes any middle ground. You either are or are not. The identity of the Japanese resides in an absolute exclusion of foreigners and in a total identification as one race and one culture. Scientific reasoning aside, the conviction of racial unity and cultural homogeneity is unshakable, leading to an ultimate belief that the unique essence of Japanese culture is transmitted genetically. Because, as the belief goes, the Japanese are one race, they are also of one culture. Any infusions of Chinese and Western culture detract not at all from the essential core of Japanese culture, even though they may have penetrated beneath the surface.

I suspect this genetic definition of Japanese culture explains the inability to include foreigners in a category of people called Japanese. Use of the term *gaijin* by the Japanese, especially by children as they point at the strangers, upsets foreigners—especially those who desire admission into the Japanese fold, have lived in Japan a long time and hope to remain, have mastered the language, and have internalized the modus vivendi of the Japanese. When their attempt to be recognized as Japanese is rejected, they become furious. They fail to realize that, in the eyes of the Japanese, they have not ceased to be gaijin. Instead, they have simply moved from the category of simple gaijin to the subcategory of *henna gaijin.*

I do not doubt that to some extent the term is used pejoratively, especially when voiced by children. We have here a classic case of mutual misunderstanding: the foreigner's wishful thinking is that internationalization can lower the boundaries separating him or her from the Japanese, whereas in reality internationalization compels the Japanese to draw a sharper line than ever before.

Homogeneity

That the Japanese are racially and culturally homogeneous is a popular idea. Chie Nakane's best-selling analysis of Japanese culture (1967) is subtitled *A Theory of a Homogeneous Society.* In a similar mode, Yoshiro Masuda invokes Japanese homogeneity in the title of his book *Conditions of a Pure Culture* (1967). This emphasis on purity and homogeneity implies that Japanese culture incorporates no foreign cultural or ethnic elements and admits of no regional variations, the differences in cultural practices from Aomori to Okinawa notwithstanding. Nor are the vast class differences observed in feudal days—from the genteel nobility in Kyoto through the humorless Confucian warriors and hedonistic townspeople to ignoble peasants—of any particular concern for defenders of the homogeneity thesis. As they see it, Japanese identity is not expressed in overt behavior or manifest customs but in fundamental premises about the culture and the people, their language and race.

The belief that Japanese is a unique language, spoken universally and exclusively by the Japanese, reinforces a thesis of cultural homogeneity. Most Japanese proceed on the assumption that the essential character of Japanese culture and expression is found and realized exclusively through the Japanese language—a cultural commodity available only to the Japanese themselves. Claiming exclusive racial homogeneity, the Japanese invoke a mythology which traces Japanese people back to their ancestral sun goddess.

While this myth may be regarded askance in contemporary Japan, the conviction of a genetic link unifying all Japanese is firmly entrenched. Belief in "Japanese blood" being carried among the Japanese is commonplace. The expression *Nihonjin no chi ga nagareteiru* has two meanings: The primary one refers to Japanese blood (in the ordinary physiological sense) circulating through the body and, by implication, streaming through generations. The second and more important meaning in this context links the idea of blood to a belief in the genetic transmission of culture and language. In this sense it carries more than red and white corpuscles and other biological substances; it carries the spiritual substance of Japanese culture. The belief in the significance of blood appears in many cultures (note the long-standing belief in the U.S. of the superiority of white to "Negro" blood), but it is especially weighted and potent in Japan.

The notion of racial homogeneity is linked to a notion that the collective identity of the Japanese is "racial-historical" (*ketsuenshi-teki*) as well as genetic. According to Kimura, who writes a piece on Japanese culture from the perspective of Japanese psychopathology, "It is an identity which exists prior to the individual Japanese—an identity out of which each Japanese is born" (1973, 13). This preexisting identity does not refer to temporal but to ontological order, that is, to the very foundation of existence and identity. For this reason, foreigners are forever excluded from the Japanese fold. So too, are those of partially Japanese descent who are less than full Japanese in the social and cultural sense.

The existence of biological and phenotypic similarity between the Japanese and neighboring peoples such as Koreans, the Chinese, and Southeast Asians does not provide sufficient evidence to destroy belief in the racial integrity of the Japanese. The racial purity of the Japanese is, as they see it, the result of genetic continuity through the generations, stretching as far back in history as they can document—at least two thousand years. They are, with ill-concealed pride, likely to call attention to pockets of Korean potters in Kyushu who have lived in Japan for over four hundred years and who are nonetheless still kept separate from the Japanese.

Another dimension of the meaning of homogeneity resides in a belief in the unity of race, language, and culture. As the Japanese see it, linguistic and cultural homogeneity persist because of the homogeneity of race (Miller 1977). Implied in this idea is the further assumption that certain core traits of Japanese language and culture are genetically transmitted (Hayashida 1976). It is no wonder that, in this context (as pointed out to me by Robert J. Smith in a personal communication), even an eminent anthropologist like Eiichiro Ishida would argue in his *Japanese Culture* (1974) that the inception of the Japanese language coincided with the appearance of the Japanese people. It should be pointed out that there is ambiguity in the meaning of the term *Nihon minzoku* (Japanese people). *Minzoku* is often translated as "race" by Japanese writers, but it also means an ethnic group possessing a distinct culture. The dictionary clearly specifies that race, culture, and language are the defining criteria for *Nihon minzoku*.

The genetic base of Japanese language and culture closes all doors to foreigners who might wish to become or be considered Japanese. Lacking a genetic base, foreigners must forswear any possibility of acquiring Japanese culture or learning Japanese as the Japanese do. They are viewed as unable to acquire the essential core of Japanese sociolinguistic competence, even though they may practice the culture and speak the language at what the Japanese would consider a superficial level. To the foreigner's slightest linguistic error, the Japanese are fond of remarking (in their presence!), "That goes to show how difficult the Japanese language is!" as if to imply that the difficulty is totally insurmountable for foreigners.

The genetic theory of language transmission applies as well to Japanese-Americans, who are expected somehow to speak Japanese without learning it. The utter amazement, nearing bewilderment, which Japanese manifest toward visiting Japanese-Americans who cannot speak Japanese is testimony to the strength of this belief. By the same token, when Japanese-Americans do learn to speak the language, the Japanese are not as charitable with their praise as they might be for Caucasians, since for Japanese-Americans, linguistic competence is implicitly assumed to be in the genes and needs only an opportunity for its phenotypic expression.

There is a related phenomenon often observed in Japan that should be mentioned. American-born-and-raised *nisei* and *sansei* living in Japan are often turned down in their applications for positions to teach English. The common excuse is that students prefer Caucasian teachers. This in itself is, of course, a blatant expression of reverse racism—a conviction that a white man has something to teach simply because he is white and that a yellow man is not qualified to teach about the white man's culture simply because he is yellow. Behind this reasoning may well lurk a genetic assumption about Japanese-Americans' linguistic and cultural competence. Their biological background stigmatizes them and diminishes the authority of their credentials as teachers and experts on matters of Western culture and language. It is probably this assumption that prevents private English-language schools from jeopardizing their reputations by hiring Japanese-Americans.

The relative difficulty of becoming a naturalized Japanese citizen according to the present civil code may also be interpreted as a legal expression of the ethos of the culture. According to a recent opinion survey, only 28 percent of the Japanese living in the largest cities (those presumably most internationalized) were willing to allow foreigners to settle in Japan or to become naturalized citizens while those in smaller cities and rural areas were more tolerant, 41 percent and 35 percent respectively. Although it is difficult to account for the differences between respondents in the large cities and the small towns, it appears that big-city Japanese—the more internationalized—are more likely to shun foreigners. (It is interesting to note that Japanese farmers, unable to get modern young Japanese women to live on their farms, are importing foreign, especially Filipino, women as brides.)

Armed with this genetic theory, or racist theory as Reischauer would put it (1977, 47), and the theory of unity of race, language, and culture, the Japanese have a secure line of defense in maintaining their separateness and distinctness even in the face of an onslaught of foreign cultural diffusion.

Minimum Essence of Japanese Culture

Japanese language and culture, when viewed as genetically based, have certain irreducible essences which define their uniqueness. Japanese cultural philosophers have explicated ad nauseam such aesthetic concepts as *iki, wabi, sabi,* and *mono no aware.* The personal character of the Japanese is epitomized by theorists of Japanese culture in such concepts as *kokoro, seishin,* and *tamashī.* Through the sharing of these and other essential and unique characteristics, the Japanese claim to possess certain uncanny nonverbal abilities to communicate with one another, often expressed as *ishin denshin* (from mind to mind) or *haragei* (belly-art) (Kunihiro 1976, 270–73). Foreigners, lacking these abilities, are said to be hindered in communicating with the Japanese.

The group orientation of the Japanese—with its hierarchies, its close psychological bonds cemented by *amae* (presuming on the benevolence of others) and woven together by the social threads of *on* and *giri*—is also considered to be unique. This group structure is said to provide a model for all kinds of concrete organizations in Japan—from bureaucratic agencies and school clubs to schools of tea ceremony and organized crime. The miraculous success of Japanese business is attributed by scores of Japanese management specialists and Western scholars to the degree to which the Japanese managerial system reflects this kind of groupism which permeates Japanese culture (Abegglen 1958; Ballon 1980; Brown 1966; Dore 1973; Hazama 1971; Inuta 1977; Iwata 1978; Ouchi 1981; Rohlen 1974; Tsuda 1977; Urabe 1978).

This is not the place to elaborate on these Japanese concepts. Suffice it to say that they are a sampling of traits defining the uniqueness of Japanese culture which the Japanese claim make their culture difficult or impossible for foreigners to understand (Kato 1962). It is interesting to note that the claim is often made by the Japanese but seldom conceded by foreigners, especially those who are specialists in Japanese studies.

This piece has been exerpted and edited from a more fully developed essay appearing in Kyoto University School of Education, Department of Comparative Education, "*Kaigai kikoku shijo no tekiō ni kansuru chōsa: Kaigai kikoku shijo kyōiku kenkyū III*" (A Study on Adjustment of Returnee Children: Research on the Education of Overseas Returnee Children III), edited by Hiroshi Mannari and Harumi Befu, *The Challenge of Japan's Internationalization: Organization and Culture,* Seminar Proceedings, 1981: 232–59.

REFERENCES

Abegglen, James C. *The Japanese Factory.* Glencoe: Free Press, 1958.

Ballon, Robert J. *Nihongata bijinesu no kenkyū* (A Study of Japanese Managerial Style). Tokyo: Pejidento, 1980.

Brown, William. "Japanese Management: The Cultural Background." *Monumenta Nipponica* 21 (1966): 47–60.

Dore, Ronald P. *British Factory, Japanese Factory.* Berkeley: University of California Press, 1973.

————. "Industrial Relations in Japan and Elsewhere." In *Japan, a Comparative View*, edited by A. Craig. Princeton: Princeton University Press, 1979.

Hayashida, Cullen T. "Identity, Race and the Blood Ideology of Japan." Doctoral diss., University of Washington, 1976.

Hazama, Hiroshi. *Nihonteki Keiei* (Japanese-Style Management). Tokyo: Nihon Keizai Shimbunsha, 1971.

Inuta, Mitsuru. *Shudan shugi no kōzō* (The Structure of Groupism). Tokyo: Sangyo Noritsu Tanki Daigaku Press, 1977.

Ishida, Eiichiro. *Japanese Culture.* Tokyo: University of Tokyo Press, 1974.

Iwata, Ryushi. *Gendai Nihon no keiei fūdo* (The Environment of Management in Modern Japan). Tokyo: Nihon Keizai Shimbunsha, 1978.

Kato, Shuichi. "Nihonjin no gaikokukan" (Japanese Views of Foreign Countries). *Shisō* 458 (1962).

Kimura, Bin. *Hito to hito tono aida* (Between One Person and Another). Tokyo: Kobundo, 1973.

Kinugasa, Yosuke. *Nihon keigyo no kokusaika senryaku* (Strategies of Internationalization of Japanese Enterprises). Tokyo: Nihon Keizai Shimbunsha, 1979.

Kunihiro, Masao. "The Japanese Language and Intercultural Communication." *Japan Interpreter* 10 (1976).

Masuda, Yoshiro. *Junsui bunka no jōken* (Conditions of a Pure Culture). Tokyo: Kodansha International, Ltd., 1967.

Miller, Roy Andres. *The Japanese Language in Contemporary Japan: Some Sociolinguistic Observations.* Washington, DC: American Enterprise Institute for Public Policy Research and Stanford: Hoover Institution, 1977.

Nakane, Chie. *Tate shakai no ningen kankei: Tan'itsu shakai no riron* (Human Relations in a Vertical Society: A Theory of a Homogeneous Society). Tokyo: Kodansha International, Ltd., 1967.

Ouchi, William G. *Theory Z: How American Business Can Meet the Japanese Change.* Reading, MA: Addison-Wesley, 1981.

Reischauer, Edwin O. *The Japanese.* Cambridge: Harvard University Press, 1977.

Rohlen, Thomas P. *For Harmony and Strength.* Berkeley: University of California Press, 1974.

Tsuda, Masumi. *Nihonteki keiei no riron* (Theory of Japanese-Style Management). Tokyo: Chuo Keizaisha, 1977.

Urabe, T. *Nihonteki keiei o kangaeru* (Thoughts on Japanese-Style Management). Tokyo: Chuo Kiezaisha, 1978.

PART II

FAMILY AND SOCIETY

The essays in this section lay to rest the idea that Japanese women can be best understood within the framework of a simplistic stereotype—that they are an oppressed group, without status, dignity, power, or personal options. They reveal the forms of respect which the Japanese confer upon women, childrearing, and the educational role of mothers. They illuminate the complexities of women's roles within the family, not as Westerners wish they were among all women, but as Japanese women understand and live them. Finally, they invite the reader to contemplate the ways in which Japanese women define liberation—within the domestic roles which they cherish and sometimes resent simultaneously.

INTRODUCTION

Families as Mirrors of Society

ANNE E. IMAMURA

An understanding of the family is one of the best ways to move beyond stereotypes in any society. Within a family, masks are difficult to maintain and emotions difficult to hide. Basic socialization occurs and sacrifices are made. Indeed, the forms of commitment reflected in the family are among the strongest indicators of the values of a society. So too are the generation gaps—lags between the values that parents are trying to instill and those of the next generation. Because the family can reflect traditional values and newly evolving ones simultaneously, it is imperative that we explore the dynamics of the Japanese family.

The family in Japan has undergone change in the postwar period. The traditional Japanese family lived in an agrarian household in which one child, traditionally the eldest son, remained to become the family head, responsible for the wellbeing of all members. The other children left. The bride of the successor came into the household as a "borrowed womb" to produce heirs, participate in the economics of the household unit, and care for the elderly generation. This "junior wife" retained the status of bride and, therefore, lowest household member until such time as her mother-in-law died or retired. Household ceremonies, for example the handing of the soup or rice ladle across generations, signaled the transformation into *shufu* (housewife) status.

In the 1960s the "salaryman family" emerged and along with it new freedoms for husbands and wives. Unlike their predecessors on family farms and businesses, salaryman families were no longer economically tied to the neighborhood, nor so deeply embedded in sticky interpersonal relationships based on *on* and *giri*. The worlds of men and women became separated. The husband spent most of his day in the work world and developed few relationships with neighbors or with parents of children's schoolmates. The wife was not likely to know her husband's work colleagues. At the same time, the couple was less likely to be living with their in-laws. Thus, the wife was in charge of the family, responsible for the running of the home and for the education of the children.

Unlike the wife in the traditional family for whom marriage meant subjugation and conformance to the training provided by her mother-in-law, marriage for the wife in the new family conferred housewife status and responsibility. The education of her children became a major focus since she no longer had the family business to tend and had fewer children and a smaller house to keep than did her rural sisters. This salaryman family transformed the quality of interdependence between husband and wife, emphasizing new spheres of responsibility and independence.

The image of the full-time housewife soon became that of the *kyōiku mama* (education mama). Becoming a partner in her children's efforts to achieve, the education mama concentrated on getting them through the difficult examination system. The emergence of the education mama coincided neatly with the democratization of educational opportunities and the expansion of a Japanese economy offering good futures to those who entered the best universities.

In the 1970s, yet another new family form appeared on the scene, reflecting, supposedly, the Japanese image of the American couple. The new family married for love. The husband was supposed to be home-centered, helping with child care and preferring to spend his free time and weekends with wife and children. In the early stages of new-family marriages—during honeymoons and when children were young—the couple more than likely wore matching clothes and dressed their children in adult look-alikes. This image of family "togetherness" became very popular in the media but soon dissolved as the couple entered their thirties and the husband became involved in the demands of an upwardly mobile career while the wife was drawn into child care and education. Repeating the pattern of the salaryman family, husbands and wives moved into separate spheres.

Even though no major change occurred in the structure of salaryman family life in the seventies, there were some significant minor changes. First, it was no longer unthinkable for a father to participate in child care. Second, the demand for family leisure facilities spawned a new industry. Family-oriented restaurants, hotels, and amusement parks developed to meet the new demand. While this was going on, women's roles were also changing.

It is easy to assume that the home is the last bastion of change and that women's roles as preservers of culture necessarily predispose them to be conservative. In particular, the commonly held Western image of Japanese women overemphasizes the conservative and is far too likely to err on the side of women's subordination to men than it is to recognize the major changes that are taking place in women's roles. On the other hand, portraying the role of Japanese women as becoming more Western does not do justice to the desire to preserve much of what Japanese women value in their lives.

One of the notable phenomena of the 1970s was the emergence of a variety of women's groups and opportunities for adult education. At the same time, women's participation in civic action groups (especially in leadership positions) received a great deal of media attention. But, to the disappointment of Western feminists, a strong women's movement did not develop.

In the article included below, "New Lifestyles for Housewives," the author discusses some of the changes in the housewife role, illustrating how it evolved and broadened from a single model rooted within the home to a multiplicity of models in which the home was a more flexible locus. The variety of roles that developed in the 1970s reflected changes in women's education and the demands of motherhood. In order to educate children and to fulfill domestic commitments, women became involved in a wide range of activities which balanced commitments inside and outside the household. The content of the housewife role was changing, but the basic values of housewives were not. Japanese women continued to consider the housewife/mother role as very important and were, for the most part, content with their lot—not only because they placed a high value on mothering but also because the long working hours of their husbands did not appeal to them; nor did mothers believe that careers and family responsibilities were easily interchangeable.

In particular, women argued that their presence at home provided the emotional security that their children needed to develop emotionally and to help them get through the demanding examination system. As Simons, in her article on the education mama, points out, mother's help may be limited to psychological support and making attractive and nutritious lunches. But the symbolic significance of this assistance should not be underestimated. While the child is studying, mother is close by rather than off doing things that interest her. Indeed, living up to the model of mother as all-sacrificing constitutes a primary motivation for success in contemporary Japanese society.

The image of the Japanese woman depicted thus far is that of one who spends most of her adult life concentrating on home and children.

However, the majority of Japanese women have always been engaged in economically productive activity. Until recently, that meant participation in the family farm and/or business.

During the postwar period, women's participation in the labor force can be graphed as an M-shaped curve with the highest peak in the women's early twenties and a second peak after children are in school. In the 1980s the midpoint of the M-curve did not drop below 50 percent, the majority of Japanese women over the age of fourteen were in the labor force, and the drop-off came after the age of sixty. These figures show only part of the picture. Many women in the labor force today (one-third of them) engage in part-time or temporary occupations; yet, year by year, women's average length of labor-force participation grows. Younger, more highly educated women indicate that they hope to continue working until retirement, and the range of opportunities for women continues to grow.

Equal employment legislation has been in effect since 1986, but it is too early yet to see how it will affect the majority of women. For a variety of reasons, including the difficulty of combining careers with family, the majority of college-graduate women who seek positions with major companies still choose traditional women's (office lady) positions. The few who choose to pursue careers in the traditional male track commonly experience difficulty with both male and female colleagues and subordinates.

On the positive side, individual companies are making efforts to retain highly qualified women by offering flex time, increased maternity and child- care leave, and assistance in finding child care. The government also offers economic incentives to companies which reemploy women who left their employ to rear children (not those who leave to care for the aged or to accompany their husbands on job transfers).

One thing appears certain. For a variety of socioeconomic reasons, Japanese women will continue to work outside the home. The cost of educating their children and maintaining a home makes women's earnings an essential part of the average family's income. As women's skills change to meet the demands of the labor market, a variety of new options will develop.

It is important to locate the family in the context of the changing Japanese economy and to place that economy in the context of international economic affairs. The growing economies of Southeast Asian countries will affect Japan and the types of jobs available for Japanese men and women. At present, the service sector is the leading employer of female part-time workers, and computer-related skills and word processing are in demand.

The changing demographic structure of Japanese society, like the changing labor market, is important for women. As the society ages and parents live longer, the prospect of caring for mothers-and fathers-in-law limits the ability of many Japanese women to participate in the labor force. At the same time, women have more time to develop interests of their own and to engage in paid work. Caught in conflicting desires and obligations—to care for aging parents and to be gainfully employed—Japanese women are, like women in other modern cultures, engaged in a search for meaning.

In sum, the family provides a very important nucleus of stability and nurturance in Japanese society. The divorce rate is approximately one-fourth that of the United States, and the importance of motherhood is recognized both informally and institutionally through mandated maternity leave and reemployment incentives. The importance of the mother-school partnership is also recognized, and as it becomes increasingly more difficult to enter a good university without additional preparation in cram school (*juku*) or through tutoring, the mother's role as supporter, selector of appropriate school and/or tutor, and provider of financial wherewithal for the tutoring becomes increasingly important.

Throughout Japanese society motivation based on individual self-interest is consistently denigrated. As the Japanese see it, motivation should reflect a desire to fulfill social roles and enhance group life. Just as husbands are depicted as working hard for the family and the company, wives' motivations should ideally reflect increased benefit to the family. To the extent that wives are perceived as engaging in activities for purely personal motives, they are described as selfish. The challenge of the nineties will be for women to continue on the path of expanded opportunities, balancing the care of an increasingly aged population and the education of the next generation in an economy that will see increasing competition from developing nations and will have a shrinking domestic labor force on which to depend.

It is likely that women will continue to sustain traditional Japanese values while preparing their children and adjusting themselves to new economic realities. As Hitoshi Fukue's article, "The Persistence of *Ie* in the Light of Japan's Modernization," suggests, the values of the family and the needs of the economy have, to date, been utterly resonant.

In the article below, Anne E. Imamura points out that the traditional housewife role is only one of the lifestyle options available to Japanese women. In the 1970s, reflecting broad changes in Japanese society, Japanese housewives moved outside the home in a variety of ways. Imamura discusses five lifestyle patterns she observed during fieldwork in the late 1970s.

New Lifestyles for Housewives

ANNE E. IMAMURA

C ommunity centers, culture centers, schooling, volunteer work, child-related groups—the list is endless. In many ways the urban Japanese housewife is becoming involved in activities outside her immediate family. Whether this is good, bad, or indifferent is a question being debated by the media, housewives, and the wider community.

Often it is suggested that such activity indicates the housewife's desire to be liberated from her housewife role. My research, however, indicates that this is not the motivation of the majority of housewives engaged in such activities. Rather, I would like to suggest that it is the status of being a housewife itself that motivates women to participate.

The Japanese housewife is also often compared to her American counterpart. This is a difficult and dubious comparison to make at this point in history since the number of full-time housewives is dwindling rapidly in the United States and because both the lifestyle and state of mind of American women has changed so radically in the last twenty or thirty years. The comparison here is actually between contemporary Japanese housewives and American housewives as they were more likely to be in the early- or mid-twentieth century. Keeping that in mind, the comparison can nevertheless throw useful light on the evolution of the Japanese housewife. I would like to suggest that the motivation of the full-time American housewife and the full-time Japanese housewife is the same: caring for her family and home and helping her husband succeed in his job. Different, however, are the activities in which the housewife engages in order to reach the goal toward which she is motivated. In this article, I will examine the role of the housewife, her life cycle, and the style of life she lives. The focus will be on the Japanese urban housewife, but an attempt will be made to compare her to her American counterpart and to consider the role of social structure in creating different patterns of activity out of similar motivations.

The Role of the Housewife

The definition of a housewife as a woman responsible for running her home, whether she performs the tasks herself or hires people to do them, is generally accepted by sociologists. This sense of responsibility for the home is expressed in Japanese society by the term used for housewife, *shufu*. There has been traditionally only one shufu to a Japanese household, and the bride had to wait until her mother-in-law died or retired from family affairs to attain shufu status. In nuclear families today most women become a shufu when they marry and become responsible for the success and care of the household. If a shufu appears to be overly involved in activities outside the home, she will most likely be warned by her neighbors or friends that she should cut back on her activities lest something happen to the home and children in her care. Housewives call this obligation "keeping the house running perfectly," and they indicate that any other activity in which the housewife may engage has to come after this primary obligation is fulfilled. Furthermore, women interviewed who were involved in volunteer activity or outside work (but particularly the former) indicated that someone, either a friend or an older woman in the neighborhood, had at some point talked to them about the importance of always keeping the home running perfectly before they engaged in too much outside activity.

An active housewife tended to arrange to do the housework early in the morning or late at night in order to manage her outside activities. There was no difference in the number of household chores done by the children of active women and women who primarily stayed at home, but a major factor was how much the husband was at home. Women whose husbands were seldom present had more freedom in terms of time and could do the housework in the evening after the children were in bed, using the daytime hours for other activities.

What about the role of the husband? Japanese housewives I interviewed defined the role of the husband as, first of all, the primary financial support of the home. His work, therefore, was to be given primary consideration in determining such things as residence, the family activity schedule, and the times during which the wife was free to be absent from home.

In addition, in the case of the male salaried employee, his work required long days and evenings away from home so that he returned only late at night, often after his children were in bed. This behavior was accepted by the housewife as necessary for her husband's success in his job. Also, the amount of time and energy that a man must invest in his work was given as a reason for the housewife's responsibility to see that her husband was not bothered by the problems of home management. In order for him to succeed in his work, then, the housewife needed to concentrate most of her energies within the home and keep it running smoothly.

In spite of all this, the women I interviewed were active outside the home. When asked about their feelings toward the statement "Men work outside, and women take care of the home," many replied that nowadays women were indeed active outside the home, citing themselves as examples.

The role of housewife is not static. Changes occur as she moves along her life cycle; changes also occur in her lifestyle that result in her dropping some roles and acquiring others. Although the general life cycle of the Japanese housewife is the same as that of her American counterpart, there are some distinctive characteristics. One striking difference is their relationship with their husbands over the span of their lives. The functioning of the couple as a unit is important throughout the life of an American housewife married to a white-collar employee or professional man. It is important not only because common friendships develop but also because the involvement of a wife in her husband's professional career is often necessary. The Japanese wife and husband will, over time, develop separate friendships, and she will not participate in the social aspects of her husband's career.

Partly as a result of these differences and the greater emphasis placed on mother-child ties in Japanese society, the Japanese woman moves quickly through what might be called the "becoming a housewife" stage of marriage, in which she tends to have her most important friendships with former work and school associates and is most likely to be involved in her husband's social life. During a second "shrinking circle" stage, she is almost entirely wrapped up in child care and may not have any friends at all except old ones whom she seldom sees. She then emerges into what is sometimes called the "full-house plateau" when she begins to make friends again, especially through association with other parents at her children's schools and through an increase in activity outside the home. She may become active in the PTA or serve as a community representative to a local children's group. If she lives in a *danchi* (subsidized housing for middle-income persons) or in company housing, which are both self-governing, she will probably become involved in governing activities.

Beyond this is the stage in which the wife takes even more decisive steps outside the home. But regardless of the type of activity, the interviewees explained them in terms relating to the housewife role. Women with part-time jobs said they really wanted to take arts and crafts classes but that the money was needed to buy a home or educate the children. Women taking classes in tea ceremony or flower arranging declared that these would make them better wives and the home more cheerful. Those involved in adult education argued that this would help them better understand their growing children. Another motivation for activity outside the home during this period of the life cycle is the need to have a network of friends in order to obtain information related to the growth and development of children.

These activities, however, must fit within the parameters of the housewife's role (readily interrupted by children's school entrance examinations or the husband's work transfers) and be flexible enough for the woman to participate in all child-related activities and to keep house perfectly. Outside activities should be scheduled only in the time the family is away, should preferably take place close to home, and should not strain the household budget.

Later, in another shrinking-circle stage, both American and Japanese housewives face the return of their husbands to the home after retirement. In the Japanese case, however, the retirement age is early, usually around fifty-five, and the husband who has gone his own way for so many years may have little in common with his wife. This contrasts, as we have noted, with American couples, who have made common friends over their lifetime. The Japanese housewife may have to deal with the uprooting of her household because of the need to evacuate company housing or because they decide to purchase a condominium or house with retirement pay. This can take her away from her old friends and make it difficult for her to make new ones. Even if she does not move, her husband is often home in the evening, spends his days around the house, and commonly requires the kind of attention that makes it difficult for her to carry on the social life she had before.

Today in Japan, activity outside the home starts earlier than formerly as more and more children attend kindergarten or other classes, such as drawing and origami. Through their children's activities, mothers may make their move outside the home quite early. Ferrying children back and forth to kindergarten daily was cited by the majority of interviewees as an opportunity for forming new friendships. There are also study groups at city facilities offering limited child-care services for preschool children while their mothers study.

One aspect of this pattern is quite different from that of the American housewife, who gradually becomes free from child-related responsibilities. The Japanese housewife gains some freedom when her children are in elementary and junior high school, only to be tied down again when the children are taking examinations for high school and then for college. Her husband's retirement ties her down for a fourth time.

Obligations to husband and children are not the only constraints on the involvement of housewives in community activities. Housing is important as well. Women who live in company housing, their own homes, or condominiums, that is, permanent housing, are more likely to engage in outside activities than those living in apartments or danchi. Involvement in outside activities depends on a housewife's need to distance herself from her immediate neighbors and to gather information about her community, and on her desire to make friends and to avoid conflict within her housing unit. Women in company housing, for example, seek friends outside the housing complexes and thereby avoid sticky relationships with neighbors, remain less conspicuous, and, since they move often, make friends more quickly, especially through their children's school connections (see below).

Women living in houses and condominiums, whether they are older or younger, have no need to work merely for money, are well educated, have free time, and value neighborhood relations. The younger ones become involved in child-related activities like the "home library" movement, the older in volunteer work. No matter which stage of life they are in, activities for these women serve a variety of functions: a means of making new friends, carrying out their role as housewives, and preserving long-term friendships. Women living in danchi avoid involvement with neighbors and make friends through their children's kindergarten connections. Some attend religious meetings. They depend on outside activities to acquire information about the community and forge friendships. Of those interviewed, women living in rented apartments were the least involved in the larger community, only participating when required in PTA. With the exception of two shopkeepers, none expected to remain and none expressed interest in outside activities.

Operating within the constraints of family obligation, the housing situation, and economic transformation, the contemporary urban housewife has developed a variety of lifestyles. With a larger range of choices than her counterpart on traditional farms and in family businesses, she may choose from a variety of models of community participation, each of which represents ways of reconciling jobs and/or community activities with the socially acceptable housewife role. Five common patterns of extradomestic involvement were characteristic of the group (excluding the one woman who had to work to earn needed cash).

Homebody

Mariko is thirty-five, lives in her own house, and has two children, ages eleven and four. Her husband is forty, university educated, and a salaried employee involved in sales. Mariko has no intention of working outside the home or of becoming involved in any classes or friendships that, in her view, would diminish her effectiveness as a "perfect house-keeper." She feels that she should commit most of her time and energy to children and home—a feeling that originated from observing her mother, a full-time teacher, who in spite of the fact that her father shared the work around the house, never really had a free moment to relax. In particular, she notes that her mother was particularly beset when her own children fell ill, having to choose between all the children waiting at school and her own family. For this reason, Mariko did not go on to college. Furthermore, her husband opposes her working outside the home, and he does nothing to help her with housework.

Mariko was content to stay at home until her second child was about two. At that time, she began to realize that her life was repetitious and static. She also anticipated the day when her youngest child would go to school and she would be alone all day long. These thoughts led her to look for some way to broaden her horizons while still not taking more than a few hours' time away from her home a week. She enrolled in a cooking course and in a municipal course on the position of women. She likes the cooking course but finds the course on women's status a bit too radical—interesting to listen to but not for her.

Mariko's lifestyle reflects that of women who seek no commitments that interfere with their primary one to the home. Women like her regard jobs, even part-time ones, as in conflict with domestic duties, reducing their time and energy for home affairs. They seek their husband's permission and advice even to pursue hobbies. They interpret the role of house-wife quite literally to mean that one should be at home to look after the household. Quantity as well as quality of time are equally important. They are completely dependent on their husbands for their present and future welfare.

Long-Range Planner

Noriko is twenty-nine and has two children, one in kindergarten and one in elementary school. She has been married nine years and her husband, a university graduate, is a white-collar employee. She is a high school graduate who, while working, went to night school to study typing and accounting and had expected to continue working after the birth of her first child, putting the child in a public day-care center.

However, she says, she took one look at the baby, decided she could not leave him, and quit her job. After he was a year old, she started taking flower-arranging lessons. She now continues the lessons and teaches flower arrangement.

When her second child was born, Noriko became interested in kimonos and now works for a kimono dealer, advising and selling, when there is a sale or exhibition. When she does this, she either leaves her children with her husband or pays a neighbor to watch them. She also studies at one of the city-sponsored classes for women and does volunteer babysitting in the nursery for mothers taking such classes. In addition, she works part-time as a housekeeper for an American woman who lives nearby. Her long-range plan, however, is to work full-time, either in a department store or for a kimono store, after her children are older. She chose kimono sales as a career because this is an area in which the older the salesperson is, the more her opinion is respected.

In general, she feels that the position of women in Japan is improving, but it is still hard for divorced and unwed mothers to get along. She disapproves of full-time work for women because it overburdens them. Rather, she believes that society could make good use of women's talents if permanent part-time work were made available during the hours that children are in school.

Community Activist

Sumiko is fifty-eight, has two grown children, and for the past twenty-nine years or so has been active in her local regional women's group. This has involved her in consumer-related activities, such as arranging the sales of fresh produce and recycling used clothing, attending yearly seminars on such subjects as the Japanese social security system, participating in the yearly bus trip for resident women, and an annual year-end program of instruction in New Year cooking and flower arranging. She has also been involved in projects to raise funds for some of these activities. She admits that this, plus PTA and involvement in the citywide group consisting of representatives from local women's groups, has kept her busy.

Sumiko is convinced of the importance of her activity outside the home for two reasons. The first is that she feels it is important to be of service to the community. However, the time and energy spent on such service must not conflict with one's duty at home. For example, she never attends any function that occurs in the evening. She does not feel it is right for her husband to eat alone. For the same reason, if an overnight trip were ever scheduled by her women's group, she would not go. She said that she made these conditions explicit to the group and that if they expected her to be involved in an evening activity, she would have no recourse but to resign. She also said that the extent of her activity was not known to her husband; he never asked what she did all day, and as long as the house was running smoothly, she saw no need to tell him. Her second reason for getting involved is that she feels it is a bad thing for a woman to have too much free time. Sitting around doing nothing only leads to complaints, which make the home unhappy.

This woman's community work, like that of several others, takes her out of the home but not too far away. Women like Sumiko make use of the absence of their husbands to complete housework, to study, and to take part in other activities without inconveniencing their husbands or interfering with their primary role as housewives. However, they tend to adopt, as some put it, a "quality of time spent" approach and become efficient at completing housework in as short a time as possible.

Self-Improver

Hisako is thirty-nine years old and has two children, ages twelve and nine. Her husband is forty-three, a blue-collar worker with a high school education. Hisako is actively involved in her local community center administration, has a part-time job at a supermarket, and is a PTA officer. She is also involved in a group studying mathematics and, as a spin-off from the PTA, is in the regional group that plans children's vacation activities, such as radio calisthenics, and that works for such goals as eliminating vending machines selling pornographic magazines. She is very busy and is out of the house most of the time. She deals with housework by rising early and getting everything done before nine o'clock. Her husband is cooperative in the sense that he does not object if she goes out to meetings or to work when he is home. They very seldom can arrange their schedules to do things as a family, which gives her a great deal of freedom.

Hisako is quite frank about her desire to be active in all her various involvements. Unlike most women, who say they are only taking an office because it is their turn, she is eager for the experience and will continue at the community center as long as she is asked to stay on the committee. She is motivated by a desire to learn. She also wishes to keep up with her children in mathematics—that is why she is studying it—so that she can help them with their homework.

This woman is representative of the housewives who use the spare time they can find or create for personal study or betterment. They incur only those obligations that are manageable within the framework of being a housewife and do not allow any conflict or competition between the two roles. They expect no lessening of their duties as housewife and see extra domestic activities as opportunities to make up for missing premarital experiences.

Purpose Seeker

Masako is forty-seven and has two children, one of whom is away at college. She is a high school graduate, and her husband is a fifty-two-year-old university graduate who is employed as a government engineer. She teaches cooking at home four to six times a month, sometimes helps a maker of Japanese confections when a spare hand is needed, and studies leather tooling as a hobby. She would like to study more things but says a housewife does not have much money to spend on lessons. Over the years she has always studied cooking or something else—driving lessons for a driver's license, various crafts, and so on. For the past several years she has worked part-time at a department store in midtown Tokyo.

Masako uses the money she earns on herself, often going on trips with friends. She is very concerned with the importance of having friends as one gets older and tries to involve other older women in her cooking classes and activities. She does not like to stay home and is looking for opportunities to get out. In her experience, younger women are content with child raising and concentrating on their own families, but when they reach her age, women have to face the question of what they are going to do with their lives.

She and her friends are annoyed with a society that offers no employment for older women. She suggests that working at wedding halls and advising young people on appropriate gifts or kimonos are jobs much more suited to the older, experienced woman than to the young woman. Her friends would all like to have their own money for their old age, but there is no way to earn it. Hence, they cultivate hobbies, seeking purpose and identity through this means. Masako wants to teach more and says that hobbies alone are not fulfilling. She believes that there should be a way, after child rearing, to develop talents, serve society, and work. However, she also thinks that men are superior to women in every field and that women have their own work—taking care of children.

Similar Motivations, Different Activities

I suggested earlier that Japanese and American full-time housewives have essentially the same motivation: to maintain a happy home and to work for the success of their husbands and children. However, they realize these goals differently. The difference in behavior patterns must be explored in the light of historical and social differences in the two societies.

Japanese women are becoming more and more involved outside their homes, but they are doing so in a way that suits the Japanese social system. Housewives in both the United States and Japan will continue to pursue somewhat different paths to attain the same goals.

This excerpt is taken from Anne E. Imamura, "New Lifestyles for Housewives," *Japan Echo* 7, special issue (1980).

Regardless of whether she is urban or rural, managing her children's education is one of a mother's most important responsibilities. (Indeed, it may well be the most important responsibility.) In this article, Carol Simons vividly illustrates the importance of this role and the worry that underlies the choice of whether or not to give children extracurricular training. Although fewer than 2 percent of the mothers choose extracurricular training for their preschool children and a maximum of 40 percent for their junior and senior high school youth, the involvement of mothers in the education of their children is nonetheless fundamental.

The Education Mother
(*Kyōiku Mama*)

CAROL SIMONS

Two-year-old Hiromasa Itoh doesn't know it yet, but he's preparing for one of the most important milestones of his life, the examination for entry into first grade. Already he has learned to march correctly around the classroom in time with the piano and follow the green tape stuck to the floor—ignoring the red, blue, and yellow tapes that lead in different directions. With the other fourteen children in his class at a central Tokyo nursery school, he obeys the "cleaning-up music" and sings the good-bye song. His mother, observing through a one-way glass window, says that it's all in preparation for an entrance examination in two or three years, when Hiromasa will try for admission to one of Tokyo's prestigious private schools.

Forty-five minutes south of the capital city by train, in the small suburb of Myorenji, near Yokohama, thirteen-year-old Naoko Masuo returns from school, slips quietly into her family's two-story house, and settles into her homework. She is wearing a plaid skirt and blue blazer, the uniform of the Sho-ei Girls School, where she is a seventh grader. "I made it," her smile seems to say. For three years, when she was in fourth through sixth grades in public school, Naoko's schedule was high-pressure: she would rush home from school, study for a short time, and then leave again to attend juku or cram school, three hours a day three times a week. Her goal was to enter a good private school, and the exam would be tough.

Her brother, Toshihiro, passed a similar exam with flying colors several years ago and entered one of the elite national schools in Tokyo. The summer before the exam, he went to juku eight hours a day. Now, as a high school graduate, he is attending prep school, preparing for university entrance exams that he will take in March.

Little Hiromasa, Naoko, and Toshihiro are all on the Japanese road to success. And alongside them, in what must surely be one of the world's greatest traffic jams, are thousands of the nation's children, each one trying to pass exams, enter good schools, and attain the prize jobs that mark the end of a race well run.

But such children are by no means independent. They are guided and coached, trained and fed every step of the way by their mothers, who have had sharp eyes on the finish line right from the start.

No one doubts that behind every Japanese student who scores high on examinations—and they are among the highest scoring in the world—there stands a mother who is supportive, aggressive, and completely involved in her child's education. She studies, she packs lunches, she waits for hours in lines to register her child for exams, and waits again in the hallways for hours while he takes them. She denies herself TV so her child can study in quiet, and she stirs noodles at 11:00 P.M. for the scholar's snack. She shuttles her youngsters from exercise class to rhythm class to calligraphy class to piano lessons. She makes sure they don't miss their swimming and martial arts instruction. Every day she helps with homework, hires tutors, and works part-time to pay for juku. Sometimes she enrolls in "mother's class" so she can help with the drills at home.

So accepted is this role that it has spawned its own label, *kyōiku mama* (education mother). This title is not worn openly. Many Japanese mothers are embarrassed or modest and simply say, "I do my best." But that best is a lot, because to Japanese women, motherhood is a profession, demanding and prestigious, with education of the child the number-one responsibility. Cutthroat competition in postwar Japan has made her job harder than ever. And while many critics tend to play down the idea of the perpetually pushy mother, there are those who say that a good proportion of the credit for Japan's economic miracle can be laid at her feet.

"Much of a mother's sense of personal accomplishment is tied to the educational achievements of her children, and she expends a great effort helping them," states *Japanese Education Today,* a major report, issued in January 1987, by the U.S. Department of Education. "In addition, there is considerable peer pressure on the mother. The community's perception of a woman's success as a mother depends in large part on how well her children do in school."

Naoko's and Toshihiro's mother, Mieko Masuo, fully feels the responsibility of the role of the education mother, although she would be the last to take credit for her children's accomplishments. This forty-six-year-old homemaker with a B.A. in psychology is a whiz at making her family tick. She's the last one to go to bed at night ("I wait until my son has finished his homework. Then I check the gas. My mother stayed up and my husband's mother, and it's the custom for me too.") At 6:00 A.M., she's the first one up in the morning. She prepares a traditional breakfast for the family, including miso soup, rice, egg, vegetable, and fish. At the same time, she cooks lunch for her husband and Naoko, which she packs in a lunch box, or o-bentō. She displays the o-bentō that Naoko will carry to school. In the pink plastic box, looking like a culinary jigsaw puzzle, are fried chicken, boiled eggs, rice, lotus roots, mint leaves, tomatoes, carrots, fruit salad, and chopsticks. No peanut butter and jelly sandwiches in brown bags for this family.

"Every morning, every week, every year, I cook rice and make o-bentō," Mrs. Masuo says with a laugh, winking at Naoko. "I wouldn't want to give her a tenuki o-bentō." Everyone knows that a "sloppy lunch box" indicates an uncaring mother.

But Mrs. Masuo doesn't live in the kitchen. She never misses a school mother's meeting. She knows all the teachers well, has researched their backgrounds and how successful their previous students have been in passing exams. She has carefully chosen her children's schools and juku and has spent hours accompanying them to classes. "It's a pity our children have to study so much," she apologizes, "but it's necessary." She says that someday she'd like to get a part-time job—perhaps when exams are over. "But at the moment I must help my children. So I provide psychological help and o-bentō help." Then she laughs.

Toshihiro says that it was his mother who drilled him in elementary school and instilled in him his good work habits. And he says it was she who forced him to go to juku from fifth grade on, even though he hated it and missed being able to play after school. And it was she who made sure the money was set aside to pay for his many lessons—up to $12,000 for two years before he took the junior high exam. Mrs. Masuo explains that her husband, who works for an oil company, didn't feel juku was necessary because he didn't go when he was young. But, like most Japanese husbands, he works late and doesn't get involved in the children's activities. "So what happened was that Toshihiro just started to go, and only afterward was the subject raised. Naoko, being the second, was no problem."

Some evenings she went with Naoko to juku. Mother and daughter walked the fifteen minutes down the hill to the train station and took the Tokyo line four stops to Yokohama, then walked past the brightly lit shops and kiosks and along the glittering lanes that make so many of Japan's shopping streets look like Coney Island. They passed sake shops and bakeries, Kentucky Fried Chicken, and a clanging pachinko parlor and turned in at the modern high-rise, where the juku occupies two floors.

Naoko studies Japanese, math, and science. In one room, the juku teacher is rapidly explaining algebra problems to fifty fifth-graders. He lectures; they listen. In a science class down the hall, a young teacher is explaining photosynthesis and pretends to be a drooping plant. Seated at long tables, the children listen attentively, occasionally giggling at his antics. It is almost 8:30 P.M. and many of them haven't been home since breakfast.

"Yes, it's difficult," says Masato Nichido, assistant director of the juku. "But most of these children like juku better than public school. These children want to study more. And whether they want to or not is beside the point. They must in order to pass exams."

It is this prospect of exams, known in Japan as "examination hell," that has prompted Yukiko Itoh to expose little Hiromasa to early training in the hope that he will get into a prestigious private school. Just over 10 percent of Tokyo's children attend private schools, some of which run from first grade through high school and even through university. Assuming there are no major mishaps, a child who enters one of these schools can pass the rest of his academic career without the fierce examinations children such as the Masuos must face.

Like most Japanese mothers, Mrs. Itoh spends most of her time with Hiromasa and her six-month-old daughter, Emi. Baby-sitters and play groups are not part of her life. She has dinner with the children well before her husband comes home from work. She takes them to the park, to swimming lessons and music, much of the time carrying her baby in a pack on her back. Indeed, a young mother with an infant in a sling and a toddler by the hand, walking along a subway platform or a city street, is a sight that evokes the very essence of motherhood to most Japanese.

This physical tie between mother and child is only a small part of the strong social relationship that binds members of the family together in mutual dependency and obligation. It is the mother's job to foster this relationship. From the beginning, the child is rarely left alone, sleeps with the parents, is governed with affectionate permissiveness, and learns through low-key signals what is expected and what to expect in turn.

Many American children are also raised with affection and physical contact, but the idea is to create independent youngsters. Discipline begins early. Children have bedrooms separate from their parents. They spend time playing alone or staying with strangers and learn early that the individual is responsible for his or her own actions. An American mother, in disciplining, is more likely to scold or demand; a Japanese mother is apt to show displeasure with a mild rebuke, an approach that prompted one American six-year-old to tell his own mother, "If I had to be gotten mad at by someone, I wish it would be by a Japanese."

Even a casual observer is struck by the strong yet tender mother-child connection. A Japanese senior high school teacher said that many wives, including his own, sleep in a room with their children and not with their husbands. At a dinner party, a businessman made his wife's excuses: "I'm sorry she couldn't come tonight. My son has an exam tomorrow." Even if the excuse were not true, the use of it says a lot.

The relationship of dependency and obligation fostered in the child by the mother extends to family, school, company, and country and is the essence of Japanese society. The child is taught early that he must do well or people will laugh at him —and laugh at his mother as well. "Most Japanese mothers feel ashamed if their children do not do well at school," said one mother. "It is our responsibility to see that the child fulfills his responsibility." Bad behavior may bring shame, but good behavior has its own rewards. One woman described a friend by saying, "Her son studied very hard in order to get into a good high school and he got in. She is very clever."

This attitude is precisely what gives education mothers such as Mrs. Masuo and her o-bento philosophy such esteem and why they take such pride in their role, even if they don't admit it. Their goal is clear: success in entrance exams, a good school, a good college, and a good job. (For daughters the goal has a twist: good schools lead to good husbands.)

For the majority of students who go the public school route, test scores become key, and it is this fact that motivates many of the eleven- and twelve-year-olds traveling home from juku on evening trains. Many try out for the elite national junior high schools which, because of the demand, grant entrance on a combination of scores and a lottery. Three years later they test again, for placement in high schools, which, unlike the egalitarian lower grades, are organized according to ability. And three years after that, they test for college.

Overcoming the final obstacle isn't easy: only about half get into college on their first try. Many try again, attending prep schools and juku and memorizing facts for a year or two before taking the exams a second time. Such students are called *rōnin,* literally "masterless samurai," and are even referred to in government statistics by this term.

But exam hell doesn't stop with college. Companies and government ministries administer highly competitive tests to prospective employees, sometimes only to graduates of the prestigious universities—a system that increases the pressure even more.

This competition at all levels has generated the "juku boom," a $5-billion-a-year industry of prep schools for rōnin, cram schools, tutors, and special courses. Over the past ten years, the number of children attending juku has increased by half—more than 16 percent of the primary schoolchildren and 45 percent of junior high students. Attending juku can cost well over two hundred dollars a month.

Even the juku compete with each other—there are now 36,000 of them in Japan. One Tokyo juku administers practice exams to 20,000 youngsters on Sundays. Some of the more famous cram schools give their own admissions tests, prompting jokes about going to juku for juku. Can a student get into a prestigious high school or college with just the information learned in public school? "Highly unlikely," said one local public high school teacher. "The exams are very severe."

In the evenings and on Saturdays and Sundays, subway platforms are crowded with students of all ages. Dressed in casual clothes or sober midnight-blue school uniforms and lugging heavy, black leather book bags, they are traveling to the thousands of cram schools tucked into office buildings, down side lanes, and in every corner of every neighborhood.

Sometimes children are launched into the system when they are barely old enough to walk. Some of them start "school" when they are still in diapers, learning to obey such commands as how to clench and open their fists. "The future of a child here begins with conception," said one Tokyo mother. "Schools, after-school schools, calligraphy, piano, exercises—Japanese mothers don't waste any time." A documentary film on nursery schools by the Japan Broadcasting Company depicted a typical week for a five-year-old named Yasukata and his mother. Every morning he went to kindergarten. Three afternoons a week he attended "special strengthening class" (five hundred dollars a month), which included rhythm exercises, simple academics, and etiquette. His mother waited two and a half hours while he took the class. On another afternoon, she took him to athletics and on another to drawing. Such preparations, the mother said, would help her son "jump the puddles" ahead of him. By the program's end, Yasukata was one of 1,066 to "challenge" the prestigious Keio private school—which continues through university—and one of the 132 first-graders to gain entrance. On the same program, a mother of twin girls, both of whom had also been accepted to a famous private school, said, "It's as though I have received a long-distance ticket to life."

Hoping for the same ticket are many of the mothers sitting on the benches in the large gymnasium at a branch of the ponderously named Japan Athletic Club Institute for Education of Infants (JAC for short), the school that Hiromasa attends. They are watching an afternoon class of about fifty four-year-olds in their regulation red-and-blue shorts and T-shirts. The children have finished exercising and are beginning a "voice obedience" session. Abreast in a straight line, the group is told to "hop forward to the beat of the tambourine, jump in place to the tweet of the whistle." It sounds easy, but not everyone arrives at the finish line at the same time, indicating a slipup in obeying the tweets and beats. Some private primary schools might use such exercises in their entrance exams, so practice is considered essential.

Watching the mothers watch their children, JAC director, Naomi Ooka, says he is dismayed by the pressure of the exams on the mothers and their children. In his view, modern Japanese mothers and children spend too much time together. "It's not good," he says.

Today, more and more educators and parents are questioning the high-pressure system that gives rise to such popular sayings as "Sleep four hours, pass; sleep five hours, fail." Educationists speak of lost childhoods, kids never getting a chance to play, "eating facts" to pass exams, and the production of students who memorize answers but can't create ideas. They cite the cruelty of students who take pleasure when their classmates fail, the increasing delinquency, and the high incidence of bullying in the schools.

Not surprisingly, Japanese mothers have been among the major critics, perhaps because they bear much of the brunt and witness the effects of the pressure on their children. "My son kept getting headaches and then he didn't want to go to school," said one mother, "so I stopped the juku." Such mothers gained an ally in former Prime Minister Yasuhiro Nakasone, whose government had been seeking ways to depressurize the education system. Nevertheless, many doubt that such efforts will have any effect in a society dedicated to hard work and competition.

On a measuring stick, the competition has surely paid off. In math and science, Japanese children rank highest in the world. They do long division before American children, take more years of a foreign language (English), learn chemistry earlier, and are overflowing with factual knowledge about history, geography, scientific formulas, and other bits of information that to many Americans would seem encyclopedic.

And the accomplishments don't stop there. A stunning 94 percent of Japanese youth go to high school. Some 90 percent graduate (compared with 76 percent in the United States) and are well qualified to take their place in the work force. At the college level, the comparison shifts: only 29 percent of Japanese high school graduates go on to college (compared with 58 percent of American graduates). It is here, at the highest level, that Japanese education is considered inferior to that in the United States. Japanese college years are often referred to as a four-year vacation, although a well-earned one since the years through high school produce students who shine.

Among the Japanese who are beginning to fight the system are the increasing numbers who have lived abroad. Quite simply, they want their children to have more time to play; they want them to learn more and memorize less; they want them to be more creative and independent. Critics say that small families, small houses, and modern conveniences lead to children being babied by mothers who don't have enough to do and that mothers themselves are stifled at an age when women should have more freedom.

Chikako Ishii claims to know a better life. She spent several years in New York City with her family and is an outspoken opponent of the education mother and the highly competitive education system. "I don't think women like this role," she says, "but the competition is pushing them into it."

Mrs. Ishii teaches Parent Effectiveness Training, an approach to learning that emphasizes the individuality of the child. It's an idea long accepted in the West but anathema in group-oriented Japan, where one of the most repeated proverbs is "The nail that protrudes will be hammered down." Her two sons go to neighborhood schools. Masahiro, twelve, is in the sixth grade and Hideaki, fourteen, is in the eighth, where he is ranked number one in his class. They do not attend juku and do not have tutors. "So far they're both doing well," remarks their mother. "I am watching to see how they develop."

Like those around them, the Ishiis have high expectations for their children, but their wait-and-see approach is baffling to many. "She's brave," said one young mother. "It's fine, I suppose," allowed another, "but what if she fails?"

This article is taken from Carol Simons, "They Get By with a Lot of Help from Their *Kyōiku Mamas*," *Smithsonian Magazine* (March 1987).

In this piece, Hitoshi Fukue describes the stability of traditional family values in post-World War II Japan, suggesting that Japan's unparalleled economic transformation has been built on a foundation of stable cultural values and beliefs that have existed for hundreds of years—rank consciousness, group orientation, emphasis on harmony, and the distinction between inside and outside.

The Persistence of *Ie* in the Light of Japan's Modernization

HITOSHI FUKUE

The year 1945 marked a radical transformation in the history of Japan. Everything prior to it was considered feudalistic, undemocratic, and premodern. After the war the country quickly adapted itself to Western democratic forms of society in almost every sphere of life. Rapid economic growth and urbanization have changed the structure of the nation; however, the value systems and cultural characteristics which were present before 1945 are still intact in the Japanese consciousness and in the social structure.

This paper examines some of the major values and principles of the traditional *ie* system that still persist in modern Japanese society. First, I would like to clarify what is meant by *ie*. *Ie* has three meanings in the Japanese language: (1) a house as a building; (2) a home, a household, and a family; and (3) a lineal family system (Takeda 1976). The third meaning of *ie* was the most important in traditional Japanese society. *Ie* as a lineal family system transcended the idea of a family as a group of living individuals:

> *Ie* was conceived as including the house and property, the resources for carrying on the family occupation, and the graves in which the ancestors were buried, as a unity stretching from the distant past to the present occupying a certain position in the status system of the village or the town. The ie

in that sense was far more important than the individuals who were at any one time living members of it, and it was seen as natural that the individual personalities of family members should be ignored and sacrificed if necessary for the good of the whole (Fukutake 1982, 18).

The lineal family, which was traditionally a male-dominated, parent-child relationship, was kept unbroken by the basic principle that the eldest son (or daughter where there were no sons) brought his bride (or groom) into his (or her) home and the young couple settled down to live in the same household with parents and grandparents. Younger sons in each generation might split off to form their own new ie, each of which thereafter continued to perpetuate itself as a "branch family" or as an original "main family," in exactly the same lineal pattern (Fukutake 1982, 25).

In this kind of family system, it is not surprising that considerable power was attached to the head of the household, who carried on the line of descent. He usually took charge of the labor of family members in the family business. The income of the family business, be it from the farm, store, or workshop, all went into the head of the household's pocket. He in turn provided money for the other members of the household. It was natural that the status of the eldest son, destined to be the next head of the household, would also be high and that he would be treated differently from his younger brothers. By contrast, daughters were inessential to their families (Fukutake 1982, 28–30).

Seen from the perspective of social anthropology, Japanese family life presents distinctive characteristics in comparison with those of other societies. Chie Nakane, in her book *Japanese Society* (1970), compares three basic patterns in family life. In English family life the most important room in the house for each member of the family is one's own individual room. Privacy is valued, and one is expected to knock at the door to get permission to enter another's room. One's room is one's castle. In the English family we find a strong consciousness of autonomous individuality. The living room or dining room is a common gathering place for the family to eat, to talk and socialize, and perhaps to discuss personal ideas in a semipublic place. However, individuals always have a room where they can go to collect their thoughts in private.

In the Indian and Italian families, members also usually have rooms of their own and feel a corresponding sense of individuality. But the common rooms (living room/dining room) are perceived to be more important than the private rooms. Much time is spent in the common room, and each person, whether young child or elder, is on an equal footing in conversations. Doors to individuals' private rooms are usually open and anyone may enter without knocking. This type of family life is also relatively responsive to outsiders and tends to flow out into the street.

In the traditional Japanese pattern, each household is a distinctly isolated unit of its own, complete with walls and a high fence around the house to insure privacy. Yet inside, walls consist of sliding doors made of paper so that privacy is kept to a minimum. The family stays together most of the time and moves from one place to the next, depending on whether it is eating, relaxing, playing, or sleeping. As stated earlier, the head of the household usually has the greatest authority. The rest of the family has to be able to adapt to his needs; otherwise, it is not easy to live together under the same roof. Although this pattern tends to create family unity, it widens the gap between the family and outsiders.

This distinctive Japanese family life, which is based on a lineal system of primogeniture and is expressed in the structure of the house, manifests several basic values or characteristics of Japanese culture. These are rank consciousness, group orientation, emphasis on harmony, and distinction between *uchi* (inside) and *soto* (outside).

Rank Consciousness

Rank consciousness arose from the distinct hierarchical order in the traditional household. In the family, children were brought up to perceive clearly their rank in the family hierarchy. This rank consciousness was even extended to the village community, where the importance of each household was rated, usually according to the length of its existence in the community. Rank consciousness permeated traditional Japanese society and exists today in interpersonal relations and in business organizations.

Rank consciousness has a powerful effect on interpersonal relationships as well. A Japanese finds his world clearly divided into three categories: *sempai* (seniors), *kōhai* (juniors), and *dōryō* (colleagues) (Nakane 1970). By contrast, in India and the U.S., lines between these categories may be quite blurred. How one Japanese addresses another is, then, regulated by which category one falls into. For instance, in a male interpersonal relationship, one would have to address Mr. Suzuki as "Suzuki-san" if the latter is the former's senior; as "Suzuki-kun" if junior; and "Suzuki" if simply a colleague. Without knowing these distinctions, one would fail in Japanese interpersonal relationships. How one speaks and behaves is regulated by vertical relationships in Japan, which Nakane calls *tate shakai* (vertical society).

Evidently, the Japanese feel comfortable with and appreciate the stability in vertical human relationships. Once a person understands his place in the hierarchy, he will feel comfortable because he will always know how to speak and behave in the group. A freshman in college quickly learns to call sophomore students sempai and establish a smooth relationship on the basis of the vertical order. (A little confusion may arise when the freshman happens to be older than the sophomore because age is usually the primary factor in determining one's place in the vertical ladder.)

There is a distinct seniority system which characterizes almost every business organization. In spite of the postwar efforts by Americans to replace the seniority system in Japanese business with a merit system, Japanese companies remained adamantly wedded to the former. They knew that the merit system would cause nothing but conflict and confusion. For the Japanese, the stability produced by the seniority system is much more important than individual merit. This system has eliminated the fear of demotion or discharge from the minds of the employees, which creates deep company loyalty. On the other hand, even though the practice of consensus decision making allows for the input of junior employees, the seniority system gives older, sometimes incompetent people unmerited freedom and privileges, often at the expense of the younger and more competent. The seniority system has nevertheless maintained a firm hold on Japanese companies, even in the process of modernization.

Group Orientation

In the traditional ie system, the household itself was considered number one in importance, more so than the concerns of any individual. The family reputation had to be defended at any cost, and the family line, which stretched from the distant past to the present, had to be maintained. This group orientation, with its roots in the agrarian society of the past, is manifest in many other facets of the culture, including interpersonal and organizational relationships.

Historically, the predominance of group consciousness was reinforced by the topographical conditions of the rural community, which necessitated collective enterprise:

> The actual creation of the rice field and laying down of the irrigation system was the first prerequisite. The maintenance of the irrigation system was not something that could be done by an individual household; it inevitably required collective labor by the villagers as a whole group. . . . The communitarian element in agriculture extended itself to other spheres of life: to mutual assistance for weddings and funerals, t o cooperative work in house building and repair. . . . People interacted with each other on a basis of real intimacy. It was very important that all decisions concerning the matters of the village

should be taken by unanimous agreement. The tight yet solid character of the village community facilitated the typical building block of the Japanese social structure in both rural and urban areas (Fukutake 1982, 33–40).

This particular type of family and community agricultural life have for centuries produced a deep sense of the group, which is firmly implanted in the minds of modern Japanese despite the deterioration of traditional family life and changes in rural social and economic structures.

For this reason, where Americans in interpersonal relationships will emphasize their feelings of independence, Japanese will do the opposite. Individuality is subordinated by feelings of group consciousness. "Cooperativeness, reasonableness, and understanding of others are the virtues most admired, not personal drive, forcefulness, and individual self-assertion" (Reischauer 1977, 135). Therefore, Americans going to Japan are often frustrated by the euphemistic expressions of the Japanese while the Japanese coming to America often become melancholic because of the forceful, direct speech of Americans.

This emphasis on group loyalty is revealed not only in interpersonal relations but in the way the Japanese relate to their employers. For the contemporary Japanese, his company is the principal focal point of his life. "A job in Japan is not merely a contractual arrangement for pay, but a means of identification with a larger entity—in other words, a satisfying sense of being part of something big and significant" (Reischauer 1977, 131). A company is "my" or "our" company, the primary community to which one belongs and which is all-important in one's life. This is the reason why lifetime employment is normal in Japanese companies. New employees are received by the company as if they were newly born family members. The company provides employees with housing; hospital benefits; family recreation; gifts on the occasion of marriage, birth, and death; and even advice for the education of their children. The company expects employees to give high priority to its goals and interests. The result is that Japanese employees who devote their whole lives to a single company become deeply and emotionally involved with it.

The Japanese affinity for collective behavior may be seen in sightseeing groups made up of school classes, work associates, village organizations, women's societies, and the like. Japanese adherence to the group has been criticized both by Western observers and by the Japanese themselves. It is said that the Japanese lack individual autonomy and originality. It has also been pointed out, however, that this kind of group orientation has made an immeasurable contribution to the process of modernization in Japan by, among other things, helping to mobilize the collective power of the society swiftly and efficiently. Therefore, it would be hard to deny that the rapid modernization of Japan is tied to the collective structure of the traditional ie family system.

Emphasis on Harmony

The achievement of harmony and the emphasis on it in family life, where children are taught to value it highly, is an integral part of the traditional ie system. As early as the seventh century this value played an important role in the political, religious, and personal spheres of Japanese thought. Prince Shotoku affirmed it in the seventh-century document called the Seventeen-Article Constitution:

> Let us cease from wrath, and refrain from angry looks. Nor let us be resentful when others differ from us. For all men have hearts, and each heart has its own leanings. Their right is our wrong, and our right is their wrong. We are not unquestionably sages, nor are they unquestionably fools. Both of us are simply ordinary men. How can anyone lay down a rule by which to distinguish right from wrong? For we are all, one with another, wise and foolish, like a ring which has no end. Therefore, although others give way to anger, let us on the contrary dread our own faults, and though we alone may be in the right, let us follow the multitude and act like them.

In this moral instruction to the court officials and the public in general, the author of the Constitution placed more importance on a tolerant attitude toward people who held different views than on unflinching commitment to a cause. Maintaining harmonious personal relationships was far more important than proving whether one was right or wrong.

This principle of avoiding personal confrontation in order to maintain smooth personal relationships—however perfunctory adherence to it by many may have been—persisted throughout the long history of Japan. It may be seen, in marked contrast to the West, in the essentially harmonious coexistence of religions in Japan. Religious warfare and dogmatic dissension are virtually unknown. "No one," says Hajime Nakamura, "has yet taken up a noteworthy controversy between Confucianism and Buddhism, but instead, there are already many who advocate the unity of these religions" (1964, 393).

One could say that the Japanese distrust of ideologies which claim ultimate truth enabled them to mobilize modern workers to focus intensely on the goal of economic growth and prosperity. A cooperative and unifying spirit in human relationships, free from political or religious ideologies, undoubtedly contributes to the generation of dynamic economic activity. Japan's process of modernization, particularly since World War II, has utilized the basic principle of harmony in order to focus all its energy on economic growth.

One could also argue that this kind of cultural ethos has minimized the value of democratic criticism and debate which in Western countries are considered essential to maintain just social organizations. Nakane puts it thus:

> One can easily observe a conversation between a superior and an inferior which is either a one-sided sermon, or the "I agree completely" style of communication, which does not allow for t h e statement of opposite views: One would prefer to be silent rather than utter words such as "no" or "I disagree." Japanese fear that such negative statements might hurt the feelings of the superior and that sometimes it could involve the risk of being cast out from the group as an undesirable member (1972, 35).

Group orientation and emphasis on harmony are naturally linked in Japanese culture as are individualism and an emphasis on justice in Western culture.

Distinction of *Uchi* and *Soto*

A typical traditional Japanese home was, and still is in many areas, fenced around with high walls of thick bushes or stone which made the house less visible. The individuals of the household unit were closely bound to each other and they formed a tightly knit human nexus. The consciousness of the distinction between *uchi,* meaning "my family," and *soto,* meaning "outsiders," was sharpened by the strong unity of the lineal family system. Whether a person was a blood relative or not was often crucial in the formulation and development of interpersonal relationships. This distinction of *uchi* and *soto* has manifested itself in Japanese psychological exclusivism toward outsiders.

The distinction of uchi and soto easily generates an attitude of exclusivism in general. In a village community, for example, villagers often made a sharp distinction between "our village" and "other villages." Similar distinction was made between "our province" and "other provinces," "our country" and "foreign countries." Today, persons from other countries often lament that they are always called *gaijin* no matter how long they live in the country. The homogeneous construction of the nation and its geographical isolation have reinforced the consciousness of *Nihonjin* (Japanese) as distinct from foreigners with a far greater intensity than most other societies.

It is also due to uchi and soto that a Japanese family rarely adopts an orphan or a child with no blood relationship. It sounds remarkable and strange to the Japanese to hear how easily (or so it seems) American families adopt children, even foreign children, and bring them up as their own. But the uchi and soto distinction has provided much for the insiders. As long as one is inside a family or an organization, one can expect its full blessings and benefits. This exclusivism meets the emotional needs of the individual who seeks security within the group founded on the family ie principle. Japan's modernization has been carried out not by changing the ie principle but by utilizing it to ensure that the material as well as the psychological security of the insiders, whether as members of a family or some other organization, is preserved.

This article is excerpted from Hitoshi Fukue, "The Persistence of *Ie* in the Light of Japan's Modernization," in *Toward Multiculturalism: A Reader in Multicultural Education*, edited by Jaime S. Wurzel (Yarmouth, Maine: Intercultural Press, Inc., 1988), 123–31.

REFERENCES

Ben-Dasan, Isaiah. *The Japanese and the Jews*. New York and Tokyo: Weatherhill, 1972.

Benedict, Ruth. *The Chrysanthemum and the Sword*. Boston: Houghton Mifflin Co., 1946.

Doi, Takeo. *The Anatomy of Dependence: The Individual Versus Society*. New York and Tokyo: Kodansha International Ltd., 1974.

Fukutake, Tadashi. *The Japanese Social Structure*. Tokyo: University of Tokyo Press, 1982.

Lebra, Takie Sugiyama, and William P. Lebra, eds. *Japanese Culture and Behavior*. Honolulu: The University of Hawaii Press, 1986.

Nakamura, Hajime. *Ways of Thinking of Eastern Peoples: India-China-Tibet-Japan*. Honolulu: The University of Hawaii Press, 1964.

Nakane, Chie. *Japanese Society*. Berkeley: University of California Press, 1970.

———. *Tekiō no Jōken* (Conditions for Adaptation). Tokyo: Kodansha International Ltd., 1972.

Reischauer, Edwin O. *The Japanese*. Cambridge: The Belknap Press of Harvard University Press, 1977.

Suzuki, Takao. *Japanese and the Japanese: Words in Culture*. Tokyo: Kodansha International Ltd., 1978.

Takeda, Choshu. *Nihonjin no Ie to Shūkyō* (Japanese Ie and Religion). Tokyo: Hyoronsha, 1976.

PART III

EDUCATION
AND CULTURAL
TRANSMISSION

The Japanese educational process, like other Japanese habits of heart and mind, reflects Japanese beliefs and values with uncommon clarity. The essays in this section seek to correct the image of these educational processes as unvaryingly military, autocratic, and deindividualized by calling attention to the exquisite sensitivity of many Japanese teachers to the motivation, needs, and learning styles of their students.

Culture and Schooling in Japan

BARBARA FINKELSTEIN

The Japanese, like Americans, invest their schools with enormous social and symbolic importance. In both societies, schools are viewed as instruments for achieving social harmony, fostering economic and social mobility, and providing civic nurture. They acquire tasks that are economic, social, political, moral, and instructional and are regarded as important agencies of cultural transmission and social control. They are both the keepers of tradition and harbingers of change.

Yet, despite the similarities, there are fundamental differences between the two educational systems arising out of equally fundamental differences in approach. From its beginnings in 1872, public education in Japan has been an instrument of national government, its curricula the product of central planning, its teachers the mediators of its content, and its students (with rare exceptions) the recipients of uniform cultural fare. In the U.S., on the other hand, public education has been controlled by state and local governments, its curricula varied, its teachers the interpreters as well as mediators of its content, and its students the recipients of diverse fare.

Equally, if not more, important are culture-based differences in the way Japanese and Americans define childhood, learning, teacher roles, and student-teacher relationships. Many Westerners have an image of Japanese education that fails to do justice to the delicacy and complexity with which the Japanese approach teaching and learning, especially in preschools and elementary schools. One such image, as Joseph J. Tobin puts it in an unpublished paper, "is that Japanese children go into preschool overindulged and undercontrolled and come out overcontrolled, unimaginative, and spiritless."

In a parallel image, Japanese elementary, junior, and senior high schools are seen as incubators of conformity, as military-like settings in which tyrannical teachers induce conformity by requiring students to wear identical dress, repeat the same slogans, learn the same facts, memorize the same textbooks, follow the same aesthetic forms, prepare for the same examinations, and otherwise learn to be like one another.

The articles offered in this section suggest that classroom practices in Japan are much more complex and subtle than these oversimplified images would lead one to believe. The role of teachers, the forms of classroom management, the quality of student-teacher relationships, the integration of moral, intellectual, and technical learning proceed from a cultural foundation which is at once more sophisticated, humane, and delicate and less militaristic than it is currently assumed to be in the popular press. The readings which follow reveal the cultural bases of educational processes at various stages of children's development from preschool to high school.

Contrary to prevailing stereotypes, the primary function of *hoikuen* (kindergarten) and *yōchien* (nursery or preschools) is not to break children's spirit or will but to help them acquire a more group-oriented, outward-facing sense of self than they received in the first three years of life.

The ideal Japanese child is not always or even usually controlled. "A well-balanced Japanese child should be able to move easily back and forth between control and emotionality," Tobin points out. In contemporary Japan, it is in the preschools that Japanese children first learn to do this.

As the first three articles appearing below suggest, the structure and pedagogy of preschools—large class sizes, a laid-back approach to misbehavior, a mixing of structure and chaos during the school day, the use of language, and even the ordering of space and time—according to Tobin, "contribute to the creation of an environment structured to help children learn to feel themselves, to be themselves, in frontdoor formal contexts as well as in interactions which are backdoor, informal, and spontaneous." In the first article in this section, Catherine Lewis suggests that teachers gradually evoke discipline and self-control by delegating authority to *tōban* or "monitors." Keeping a low profile themselves, Japanese nursery school teachers (1) organize activities which reward cooperation, (2) create groups through which the identity of each child is defined, realized, and rewarded, (3) provide ample opportunities for children to succeed, and (4) rarely assume that children misbehave intentionally. They seem to regard unfortunate behavior as a consequence of misunderstanding rather than an oppositional will.

Similarly, Lois Peak's article examines the processes by which Japanese preschool teachers transform indulged children into manageable, tractable, and efficient group members and prepare students to function without being pressured by a talkative, intrusive teacher. Taken together, the articles by Lewis and Peak suggest that the tapestry of Japanese school discipline and achievement are woven through the gentle thread of sensitive guidance in the early years.

In an interesting variation, the article by Joseph Tobin et al. on class size and student-teacher ratios suggests that large classes in Japanese preschools—like the quiet authority of teachers, the emphasis on group activity, and the commitment to practice, perfection, and form—are designed to reflect, reinforce, and advance Japanese culture as the Japanese want it to be.

Professor Singleton's piece focuses on the forms by which elementary and secondary school teachers reinforce a spirit of persistence, commitment, and group cohesion. *Gambare* is a rallying cry, a call for courage, an inducement to greater effort. It reflects a deep sense of conscientiousness and a reciprocal sense of responsibility toward the group. The spirit of gambaru evokes an exquisite and sometimes explosive spirit of intense commitment which suffuses home, school, and work cultures.

No matter what the setting, Japanese teachers are moral and aesthetic overseers responsible for habit formation as well as intellectual guidance. Contrary to prevailing stereotypes and despite the existence of schools like Tojo High as described by Nobuo Shimahara in his article in this section, teachers are not simply drillmasters. Rather, as Shimahara observes in an earlier work, Japanese teachers, unlike American teachers, assume fundamental responsibility for moral education and character development and manage classrooms in a manner that elevates and reinforces the importance of the group (Shimahara 1986).

The commitment to moral and aesthetic oversight exists in elementary, junior, and senior high schools where the curriculum is relatively uniform, the amount of memorization enormous, the concern with examinations often preeminent, and the intellectual overseer role obvious. As Professor Shimahara points out, the moral dimension of schooling is so basic that the Monbusho (Japanese Ministry of Education, Science, and Culture) defines habit formation as a fundamental teacher responsibility.

It should be a basic principle that moral education in the school be provided throughout all the educational activities of the school.... Proper instruction for moral development should be given not only in the hours for Moral Education, but also in the hours for each subject and special activities.... In carrying out moral education at school, due consideration should be given to establishing closer human relationships between teacher and students and among students themselves, and to guiding thoroughly the practice of moral codes ... in cooperation with the home and the local community concerned.

The conduct of classroom education is molded by the policy environments within which teachers and students teach and learn as well as by the spirit of gambaru. Professor Shimahara, in the article included here, provides a conceptual link between classroom and school practices and education policy in Japan.

The Japanese examination system, which he describes with striking clarity and insight, involves the teachers in the moral education called for by Monbusho. It sorts, labels, tracks and stimulates group affiliation and is reinforced by an array of teacher-driven activities which simultaneously bind group commitments and prepare students to compete for places in prestigious high schools and colleges.

REFERENCES

Shimahara, Nobuo. "The Cultural Basis of Student Achievement." *Comparative Education* 9, No. 1 (1986): 19–26.

In this article, Catherine Lewis makes use of cross-cultural communication theory in an effort to describe Japanese preschool practices. This excerpt does not do justice to the elegance of her wedding of theory and empirical analysis. It does, however, portray the transitional roles which preschool teachers play as well as the gentle nonmilitary qualities of Japanese preschool teaching.

Nursery Schools: The Transition from Home to School

CATHERINE LEWIS

Cultural traits as diverse as respect for nonverbal communication or the commitment to permanent employment have been attributed to Japanese child rearing. Yet, there is remarkably little literature in English on early socialization in Japan. This article provides observational data from fifteen Japanese nursery schools. It is not my intention here to draw generalizations about Japanese nursery schools or to demonstrate differences between Japanese and American schools. The substantial variability in nursery schools within each country makes such systematic comparison an ambitious undertaking. Rather, the behavioral and ethnopsychological data of the present paper are intended to identify potentially interesting areas for future research on nursery school socialization and to stimulate American thinking about two aspects of early education: school practices which influence the development of cooperative behavior in children and adult strategies for controlling children's behavior.

Nearly two-thirds of the five-year-olds in Japan attend preschool (*yōchien*). Researchers have studied the early Japanese parent-child relationship and the socialization of values by Japanese elementary and secondary schools (Caudill 1972; Caudill and Schooler 1973; Shand 1978; Cummings 1980). Studies seeking the roots of Japanese educational achievement have investigated the period between ages two and a half and six (Doi 1974), but social development during this period remains largely unstudied. This is a tantalizing gap. Accounts suggest that Japanese children must make a transition from the undisciplined, indulgent child rearing of the home to an elementary school classroom where forty to fifty children share one teacher and where subordination of personal needs to group goals is the dominant norm (Cummings 1980). For most Japanese children, nursery school is that transition. Nursery school generally commences at age three or four and continues until age six, when elementary school begins. Of the almost fifteen thousand nursery schools in Japan, approximately 60 percent are private, 40 percent public (city, ward, etc.), and fewer than 1 percent national (supported by the national government). Of the fifteen schools in the present study, six were private, seven public, and two national.

In this article, cooperation refers to an orientation to seek mutual benefit rather than individual benefit when the two conflict. Japan presents an interesting arena for studying socialization toward cooperation. In Japan, as in other highly industrialized countries, a large number of individuals compete on objective examinations for a limited number of educational and occupational opportunities (Vogel 1979). Yet, contemporary Japanese institutions often preserve traditional sanctions against face-to-face interpersonal competition (Nakane 1970). For example, Japanese workers' willingness to subordinate individual goals to group goals is frequently cited as a reason for the success of Japanese work groups (Cole 1979).

Until recently, psychologists widely accepted the view that firm control by parents (i.e., consistent enforcement of clear rules) promotes internalization of values by children (Baumrind 1973; Maccoby 1980; Lewis 1981). Accounts of Japanese child rearing challenge this American view of firm control. Japanese mothers apparently do not make explicit demands on their children and do not enforce rules when children resist; yet, diverse accounts suggest that Japanese children strongly internalize parental, group, and institutional values (Vogel 1979).

Method

Observations of fifteen Japanese nursery schools were conducted from May through July of 1979. At each school, one class of five-year-olds was observed for two days. During the first day, the author noted the materials and equipment in view at the school, the schedule of activities engaged in by the children, and any incidents related to control or cooperation. Initially, the major purpose of the first day's observation was simply to accustom children and teachers to the presence of a foreigner in the classroom. However, these unstructured observations and teachers' subsequent interpretations of what occurred proved remarkably interesting and are the primary data of this report. On the second day, the author conducted spot observations every twenty minutes, noting the locations and activities of all children and teachers. In addition, a ten-minute running account of teachers' behavior was dictated into a small hand-held tape recorder every twenty minutes. After observations on both days one and two, teachers were interviewed about specific incidents which had been observed, about usual classroom practices, and about the concepts of child development which lay behind teachers' practices.

Small Groups within the Classroom

Small fixed-membership groups were a striking feature of most nursery schools visited; thirteen of fifteen classrooms had such groups. Groups had their own tables and were frequently the units for chores, teacher-initiated special projects, lunch, and the children's own informal play. Groups of six to eight children were most common, with group size ranging from four to ten. Teachers selected the groups. Nine of eleven teachers reported that they based the groups on children's own friendships, choosing as a core for each group children who played well together. Only one of eleven teachers mentioned that best friends were split up in constructing groups. Distributing able children among groups was a second strategy, spontaneously mentioned by six of eleven teachers. Abilities mentioned as important to distribute among groups included leadership and social skills, athletic skills, and artistic ability. Same-sex and mixed-sex groups were both seen. The tenure of the small groups depended on how well children played and carried out tasks together.

Teachers planned to maintain the same groups for periods ranging from one term (four months) to two years; most teachers expected to maintain the groups without major changes for at least one year. When teachers made changes in the groups, it was sometimes a de facto recognition that children were not functioning well together as a group: "We don't change the groups; the groups change [themselves]." Children were frequently referred to collectively by group name. Dismissal and other rewards were sometimes conferred by group, and group murals with the names of each group member were in evidence in many classrooms. Teachers planned activities which required children to work collaboratively. For example, in one classroom, the teacher asked each group to make a *kamishibai* (paper theater) by having all children in the group make pictures which fit together in a continuous story. This task required children within the group to agree on a story line and to divide up the story among group members. The teacher in this classroom used an interesting technique for physically orienting group members toward one another. Before starting the project, all groups were asked to find their members, sit down, hold hands in a circle, lie back in a pinwheel, and then sit up. As the groups planned the paper theaters, the teacher circulated through the room, physically orienting toward their groups any children who were turned outward. In addition, the teacher deflected children's questions to their fellow group members, telling children, "Ask the other children in your group what they want to make" and "Remember to make pictures that fit together in a story, not the same picture."

Play Materials and Cooperation

Foreign visitors to Japan are accustomed to seeing familiar objects miniaturized to fit an environment where space is a precious resource. An interesting exception to this was the oversized, heavy wooden blocks, three feet or longer, which were observed in eight of twelve schools. Such blocks are extremely difficult or impossible for one child to manipulate without help. These large blocks seem to demand cooperative play.

Observation notes suggest also that classroom materials may be distributed in a way that facilitates cooperation. For example, a teacher in one classroom placed paints on each group's table, providing fewer brushes than children and asking the children to consult each other about paint use so the paints would not be spilled. A subsequent interview with the teacher confirmed that the teacher had deliberately chosen to provide fewer brushes than children and to place the paints in a location (the center of each group's table) where they would be spilled if children failed to confer about their use. Other teachers spontaneously mentioned that they withdrew toys as children became older to help children learn cooperation. Teachers viewed scarce, not plentiful, resources as a means for promoting cooperation among five-year-olds.

Minimizing Competition for the Teacher's Attention

With thirty to forty children per classroom and only one adult, teachers could hardly minimize competition by giving close personal attention to all children. During interviews, several teachers commented on the use of aides and parent helpers in American nursery schools and expressed envy of the greater flexibility this would allow classroom teachers. However, these teachers also remarked that the presence of such helpers in the nursery class could undermine children's formation of friendships with other children.

Neither did teachers choose to minimize competition by interacting with the class as a whole. In only 22 percent of spot observations did teachers interact with the class as a whole. However, hand waving and other forms of competition for the teacher's attention were not in evidence, perhaps because much classroom authority was delegated to children. As we will see below, children were encouraged to consult other children, not the teacher, on matters ranging from what to draw to how to settle a playground fight.

Strategies for Controlling Children's Behavior

How is a transition made from the indulged, undisciplined, early child rearing at home to a nursery school structure which must, at the very least, ensure the safety of thirty to forty children? As noted above, a growing research literature suggests that external controls—beyond those necessary to elicit compliance with a request—tend to undermine children's internalization of the norm involved in the request. On the other hand, control strategies which elicit compliance using minimal pressure tend to foster internalization of norms. From this point of view, four aspects of teachers' control strategies were particularly interesting: (1) minimizing the impression of teacher control, (2) delegating control to children, (3) providing plentiful opportunities for children to acquire a "good-girl" or "good-boy" identity, and (4) avoiding the attribution that children intentionally misbehave.

Minimizing the Impression of Teacher Control

One way to minimize the salience of teacher control in the classroom is simply to tolerate a wide latitude of child behavior. The observations suggest that Japanese nursery school teachers may do just that. In view of previous suggestions that the behavior of Japanese children in nursery school is somewhat regimented (Bedford 1979; Bettelheim and Takanishi 1976), the noise level and apparent chaos of the Japanese nursery schools was perhaps the single most astonishing aspect of the observations. Very high levels of spontaneous background noise from children (shouting, laughing, etc.) partially obscured teachers' voices, even though the tape recorder was held directly to the observer's mouth and the children were rarely within two feet of the observer. One possible explanation for the noise level is that Japanese adults positively value children's *genki* (vigor). Thus, considerable classroom noise does not necessarily reflect negatively on the teacher (Turner 1979).

The spot observations also suggest that teachers kept a low profile as classroom authorities. In only 53 percent of the spot observations were all children even within the teacher's sight. In 13 percent, none of the children in the classroom were within the teacher's sight. These percentages do not include situations in which another adult was responsible for watching the children, or in which all children were in an area, such as the playground, where supervision was not required. (Subsequent questioning also confirmed that teachers did not expect the observer to watch the children in the teacher's absence.) Nor was it the case that classrooms had been child-proofed to obviate the need for adult presence. In six of ten schools one or more of the following were within reach of the children: sharp scissors, razor blade knives, leather punches, or nails. Teachers recognized that children could hurt themselves with these objects but believed children would only use them under supervision. My questions about whether they would purposely use these objects to hurt other children elicited puzzlement. Perhaps, as we shall see below, the puzzlement centered on differences in attribution about intent (Hess et al. 1980). Teachers stated that the children were capable of self-supervision on occasions when the teacher was called out of the room.

Teachers also maintained a low profile in their response to misbehavior. There were numerous incidents, such as the following, in which teachers made requests but did not enforce the requests or check to see whether children complied:

> Yuki is throwing sand and calling it "snow." Teacher asks Yuki to stop throwing sand. Yuki continues. Teacher repeats request two more times. Yuki continues. Teacher tries to turn child's attention to building a race track, but he brings more sand to throw. Teacher: "If you fill up the tunnel with snow, you can't have a race." Teacher turns to student teacher and says, "It's no use. He wants to make it snow no matter what you do."

Interviews with teachers about these incidents and others suggested that their goal was not necessarily to make children comply but, rather, to make them understand what was proper behavior. In another incident described in the field notes, boys had been dropping clay bombs on the fish in an aquarium. The teacher explained that the clay could hurt the fish but did not specifically tell the boys to stop (nor did they). In her announcements to the whole class at the end of the school day, the teacher explained that some boys in the class thought they were helping the fish by throwing in clay "food" but that actually the boys were harming the fish. When I subsequently interviewed the teacher about the incident, our exchange was as follows:

INTERVIEWER: Did you really think the children were trying to help the fish by throwing the clay pellets?

TEACHER: Yes.

INTERVIEWER: Don't you think the boys understood they might hurt the fish by throwing the clay pellets?

TEACHER: If they understood it was wrong, they wouldn't do it.

An incident from the observation notes suggests that an attempt to impart understanding may sometimes take precedence over performance as a teaching goal.

Child is sitting on steps, having just put his shoes on in order to play outside. Shoes are on wrong feet. Teacher notices and says to child, "Do you feel anything funny?" Child fails to recognize problem. Teacher says, "Do your shoes feel funny?" Child still doesn't understand. Teacher says, "Look at Taro's shoes. Do they look the same as yours or different?" Child still does not understand. Teacher continues this line of questioning for approximately three minutes. Child still doesn't understand. Teacher says, "Oh well, just go ahead and play." Child goes off to play with shoes on the wrong feet.

While systematic evidence is needed on teachers' monitoring and enforcement of requests, the preceding interview material suggests a philosophy of child development coherent with minimal use of control: if children understand what is proper behavior, compliance will naturally follow. Thus, understanding, not compliance, becomes the teacher's primary goal.

Delegating Control to Children

Frequently, children were responsible for calling the class together, overseeing class projects, and even managing disagreements. For example, in one class thirty-eight children initiated preparations to go home on the basis of one quiet remark made by the teacher to a few children playing near her. When interviewed, the teacher indicated that ideally she should not need to mention going home even to a few children since they should keep an eye on the clock and remember it spontaneously. Similarly, when classes assembled for some program (such as a puppet show or singing), it was common for the teacher to make only one quiet statement to a few children. Sometimes children would be asked to see if their friends or group members had assembled; frequently teachers themselves did not attempt to find or involve children who did not appear for lunch, dismissal, or other class activities. Children were frequently seen searching for missing classmates, reminding isolated or distracted classmates about class activities, and improvising noisemakers to summon or quiet classmates for an activity.

Examples from the observations and interviews suggest that teachers often encouraged children to manage their own and other children's problems without teacher intervention. For example, when a child reported to the teacher that members of the "tulip" group were throwing stones out of the playhouse window, the teacher did not herself investigate the situation but said, "Tell the tulips it's dangerous." In another example from the field notes, a teacher asked two girls to encourage a boy to finish his lunch. The girls sat with the boy, helped him assemble scattered grains of rice and urged him to eat, and finally reported to the teacher that he had eaten. Interviews and observational data also suggest that teachers preferred not to intervene directly in classroom aggression but to have the children themselves manage it.

> When I see kids fighting, I tell them to go where there isn't concrete under them or where there are mats. Of course, if they're both completely out of control, I stop it. Fighting means recognizing others exist. Fighting is being equal in a sense. We let them fight a bit, not to the point of biting, etc. We have to let them experience pain to a small extent but not to the extent of hurting themselves. I tell children to cry if they're being hurt because the opponent will bite or pull until they cry. If they work hard to keep from crying, they'll get hurt more in the end. If children can solve fights on their own without people getting hurt, I let them do it themselves and ignore it. Kids start out rooting for the weak kid if the teacher stays out of it. If I can, I let them solve it.

The fact that there isn't more fighting among children is considered a problem by many teachers and parents. As a spur to cooperation, teachers might decrease the number of toys for five-year-olds, induce conflict, and encourage the children to take responsibility for each other's quarrels. "We encourage children to look when someone's crying and to talk about what the child is feeling, thinking, etc."

In one of the few aggressive episodes recorded in the field notes, two boys had a fight which progressed from sand throwing to hair pulling and hitting. The teacher did not directly attempt to stop the fight; in fact, she cheered on the smaller boy, saying, "Give it your best" and "Look, Taro's gotten strong; now he can fight without crying." When asked by a child why the two boys were fighting, the teacher said, "You'd better ask the fighters."

The teacher encouraged two bystanders to question the fighters about the problem and then asked each bystander to report what had been learned. After hearing the reports, the teacher said, "You're the caretakers, so you should decide what to do" and turned her back. The caretakers tried to get each fighter to apologize but failed. The caretakers then became frustrated and abandoned their mediation efforts. The fighting resumed, and the teacher asked a girl watching the fight to help the two fighters make up. At the same time, the teacher said, "I am washing my hands of this" and walked away. The girl and a second one nearby began to question the fighters, saying, "Are you mad? If not, say 'I'm sorry.'" Meanwhile, the teacher drew a circle around the fighters and children solving the fight and asked the rest of the children to start cleaning up to go home. The two girls succeeded in getting the fighters to apologize to each other. Each girl held hands with one fighter and brushed the sand off him, and then the two girls joined hands, forming a chain with the two fighters. From a distance, the teacher said, "Great! The problem has been solved because of the two girls." Noticing that one boy was still crying, the teacher said, "Now it's your problem alone if you've already made up."

Although class dismissal time had been delayed fifteen minutes by the fight, the teacher discussed the incident with the whole class. The teacher named the fighters and described in detail how they had thrown sand, pulled hair, and hit. She also named all four mediators and praised them for helping solve the class's problem. Parents picking up their children were kept waiting for about twenty minutes beyond the normal dismissal time.

The number of aggressive episodes observed was too small to permit generalization. However, the limited data available suggest that teachers are less interested in stopping aggression than in developing children's own ability to stop aggression. Seemingly, teachers preferred not to isolate or hide incidents of aggression but to involve other children, using aggressive episodes as grist for fostering peer management skills.

Providing Opportunities to Develop a Good-Child Identity

In addition to children's informal involvement in classroom management, fourteen of fifteen schools had a formal system of daily rotating *tōban* (monitors). Tōban were responsible for such visible leadership roles as leading the class in greetings and distributing tea at lunch. The tōban's authority might include deciding which group to dismiss first, deciding which group was quiet enough to have lunch, giving permission to individual children to go outside after lunch, and finding children who were missing at lunch time or other assembly times. Tōban were addressed as *san,* a higher honorific than that normally used to address kindergarten children.

Some schools had a tōban from each group while others had one or two tōban from the class as a whole. The tōban changed daily, and picture charts showed when each child's turn would come up. Although all children became tōban automatically in turn, considerable pomp and circumstance were attached to the position. In most schools, at the beginning of each day, a song or ceremony identified the new tōban and a badge was conferred. At the end of the day, the tōban received formal thanks from the whole class. The honor was keenly appreciated by the children: teachers reported parents had difficulty keeping ill children home from school if it happened to be their tōban day. The tōban system afforded each child an opportunity to develop an identity as a classroom leader and authority figure.

Although the tōban system existed in fourteen of fifteen schools, individual teachers took pains to explain how the system emerged naturally from the children's wishes.

> Tōban grows naturally out of children's helping. It is not required for three-year-olds; for them, the children who want to help do help. For the older children, the tōban system allows even a child who can't normally be a leader a chance to be one. The children who are least able to lead others in daily encounters are often the ones who work most carefully when they are tōban. Children think up the jobs that need to be done in the classroom; then they decide who will do them. Usually they take responsibility to do them, since they've mentioned the job themselves. If they don't, the teacher may do the job for a while.

In the view of the teachers, the tōban system and the chore groups (which were often the same as the children's fixed groups) helped children learn cooperation: "You understand how hard people can make it for you and how much better it is to have help."

One teacher recounted her ongoing efforts to encourage the children to adopt a new chore. Each day for several months the teacher had asked the class to thank Ken for closing the classroom door. She mentioned that this prevented neighborhood cats from entering the classroom at night. So far, the children had not picked up the teacher's hint to make door closing a regular chore. The teacher justified her plan to continue hinting rather than making an open request: "Children can't be told those things; they must learn them by doing."

Similarly, teachers took pains to see that classroom decisions emerged from the children; if even one child objected, teachers might refrain from enforcing a new policy:

Boys are putting blocks in a box and carrying it to another class. About six boys are all carrying the box together, and several boys are complaining that the other class gets the blocks. The teacher says, "We've had them for a long time, so we'd like to lend them to the other class. Do you think that's a bad idea?" Most of the boys say it's not a bad idea; one boy says it's a bad idea. Teacher says, "Then please stop moving them. We need to ask how the whole class is feeling about this."

A further incident from the field notes suggests that teachers helped children find peer-based, not teacher-based, methods for dealing with breakdowns in cooperative work. In the course of asking groups to report to the class on their chores, a teacher was told by the "bird" group that they did not finish their chore because they "began playing in the middle." The teacher solicited suggestions from the whole class about what to do if a group could not assemble to work. The teacher passed over suggestions that the group members be punished, saying, "It's not a good situation when people work because they are forced to." The teacher appeared satisfied when one child finally suggested that the group members ready to do chores could "get together and shout to call the people who aren't there." This solution focuses not on punishment or reward for behavior but on a pragmatic strategy for eliciting cooperative behavior.

Avoiding the Attribution That Children Intentionally Misbehave

As illustrated in the case of the boys who did not "understand" not to bomb the goldfish, teachers frequently attributed children's misbehavior to something other than malicious intent. For example, children had "forgotten their promises" or did not "understand" what was right. Misbehavior was often described as "strange" behavior. Frequently, discipline consisted of a simple explanation of appropriate behavior or a series of questions which assumed the child would not knowingly commit wrongdoing. For example, a boy who hid the shoes of another boy while he was washing his feet was asked these questions: "Did Ben ask you to move his shoes?" "What happens when you finish washing your feet and your shoes aren't there?" "Do you know it would be nicer to help Ben?" The teacher's questions concluded with, "This time is over, but remember these things next time." Similarly, a boy with his hand cocked back about to throw a large rock was asked to "lend" the rock to the teacher who demonstrated, by touching the child's head with the rock, how he could be hurt if such a rock hit the back of his head. The teacher then returned the rock to the child, asking him to carry it carefully. The teacher did not ask the child to put down the rock or imply that the child intended to throw it. Parenthetically, it is interesting to note that the use by teachers of naive questions as a form of discipline may have shaped children's responses to my interaction with them. When I was not carrying out observations and was free to interact informally with the children, they apparently interpreted my (genuinely naive) questions about game rules as a signal that they were behaving improperly.

When questioned about children's misbehavior, teachers frequently volunteered that enjoyment of school was the key to good behavior for children. An emotional attachment to the teacher and friendships with children were considered critical elements in the child's enjoyment of school. Techniques for building the teacher-child relationship included keeping the same teacher for two or more years (seven of nine schools) and teacher visits to the children's homes (four of eight schools). Some schools offered special preparatory classes for children who had cried during their nursery school interviews; prior to the school year, these children visited the nursery school as frequently as was necessary to adjust to the new setting. Teachers' elaborate efforts to construct children's groups which successfully played together were described above. One school even held regular meetings with mothers whose children were in small groups together. These parallel maternal networks were intended to strengthen the children's groups.

The Role of Small Groups in Socialization

While previous accounts of Japanese nursery schools have focused on the restrictiveness of group activity, the role of small groups in promoting cooperation, empathy, and self-management among nursery schoolchildren is largely unexplored. One researcher found that children trained in constant membership groups are more cooperative when grouped with new children than are children trained in changing membership groups. The present observations suggest two possible interpretations of this finding. First, retributive justice may more often prevail (e.g., children who commit aggressive acts may be punished, children who shirk work may be discovered, etc.) in groups which continue over time. This may be particularly true if group activities demand cooperation and accommodation and if children focus attention on ways of achieving cooperation rather than avoiding punishment or obtaining external rewards. Second, sustained interaction with the same group may accelerate children's understanding of others. These hypotheses need to be tested by future research that more fully explores the role of long-term, small-group membership in children's early socialization.

Delegating Authority to Children

Children in Japanese nursery schools receive encouragement to be their brother's keeper. Peers, not teachers, may have authority to manage aspects of classroom life ranging from participation in class events and finishing one's lunch to fights with other children. While peer management of classroom behavior by older students has been studied, little is known about consequences of peer management in nursery schools. Research on children's moral judgments suggests that peer justice may be unduly harsh (Johnson 1982), but little is known about how these moral judgments translate into actual behavior.

What are the likely effects of peer versus adult enforcement of rules on children's internalization of rules and their attitudes toward authority? Several speculations are in order. First, delegating authority to children allows teachers to make few behavioral demands on them. In the Japanese schools observed, as noted, peers assume much of the authority for checking that children complete their chores, finish their lunches, behave nicely toward other children, and so forth. This delegation of authority may enable the teacher to remain a benevolent figure to whom children have a strong, conflict-free, positive attachment.

A second speculation is that delegation of authority allows children to experience negative sanctions as intrinsic consequences of their acts. When the tōban fails to realize it is time for lunch and is hit on the back by hungry group mates attempting to redirect his or her attention (to take an actual example from observations), the child may experience this very differently from a teacher's reprimand. Children's sanctions may appear less contrived and external and more like the direct, natural consequences of the child's own acts, thus fostering greater behavioral change.

Finally, it may be that peer criticism, in comparison with adult criticism, poses less of a threat to the child's identity as a good child. Research on moral judgment suggests that, in the mind of a five-year-old, morality and adult authority are inextricably linked (Kohlberg 1976). Thus, criticism by adults may, to a much greater degree than peer criticism, cause the child to feel like a bad child. The "good-child" identity may, in turn, be a critical determinant of the child's subsequent willingness to obey rules (Lepper 1980).

But how is a transition made from the indulged, undisciplined early child rearing at home to a nursery school structure which must ensure the safety of thirty to forty children? The present data suggest several answers. Teachers may tolerate, at least initially, a wide latitude of behavior by children. Compliance, orderliness, and classroom harmony may be viewed as consequences which naturally follow when children understand what proper behavior is. Since it is frequently the peers who are responsible for eliciting proper behavior, there is reduced need for the teacher to exercise authority. Further, teachers provide plentiful opportunities for children to shape classroom rules and to assume positions of authority. The attribution theory discussed above suggests that providing children with opportunities to cooperate and act in accordance with classroom rules, without salient external pressure from the teacher, will promote strong internalization of classroom values. Thus, these Japanese nursery school practices may cultivate the incorporation of values and, ultimately, high compliance while maintaining the role of the teacher as a benevolent, though perhaps not quite indulgent, figure.

This article is excerpted from Catherine Lewis, "Cooperation and Control in a Japanese Nursery School," *Comparative Education Review* 28 (February 1984): 69–84.

REFERENCES

Baumrind, D. "The Development of Instrumental Competence through Socialization." In *Minnesota Symposia on Child Psychology* 7, edited by A. D. Pick. Minneapolis: University of Minnesota Press, 1973.

Bedford, Leslie C. "*Rakuto* Kindergarten: Observations on Japanese Preschooling." *Harvard Graduate School of Education Association Bulletin* 23 (Spring 1979): 18–20.

Bettelheim, Ruth, and Ruby Takanishi. *Early Schooling in Asia.* New York: McGraw-Hill, 1976.

Bronfenbrenner, Urie. *Two Worlds of Childhood: U.S. and U.S.S.R.* New York: Pocket Books, 1973.

Caudill, William A. "Tiny Dramas: Vocal Communication between Mother and Infant in Japanese and American Families." In *Mental Health Research in Asia and the Pacific* 2, edited by W. P. Lebra. Honolulu: East West Center, 1972.

Caudill, William A., and Carmi Schooler. "Child Behavior and Child Rearing in Japan and the United States: An Interim Report." *Journal of Nervous and Mental Disease* 157 (1973): 323–38.

Cole, Robert E. *Work, Mobility and Participation: A Comparative Study of American and Japanese Industry.* Berkeley: University of California Press, 1979.

Cummings, William K. *Education and Equality in Japan.* Princeton: Princeton University Press, 1980.

Doi, Takeo. *The Anatomy of Dependence: The Individual Versus Society.* Tokyo: Kodansha International Ltd., 1974.

Hara, Hiroko, and Hiroshi Wagatsuma. *Shitsuke*. Tokyo: Kobundo, 1974.

Hess, Robert, and Hiroshi Azuma. "Family Effects upon School Readiness and Communication Skills of Preschool Children in Japan and the United States." Data Reports 1–6. Stanford University Graduate School of Education and University of Tokyo Faculty of Education, n.d.

Hess, Robert, et al. "Maternal Expectations for Early Mastery of Developmental Tasks in Japan and the United States." *International Journal of Psychology* 15 (1980): 259–70.

Johnson, R. "A Study of Children's Moral Judgments." *Child Development* 23 (1982): 327–54.

Kohlberg, Lawrence. "Morals and Moralization: A Cognitive Developmental Approach." In *Moral Development and Behavior,* edited by T. Lickona. New York: Holt, Rinehart and Winston, 1976.

Lepper, M. "Social Control Processes, Attributions of Motivations, and the Internalization of Social Values." In *Social Cognition and Social Behavior: Developmental Perspectives,* edited by E. T. Higgins, D. N. Ruble, and W. W. Hartup. San Francisco: Jossey-Bass, 1980.

Lewis, Catherine. "The Effects of Parental Firm Control: A Reinterpretation of Findings." *Psychological Bulletin* 90 (November 1981): 18–20.

Maccoby, Eleanor. *Social Development: Psychological Growth and the Parent-Child Relationship.* New York: Harcourt Brace Jovanovich, 1980.

Nakane, Chie. *Japanese Society.* Berkeley: University of California Press, 1970.

Shand, Nancy. "Cultural Factors in Maternal Behavior: Their Influence on Infant Behavioral Development in Japan and the U.S." Progress Reports I and II. Menninger Foundation, 1978.

Taniuchi, Lois. "The Creation of Prodigies through Special Early Education: Three Case Studies." Paper of the Van Leer Project, Harvard University Graduate School of Education, n.d.

Turner, Christena. Personal communication, July 1979 (dissertation in progress, Stanford University).

Vogel, Ezra. *Japan's New Middle Class.* Berkeley: University of California Press, 1971.

———. *Japan As Number One.* Cambridge, MA: Harvard University Press, 1979.

In this article, Lois Peak explores the manner in which Japanese teachers create a learning environment calculated to inspire students to (1) learn a specific skill and become dedicated members of a community, (2) organize occasions to practice basic component routines until the routines become automatic, and (3) monitor their own performance. Her description, which focuses specifically on the Suzuki method, suggests that teachers pay very close attention to children's evolving competence while at the same time quietly manipulating the environment around them. Teachers appear to help students acquire skills of craft without intruding or imposing directly and without punitive intent.

Training Learning Skills and Attitudes in Japanese Early Education Settings

LOIS PEAK

It is a commonly agreed-upon principle in the comparative study of education and child development that cultural and environmental influences play an important role in determining both the abilities that children develop and the rate at which they achieve competence. Cultures that require children to master the skills required of daily life encourage the early development of complex skills that adults in other cultures might assume to be beyond a given age group's capabilities. A classic example is Margaret Mead's description of the degrees of competence in canoeing and swimming that were achieved by five- and six-year-old children among the Manus of New Guinea. Because the Manus lived in houses raised on stilts above the water of a tidal lagoon, water was a more salient aspect of their environment than dry land. Exposed from infancy to swimming as an everyday means of locomotion, children quickly mastered the abilities necessary for life in this environment.

A child's knowledge of a canoe is considered adequate if he (or she) can balance himself, feet planted on the two narrow (one-inch) rims and punt the canoe with accuracy, paddle well enough to steer through a mild gale, run the canoe accurately under a house without jamming the outrigger, extricate the canoe from a flotilla of canoes crowded about a house platform or the edge of an islet, and bail out a canoe by a deft backward and forward motion which dips the bow and stern alternately. Understanding of the sea includes swimming, diving, swimming under water, and a knowledge of how to get water out of nose and throat by leaning the head forward and striking the back of the neck. Children of between five and six have mastered these necessary departments (Mead 1975, 35).

Western students of child development who rarely spend significant amounts of time in cultures outside of the industrialized West have few opportunities to be so graphically reminded of the central role of environmental influence and cultural expectations in shaping the development of early abilities. In studying the progress of children developing within our own familiar cultural environment, we often imagine that the rates of development typical of children in this particular culture reflect pan-human, age-related competencies rather than the priorities and environmental demands of our own culture. Although the Manus case represents the early development of a largely physical ability in response to environmental demands, the development of more abstract cognitive abilities is also considerably influenced by the cultural environment. Gardner (1983) has recently presented detailed evidence on the interrelationship of cultural expectations and priorities and the development and selection of a broad range of human abilities.

As LeVine (1980) has observed, without the perspective gained by evidence concerning child development in other cultures, Western educators and psychologists run the risk of elevating Western folk assumptions about children's learning potential to the level of academic theory. Recommendations concerning age-appropriate learning activities, appropriate methods of teaching preschool children, and the proper goals of early education can thus become limited to a narrow range of alternatives derived from commonplace Western assumptions and folk practices.

Japanese early educational beliefs and practices present an interesting case study for consideration from this point of view. As a fully modern, industrialized society that has received a substantial educational influence from the West, the overall structure and content of the formal education system resembles that of the United States (Vogel 1979). However, closer investigation reveals that the familiar external appearances conceal very different beliefs and practices that are deeply rooted in a highly sophisticated non-Western cultural and historical educational tradition. Modern Japanese children's superior performance on international tests of mathematics and science achievement (Comber and Keeves 1973; Husen 1967; Stigler, et al. 1983) demonstrates that these different

educational beliefs and practices are also associated with high competence in academic subjects and abilities relevant to classroom learning.

This article focuses on one aspect of the Japanese educational approach—the inculcation of basic learning skills and attitudes in novice
learners, particularly training that develops basic cognitive support skills
in early learning situations. This topic is particularly relevant to the
discussion of the role of early experience in the development of competence for two reasons. First, this careful basic training in learning strategies and consequent thorough, reflective approach to learning tasks has
been cited by Japanese psychologists (Kojima 1985; Nagano 1983) as
an important ingredient in Japanese children's educational success. Second, the goals of this training and the manner in which it is carried out
are foreign to American cultural beliefs about appropriate educational
goals and teaching methods for preschool-age children. For these reasons
it may spark reflection on our cultural assumptions concerning early
education.

The data presented in this article were collected in 1983 and 1984,
during eighteen months of ethnographic fieldwork in Japanese early
learning environments, such as preschools, various types of enrichment
lessons, and first grades. Data were collected through intensive classroom observation, teacher interviews, and curriculum analysis through
the first three months of the school year in each of two preschools, four
first-grade classrooms, and one program of early music instruction. Supplementary interviews with principals and parents, questionnaires,
analysis of popular books and magazines about early education, and
briefer observation of a broad sample of other preschools, first grades,
and other enrichment lessons were also conducted.

Introduction of Novice Students to Learning Situations

Both traditional and contemporary Japanese education places an extremely high priority on the careful structuring of novice students' introduction to learning situations. Typically, the period of transition from
initial applicant to fully accepted beginning student is considerably pro-
tracted, encompassing several months or more. During this period the
new student undergoes systematic training in the basic attitudes and
cognitive support skills fundamental to the medium to be learned. This
preliminary training requires a long period of diligent study and thorough mastery of precisely defined basic routines before the student is
allowed to engage in the medium itself. This training is combined with
the calculated arousal of the learner's motivation to study and training
in concentration and self-monitoring skills.

The training involved in this preparatory period shares some similarity to the introduction of new students to learning situations the world over. However, the sophistication and detail of the procedures used in the Japanese case, their pervasiveness throughout a broad range of traditional and modern educational settings, and the unassuming ease with which they are used by even a pedagogically naive Japanese point to a highly elaborated indigenous cultural structuring of the educational process. Typically, these techniques are a part of the training of novice learners of any age in a broad range of settings, such as the induction of new employees into Japanese banks (Rohlen 1974), studying traditional archery (Herrigel 1953), and entering the first grade of a public school (Taniuchi 1985a). However, the techniques are more clearly defined and heavily emphasized in the teaching of very inexperienced learners such as preschool children. Across a broad range of different types of early learning environments, the following training practices were universally observed during the initial period of induction into the learning situation:

- Calculated arousal of learner motivation to acquire a specific skill and to become a member of its social setting
- Repeated practice of precisely defined component routines until they become automatic
- Development of self-monitoring of learning performance

Japanese teachers and parents believe that careful establishment of these habits and attitudes is the first requirement for minimal teachability and one of the most important determinants of future success in learning endeavors. In all settings studied, the presentation of regular curriculum content is delayed for one to six months until students are judged to have developed the appropriate basic attitudes and habits. Once these are established, however, teaching shifts to an increasingly straightforward and rapid presentation of curriculum content with minimal need to slow the pace of instruction for the slow learner.

The effectiveness of these practices is evident in comparative studies of both Japanese children's approach to learning tasks and studies of classroom discipline. Salkind, Kojima, and Zelniker (1978) report that five- to seven-year-old Japanese children are significantly more reflective and more accurate than either American or Israeli children on tests of cognitive style such as the Matching Familiar Figures Test. This test requires children to identify which of six slightly different pictures exactly matches a certain model picture, making careful, repeated comparison of one picture after another before forming a judgment. Although at ages five, six, and seven, Japanese children are the slowest of the three groups, by age ten they have become faster than both American and

Israeli children. Japanese children make the fewest errors at all ages, until a measurement ceiling effect is reached at age eight among Japanese and at age ten among American and Israeli children. These results exemplify Japanese teachers' emphasis on a slow, careful approach to learning tasks during the early years that speeds up as children acquire facility and confidence.

Careful training in learning routines and development of concentration skills also pay off in better classroom management and less wasted time. Stevenson (1985) reports that Japanese first-grade children attend to the teacher when he or she is speaking better than their American counterparts (60 percent of the time as opposed to 45 percent) and display inappropriate behavior less frequently (12 percent of the time as opposed to 20 percent). This better classroom discipline, combined with more efficient routines for managing transitions between activities, allows Japanese teachers to spend almost 50 percent more time per hour imparting information. A few months of extra effort at the beginning of first grade appear to produce considerable benefits in making Japanese students both more attentive and easier to manage.

How is this initial training in learning skills and attitudes accomplished? This article describes the process using examples from both modern, formal early learning situations, such as preschool and first grade, and a more traditionally structured, informal setting, such as the Suzuki method of music instruction. In fact, the Suzuki method is a good case study for examining this training process because it exhibits in simple, straightforward form the cultural beliefs and practices used to develop proper learning skills and attitudes in other Japanese early educational settings. In addition, its similarity to traditional Japanese methods of teaching and learning (Taniuchi 1985b), its relatively discrete focus of instruction, and its individual approach make it an ideal prototype against which to compare the more complex and diverse practices of Japanese preschools and elementary schools.

Before focusing in detail on the process by which these various early learning situations train novice students in basic learning skills and attitudes, a brief description of the Suzuki method is in order. The Suzuki method is a system of teaching musical instruments to children founded by Shinichi Suzuki, a Japanese violinist. Developed shortly after World War II according to very traditional Japanese patterns of teaching and learning, it has now been adopted in somewhat modified form in twenty-three countries, chiefly in North America and Europe. Children begin lessons very early, usually during their third year, using instruments scaled down or modified in size. Initially, students learn the classical musical repertoire solely by listening to records at home, in the same manner in which they acquire their native language. The child's mother is the central figure in the learning process, and the teacher's task is to teach the mother how to train her own child at home. Mothers study the instrument themselves in the beginning stages, starting lessons a few weeks before the child. They attend all lessons and lead all home practice sessions according to the teacher's directions until the child reaches upper elementary school age, at which time responsibility is gradually shifted to the child. Although most families in the program have had no prior musical background, children's progress is usually surprisingly rapid, and students are quickly able to play a difficult professional repertoire. Average violin students master Vivaldi concertos at age seven or eight and Mozart concertos at age ten or eleven. Faster students perform these works at ages five or eight, respectively.

Arousing Learner Motivation

The manner in which a prospective Suzuki student is inducted into the lesson process exemplifies the Japanese practice of calculated inflation of learner motivation for a considerable period before training begins. When new students arrive to request piano or violin lessons, they and their mothers meet with the teacher, who describes the method and assigns them to a class of four or five other recent beginners and their mothers. For the first month or more, the child and mother come once or twice a week and observe the other children's lessons and group activities, meanwhile listening daily at home to a recording of the first songs in the repertoire. As the child and the mother watch from the back of the room, the teacher and other mothers tell the new student how much fun it is to learn to play the piano. The mother explains that if the child is very good, he or she may someday be allowed to join in the fun.

Once the child's interest has been visibly aroused, the mother begins lessons and daily home practice sessions. The child is required to wait a few weeks longer, watching alone from the back of the room during weekly group lessons and hearing and seeing the mother practice at home the same exercises that the child will soon learn. At this point, it is a rare child who does not daily beg to be allowed to practice the instrument too. When the mother and teacher see that the child's motivation is at fever pitch, the first lessons begin.

This period of observation is the time-honored *minarai kikan,* or period of learning through watching, so typical in Japanese educational and social institutions as varied as Zen temples, junior high school tennis clubs, and places of employment. In the Suzuki method, the goal of this preliminary period is obviously to awaken in the child a sufficiently high level of motivation that he or she is willing to undertake the difficult process of daily coaxing the fingers and body to learn the new and difficult combinations that constitute learning to play an instrument. However, interviews with master teachers reveal that they also have a less obvious goal in mind. The observation period continues not only until motivation is sufficiently aroused but until the child has become able to listen quietly and attentively to three or four consecutive lessons and can understand that the lesson situation is one in which quiet focusing of attention is required. This step may take from three to twelve weeks, depending on the age and personality of the child. Once the child has developed the ability to listen quietly, the first lesson in arousing motivation and training concentration has been accomplished.

In preschools and elementary schools, this period takes the form of several occasions on which incoming students are invited to observe the life of the school and see the older students in action. The incoming students are treated as special guests, and they watch from the sidelines at the yearly sports day and are invited to meet the teachers and older students, sit in the desks, and see their future classroom several weeks before school begins. Teachers and older children welcome the prospective students individually and give the children handmade gifts. As the first day of school approaches, new students receive uniforms or other identical clothing and regulation equipment that clearly mark their new status as members not only of a given school and class but also of a new social age group.

In Japan, beginning virtually any type of lesson involves the process of gaining membership in a new social group. The minarai kikan also involves long hours of standing on the sidelines and waiting to be accepted by the teacher and one's older peers. Although in formal settings, such as preschool and elementary school, this acceptance is eventually bestowed automatically, there is still a clearly defined period of watching as an unskilled outsider the graceful execution of school activities and routines by older peers before assuming a new social identity and gaining membership in the group. In this manner the cultural structuring of the process of group membership and activities serves to arouse and maintain individual motivation to participate in the learning process.

Inculcation of Basic Routines

The next step in the process of learning Suzuki piano or violin epitomizes the process of training the novice in basic routines that form both the components of the skill to be learned and a cognitive support system for the learning process. When the teacher determines that the child has developed sufficient concentration and motivation to join the lesson group, the child is called from the observer's seat and asked if he or she would like to take lessons along with his or her mother and the other children. With the proud mother looking on, the teacher introduces the child to the rest of the group, and the first lesson begins. The first lessons focus exclusively on training in basic routines and the development of learning skills having nothing to do with making sounds on the instrument. In the Suzuki method this begins with the process of teaching the child to bow in the style of traditional Japanese greeting. In a carefully choreographed ritual similar to a ballet routine, the child is taught to put the feet carefully together, place the hands on the thighs, straighten the body, and then incline the torso at the correct angle and hold for a count of three. On straightening, the child looks at the teacher and says clearly, "*Onegai shimasu*"—which could be loosely translated as "Please teach me." One step at a time, the act of bowing is broken down and taught as a ritualized dance: Feet, one, two. Hands on thighs. Bend, one, two, three. Straighten. "Onegai shimasu." The first lesson ends with the teacher asking the child to promise to practice carefully every day according to the mother's instructions until he or she can perform the bow smoothly at the next lesson.

This apparently simple task is in fact very complex. Besides posing a considerable challenge to the physical coordination of a two- to four-year-old, it forces the child to consciously monitor and adjust body movements according to a verbally cued model. This is initially practiced on a large-motor scale involving the torso, legs, and arms, before proceeding to control the wrists and fingertips on the instrument itself. This initial stage of lessons is considered extremely important in developing a proper attitude toward the learning task itself. Beginning each lesson with a properly respectful request for instruction requires the child to reaffirm his or her commitment to the learning process and is seen as important in establishing a serious mindset. Also, the child begins the establishment of a habit of careful, daily home practice or study immediately on induction into the lesson situation and learns to accept practice as a responsibility concomitant with the lesson process.

This stage of learning is almost exactly replicated in most early educational settings, particularly first-grade classes. During the first few days of school, the class practices countless times how to stand, bow, and recite "Good morning, teacher" in unison. The process of standing up, bowing, and sitting down again is similarly choreographed into a series of tiny precise steps in which every move is calculated—even whether one arises from the right or left side of the chair. Every routine basic to daily classroom life is broken down into a similar series of careful steps, painstakingly practiced again and again until it becomes second nature, and then speeded up until it becomes an automatic, smoothly executed part of the school day.

First-grade students practice how to prepare their desk tops and come to order before class starts. For several days before actual instruction begins, students practice together a routine in which they place their textbook on the left side of the desk, notebook in the center, and pencil and eraser horizontally at the top right of the desk. Each desk is identically arranged according to a diagram drawn on the board. Then the students sit with backs straight, hands on knees, and eyes on the teacher waiting for a signal to end the drill. After several consecutive days of repeated practice of this routine, students accomplish it automatically with the speed and assurance of a drill team, and the cuing is delegated to the daily student monitor.

Although the explicit training of such detailed routines seems uncomfortably rigid and authoritarian to the unaccustomed Western eye, in practice it actually reduces the amount of authority and control teachers must exercise on a daily basis. By carefully training students in the behavior expected of them and having students practice until it becomes an individually maintained habit, teachers avoid the necessity of using their own authority to bring the class to order and to personally direct the preparation of lesson materials. By expending extra time and effort in establishing learning routines at the beginning of a child's school career, for the rest of the child's public school life, within seconds after the teacher enters the classroom, the class calls itself to order and sits with all lesson materials prepared, ready for the teacher to begin.

Elementary schoolteachers share with Suzuki teachers the cultural belief in the importance of establishing the habit of conscientious daily home practice or study before introducing the main curriculum content. The guidelines distributed by local public elementary schools to parents of children entering first grade routinely describe the importance of training children in the habit of regular home study. In a typical memorandum from one school, parents are requested to begin training this habit six months before the first day of school by having the children write their names five times each day in their best handwriting in a blank notebook. This practice is to be continued each day without fail in the same notebook until the first day of school. This practice develops the habit of daily home study before the child reaches school, and it also allows the child to realize the importance of sustained diligent practice in improving performance by seeing the improvement in handwriting that occurs over the six-month period. Teachers assert that once students have thoroughly understood the effectiveness of diligent practice and developed the necessary daily habits, they become much more disciplined, self-motivated learners. For this reason, five to ten minutes of daily homework is commonly assigned to Japanese first graders.

Developing Concentration Skills

Once a new Suzuki student has learned to execute a proper bow, the next steps in the training process attempt to strengthen the child's ability to concentrate. This is done by carefully structuring the way in which the child mentally and physically prepares to play the instrument. Through a similar precisely choreographed ritual, the child learns to properly orient the body to the keyboard and hold the hand in the correct position above the keys. Next, the mind is focused as well. The child is taught to focus the eyes on the back of the hand held over the keys and to concentrate for a slow count of three. Then a one-and-a-half- to two-minute recording of the first song the child will learn is played, and the child holds the "ready" position with the eyes on the back of the hand until it is finished.

This task is challenging for a three-year-old and usually requires from two to six weeks, depending on the child. It requires learning to focus the child's mind on the task and ignore distracting thoughts and outside influences while on the piano bench. It is always approached in the manner of a personal and pleasurable challenge. The teacher gradually encourages the child to hold his or her concentration for slightly longer—a count of five instead of three, or for two phrases of the song instead of one. Each week generous praise greets slightly longer concentration ability, and the child is encouraged to compare this week's progress to that of the past week and to take personal pride in his or her increasing ability to accomplish a difficult task. Japanese teachers of all disciplines view the ability to concentrate as a skill that is developed through practice, rather than as a function of personality or the child's tendency to be obedient. Good concentration is always praised as *jōzu*, or skillful, never with the observation, "You're being a good boy (or girl)." Children whose attention wanders easily are believed to be in need of concentration practice rather than discipline.

Similar concentration games and exercises were observed in preschool and first-grade classrooms. In the manner of a coach encouraging a group of beginning athletes, the teacher always structured the game in such a way that its daily repetition left a clear record of the class's growing skillfulness. Initial demands were always short but required complete immobility and quiet. Gradually the challenges lengthened until after several months, the entire class of first graders could stand at attention in school assemblies without moving or talking for as long as ten minutes.

Self-Monitoring of Performance

In the Suzuki method, learning to play the first note comes almost as an anticlimax. After two to six months of careful preparation, the child is judged to have completed the prerequisites necessary to actually begin to make sounds on the piano or violin. However, the child's first production of sounds is structured in such a way as to establish a long-term habit of careful evaluation of his or her own performance. After the child properly orients body and hand to the instrument and rests the eyes on the hands, the teacher commands, "Listen," and plays the first note of the first song on the record, and there is silence for a count of three. Then the child is instructed, "Ready"; then there is another silence for a count of three; then "Play." The child plays the note and then there is an evaluative silence for a count of three, then again, "Listen"; the teacher plays; silence; "Ready"; silence; "Play"; silence. This sequence is repeated several times with the same note, and then the teacher stops and praises the good points of the child's performance and clearly tells the child what to change in the next attempt. Then the process begins again.

This procedure is maintained for every note that the child plays for the next several months and inculcates the habit of mindful concentration: first, to form a mental model of what will be produced, then to carefully prepare, then to execute, then to evaluate. Never is the child allowed to approach the instrument in a lackadaisical, half-attentive manner. In addition, the teacher clearly verbalizes the strong and weak points of the child's performance in such a manner that the child is encouraged by his or her growing ability but knows also what to work on.

To an American observer entering the lesson at this point, the tiny three- or four-year-old child perched on a high stool in front of a huge piano displays an almost unbelievable ability to concentrate. In the manner of a serious adult ten times the child's age, he or she responds quickly and accurately to the teacher's instructions, with eyes never leaving the keyboard. Both teacher and student are completely absorbed, and the lesson is surprisingly businesslike, with a minimum of the fun and games and sugar-coated sweetness Westerners usually associate with the training of preschool children. However, to the charge that the lessons do not seem "fun" in an American sense, Japanese Suzuki teachers point out that the children listen carefully, try hard, practice willingly and well, and the enjoyment they derive is the personal satisfaction of competent execution and growing ability. Developing this attitude and the prerequisite learning abilities in children is the criterion for successful introduction to learning situations in Japanese teaching theory.

Preschools and first grades reflect this pervasive cultural emphasis on mindfulness in task preparation and evaluation. Initial speed in task performance is actively deemphasized in favor of extreme care and precision of execution. Throughout the school day, children are reminded again and again to take inventory of their materials and to be prepared for a new transition. Once the new task has begun, sloppy preparation is not cheerfully overlooked. In hundreds of hours of classroom observation, the only instances in which individual students were observed to be punished by being forced to stand or refrain from group participation were as a result of forgetting materials. Once a task has been executed, evaluation, or *hansei,* is a typical ritualized final step in the process. Group activities, ranging from daily cleaning of the classroom to the yearly class trip, end with a formal student-led period of hansei. Remedial pedagogy and discipline both focus on trying to get the student to reflect on and understand his or her inappropriate behavior and to develop an independent ability for self-evaluation.

Conclusion

Certain elements of these Japanese methods of training basic learning skills and attitudes bear some resemblance to individual aspects of various pedagogical techniques developed in the West. However, in the Japanese case, they represent a pervasive, universally recognized and almost unconscious cultural structuring of the basic goals and practices of early education. As a product of a long historical process of development, they form an integral part of the values by which Japanese adults unconsciously structure their own daily lives, as well as the ways they organize the process of cultural transmission to the young. Growing up in this environment, Japanese children receive both naturally acquired experience and consciously structured training in the development of proper attitudes and cognitive support skills for the learning proces.

Recent Western interest in Japanese education has tended to focus on easily measurable aspects such as test scores, administrative organization, and curriculum content. However, closer observation reveals the existence of a fascinatingly different and yet highly sophisticated and effective indigenous educational ethno-psychology. The preliminary evidence presented in this article focuses on one aspect of this indigenous approach—training to facilitate the development of appropriate learning attitudes and cognitive support skills. It suggests that given appropriate training and environmental support, children may be able to develop sophisticated control of their learning behavior much earlier than is believed in the West. Perhaps this example will encourage Western educators and psychologists to reflect on the manner in which our own cultural assumptions about the teaching and learning process restrict our understanding of the limits of early experience and the development of children's abilities.

This article is from *Early Experience and the Development of Competence, New Directions for Child Development 32*, edited by W. Fowler (San Francisco: Jossey-Bass, 1986), 111–23.

REFERENCES

Comber, L. C., and J. Keeves. *Science Education in Nineteen Countries: An Empirical Study*. New York: Wiley, 1973.

Herrigel, E. *Zen in the Art of Archery*. London: Routledge and Kegan Paul, 1953.

Husen, T., ed. *International Study of Achievement in Mathematics: A Comparison of Twelve Countries*. New York: Wiley, 1967.

Kojima, H. "A Cultural Background of Learning and Problem Solving in Japan." Paper presented at the Conference on Child Development in Japan, Ann Arbor, Michigan, April 1985.

LeVine, R. "Anthropology and Child Development." In *Anthropological Perspectives on Child Development, New Directions for Child Development 8*, edited by C. M. Super and S. Harkness. San Francisco: Jossey-Bass, 1980.

Mead, M. *Growing Up in New Guinea*. New York: William Morrow, 1975.

Nagano, S. "Docility and Lack of Assertiveness: Possible Causes of Academic Success in Japanese Children." Paper presented at Stanford Conference on Childrearing in Japan, March 1983.

Rohlen, T. *For Harmony and Strength*. Berkeley: University of California Press, 1974.

Salkind, N., H. Kojima, and T. Zelniker. "Cognitive Tempo in American, Japanese, and Israeli Children." *Child Development* 49 (1978): 1024–27.

Stevenson, H. "Classroom Behavior and Achievement of Japanese, Chinese, and American Children." In *Advances in Instructional Psychology*, edited by R. Glazer. Hillsdale, NJ: Erlbaum, 1985.

Stigler, J. W., S. Y. Lee, G. W. Lucker, and H. W. Stevenson. "Curriculum and Achievement in Mathematics: A Study of Elementary School Children in Japan, Taiwan, and the United States." *Journal of Educational Psychology* 74 (1983): 315–22.

Taniuchi, L. *Classroom Discipline Management in Japanese Elementary Classrooms*. Washington, DC: United States Study of Education in Japan, National Institute of Education, 1985a.

———. "Cultural Continuity in an Educational Institution: A Case Study of the Suzuki Method of Music Instruction." In *The Cultural Transition: Human Experience and Social Transformation in the Third World and Japan*, edited by M. I. White and S. Pollack. London: Routledge and Kegan Paul, 1985b.

Vogel, E. *Japan As Number One*. Cambridge, MA: Harvard University Press, 1979.

In a revealing examination of teacher and student classroom practice, Tobin, Wu, and Davidson demonstrate important cultural distinctions between Japanese and American teachers. The authors discuss a method of using film and discussion to reveal culture-based educational practices. The focus here is on student/teacher ratios, but the article also reveals that educational practices in Japanese preschools are neither militaristic nor authoritarian.

Forming Groups

JOSEPH J. TOBIN, DAVID Y. H. WU, AND DANA H. DAVIDSON

A merican preschool teachers, parents, and scholars universally believe that small class size and student/teacher ratios are desirable. Advisory groups in the U.S. push state regulatory agencies to lower student/teacher ratios for four-year-olds from eighteen to one to fourteen to one. American parents shopping for a program for their three-year-olds are likely to begin their questioning of a preschool director by asking how many children there are in each class. If they can afford it, these parents are likely to select a school with a ratio of eight children per teacher over a school with a ratio of twelve to one.

What, then, are we to make of the typical ratios of thirty students per teacher in Japanese preschools attended by three-, four-, and five-year-olds? Japan is a wealthy country, one that assigns great importance to education, and one whose students outperform Americans (and most of the rest of the world) on international academic achievement tests (Husein 1967; Stigler et al. 1983). Indeed, Monbusho, the Japanese Ministry of Education, allows up to forty children per class in yōchien, which are comparable to U.S. nursery schools and kindergartens.

Recently, American studies of Japanese preschools have begun to examine the techniques of classroom management employed to keep classes of thirty or more children in line and learning. We came to understand the rationale behind the large group size and the high student/teacher ratios of the Japanese preschool only when we showed Japanese teachers, parents, and administrators videotapes of class conduct in a selection of American and Japanese preschools, the latter located in Kyoto, and asked them to explain and evaluate what they saw. The view of Japanese preschools we derived from their explanations and evaluations challenges us to rethink the issues of student/teacher ratio and class size.

Small Classes/Large Classes

In 1985 we returned to Kyoto to show children, parents, and staff of Komatsudani Hoikuen and Senzan Yochien edited versions of the tapes. We expected our Japanese informants to tell us why they preferred large classes with high student/teacher ratios to small classes with low student/teacher ratios. We were therefore puzzled and a bit worried by the first responses we received after showing the Senzan teachers a tape of an American preschool with a student/teacher ratio of eight to one. Saito-sensei, a teacher, began the discussion with a sigh: "Gee, it must be great to teach in a school with such small classes." Tanaka-sensei, another teacher, said "I envy the way the American teacher in the film plays with the children in such an uninhibited, 'barefoot' way." Seeing our hypothesis unraveling before our eyes, we desperately sought clarification: "You're saying you would like to have smaller classes in your school?" "Sure," the teachers all agreed, "it would be much easier to teach a smaller class." Before abandoning our hypothesis, we tried one last question: "We want to make sure we understand this. You're saying it would be better to have a class size of ten students instead of twenty-five or thirty?" Saito-sensei, looking a bit puzzled, responded: "No, we didn't say better. Well sure, better for the teacher, but it wouldn't be better for the children, would it? Maybe I'm wrong, but it seems to me that children need to have the experience of being in a large group in order to learn to relate to lots of children in lots of situations."

Tanaka-sensei, who had commented favorably (or at least her comments had seemed to us to have been favorable) about what she had called the barefoot play style of the American teacher in our tape, then explained:

> I envy the way the American teachers, with such small classes, have time to play so affectionately with each child. That's how I like to play with my nieces and nephews. That's a good way for aunts and uncles and parents to play with their children. But I don't think that's necessarily the best way for a teacher to relate to children. Teaching is different from being a parent or aunt or friend to a child. Sometimes I feel like playing very warmly in a

down-on-the-floor, barefoot sort of way with my students, and sometimes I feel like hugging some of my students or having an intimate chat with one of the little girls. And sometimes I do these things, of course. I'm a human being as well as a teacher, and I'm not suggesting that teachers should be cold or formal. What I am trying to say is that I believe a teacher should emphasize relating to the class as a whole rather than to each student, even if this is a little sad for the teacher sometimes.

Comments like these from Japanese teachers viewing our tapes of American and Japanese preschools suggested to us that, behind the disparity between the United States and Japan in the preferred student-teacher ratios, lie very different notions of the function of the preschool teacher and the role of preschools in educating and socializing young children.

Teaching and Mothering

Americans expect consistency in approaches to child care and in children's behavior at home and at school. For example, Barbara Culler, a day-care center director in Honolulu, told us:

We feel it's crucial that children get the same sort of messages at home as at school. If we teach children here at school to use words instead of hitting to deal with disagreements and then these children go home and get slugged by their parents, it undoes what we are trying to accomplish. When situations like this arise, we ask parents to come in to talk about our different approaches to discipline. If we can't resolve our differences, we occasionally have to counsel parents to change schools.

Our discussions with Japanese parents, teachers, and administrators suggest, in contrast, that the worlds of preschool and home, of teacher and mother, are viewed as largely discontinuous. As Tanaka-sensei suggests, teachers are not parents, and to the degree a Japanese teacher allows herself to slip into a motherlike stance toward a child, she has compromised her role as a teacher.

We can see in these different views of the teacher's role larger cultural differences between Japan and the U.S. In the U.S. where one-on-one relations are emphasized over group relations, any relationship between an adult female and a small child (as, for instance, between preschool teacher and student) cannot help reflecting in important ways the mother-child bond. Conversely, in Japan, where group relations are emphasized, a preschool teacher is less likely to play a motherlike role.

Most Japanese preschool teachers are hired directly out of college or junior college at twenty or twenty-two years of age, and they generally work only three to five years before retiring to marry and start a family. Unmarried young women, including preschool teachers, are expected to be energetic, cheery, cute, and girlish. A Japanese preschool teacher is likely to appear to the children in her class to be more like a (much) older sister than a mother. It is precisely at that point in her career when she begins to tire of her girlish role and to desire a child of her own that a Japanese teacher is most likely to retire from preschool teaching. The average age of the Japanese teachers in our study was twenty-four, compared to twenty-nine in the United States.

The child's transition from the small world of home to the larger world of school and society is facilitated not by offering teachers who are mother substitutes but rather by offering a program of large class size and high student/teacher ratios, limiting emotionally intense interactions between children and teachers.

These points were borne out in the reactions of the Japanese parents and teachers who watched our tapes. Most of them praised the creativity and warmth of the American teachers in our films, but many also wondered if there was not, perhaps, too little chance for children to enjoy spontaneous, unsupervised child-child interactions and too much emphasis on the child-teacher relationship. For example, a yochien mother in Tokyo said of the American film:

> The teacher is so stimulating and creative! The children look happy and bright. Everything looks so exciting. But as I was watching, I found myself wondering if it might sometimes not get to be too much. I wonder what it is like for a child to be in a class where the teacher is always so fun and creative and exciting, and so important to the children. Wouldn't the children get to be too dependent on the teacher always being there to organize their play and show them how to have fun?

Kumagai-sensei, the assistant principal of Senzan Yochien, explained:

> Teachers in our yochien have thirty children to watch at once, and that's not necessarily a bad thing because it forces children to learn to deal with problems and disagreements on their own. Children get spoiled these days at home. They are used to having their mothers' undivided attention. It's good for them to have the experience of interacting with other children without their mothers around.

Large Classes and Benign Neglect

On the day we visited Komatsudani Hoikuen, the noisiest and most disruptive of the thirty children in the Peach Class, four-year-old Hiroki, was at his wildest in a scene we taped as lunch drew to a close:

About two-thirds of the children in the class are sitting at their low tables, eating and chatting. Other children are running around in the hallways or playing on the balcony that adjoins the classroom. Midori runs over to Fukui-sensei, who is sitting with some children at one of the tables, and announces that Hiroki is throwing flashcards off the balcony. Fukui-sensei says matter-of-factly to Midori, "Hiroki's throwing cards, is he? What do you suppose can be done about that?" Meanwhile, on the balcony, Hiroki punches Satoshi. Satoshi holds his wounded arm out in front of Hiroki and says, "Look what you did." Hiroki, with a trace of a smile, stomps on Satoshi's hand, sending Satoshi off in a gale of tears. Midori, returning from telling on Hiroki, sees Satoshi crying and takes him by the arm and leads him to a quiet corner. She comforts Satoshi, asks him to tell her what happened, and then says, "What a shame. That always happens when you play with Hiroki, doesn't it? Maybe you should play with someone else next time."

When we returned to Komatsudani two months later with an edited version of the tape, we wondered if Fukui and her supervisors, Higashino and Yoshizawa, would be surprised or disturbed by the fight scene.

As we watched the fight scene with them, we asked if this looked like a typical day. Fukui responded: "Your being here with the camera made the children excited and I was a bit camera shy, but I'd have to say the way things look on the tape is pretty typical. Hiroki always acts like that. The fight is certainly typical Hiroki, and the tape pretty well shows the approach I usually take to dealing with him." Higashino added: "As you see in Fukui-sensei's treatment of Hiroki, we try never to confront or criticize children directly. Hiroki is a very difficult child. What we think works best with him is to be as patient as we can be. We try to ignore his behavior with the hope that gradually he'll begin to notice the effect he is having on other children and his interactions with others will help him come around." When asked if the large class size makes it difficult for teachers like Fukui-sensei to break up or head off fights between children, Principal Yoshizawa said:

It is no doubt true that if we had smaller classes, as in the United States, our teachers would be able to break up many of those kinds of fights more easily. But would that be a good thing? Perhaps one reason we have big classes is precisely to assure that there will be fights of this kind. Does that sound strange? At home these days children are supervised very closely by their mothers. Many have no siblings. They live in small apartments, for the most part in a world of only mother and child. They have little opportunity to play naturally with other children, in a childlike way, out of the sight of adults. That's why I say that children's fighting isn't a real problem. If there were no fights, now that would be a problem. We don't encourage children to fight, but if fights occur, well, that may be for the best, and the best thing we can do might be not to rush in to break them up.

When class size is small, preschool teachers can take a much more active approach to helping children arbitrate their disputes. A teacher can work with children individually or in groups of two or three on developing the ability to share, to empathize, and to verbalize needs and feelings. But Japanese preschool teachers and administrators generally are ambivalent about this sort of high-profile approach. While they value the teaching of *omoiyari* (empathy), the emphasis on feelings they saw in our tape, many of the Japanese suggested that such a direct, interventionist approach is too didactic and emotionally intense for young children. In the tape there is a scene from an American preschool in which a fight breaks out between two children over a toy. Before matters can escalate further, the teacher quickly comes over and says, "What's going on here, boys? Jimmy, can you use words to tell Danny how you felt when he grabbed the truck out of your hands? Danny, can you tell Jimmy how you are feeling right now? Are you feeling angry? Sad?" When we stopped the tape at this point and asked the staff of Senzan Yōchien in Kyoto for their reactions to this scene, Tanaka-sensei was first to respond:

TANAKA: Wow, that's amazing. In America, even young children are encouraged to talk directly about their feelings.
TOBIN: Do you approve of this approach?
TANAKA: For Americans maybe, but to me it's a little too heavy for children. It reminds me of marriage counseling.

Developmentally Appropriate Chaos

A key distinction between the worlds of home and school in Japan is the level of chaos. The home of a young Japanese child at times may be noisy and disheveled but never as chaotic as a yōchien or a hoikuen. Americans believe that large class size and high student/teacher ratios create the potential for chaos, which leads teachers to become authoritarian and rigid in their approach to children (Clark-Stuart and Gruber 1984). But the Japanese teachers with whom we spoke view chaos in preschools as normal and even desirable, an important transitional experience between the sheltered life of the homebound toddler and the tumult of the real world. Japanese teachers, who believe that a healthy environment for young children includes periods of chaos, can teach large groups of children without feeling compelled to become too authoritarian or rigid in an attempt to maintain tight control of the classroom. When we asked Higashino-sensei, the assistant principal of Komatsudani, "Doesn't the noise and chaos ever get to you?" she responded: "Aren't children in America wild and noisy? The purpose of preschool is to give children a place to be children. To be a child is to be wild and noisy. Children growing up in Japan these days too often miss a chance to get to be real children. I think preschools should give them this chance."

Teaching Group Mindedness in a Changing Japan

In explaining their philosophy of preschool education, several Japanese teachers and administrators agreed with Higashino. Demographic and cultural changes in postwar Japan have led to profound changes in the Japanese family, which are reflected in the way the Japanese think about their preschools in reference to class size.

In the last hundred years, and particularly since the war, there has been a rapid urbanization and nuclearization of the Japanese family (Koyama 1962). The numbers of children per family have dropped (Iritani 1979). Young people have moved from the country to the city and from the city to the suburbs, leaving grandparents and other kin behind (Linhart 1975; Taeber 1958). The salaryman lifestyle of commuting, white-collar husband and nonworking, stay-at-home wife has become the ideal typical family structure in contemporary Japan (Vogel 1971). In the context of these changes, Japanese preschools have grown and flourished, taking over the child-rearing and child-minding functions traditionally performed less by mothers than by the extended family and the community by the *seken,* the ever-watching, supportive, and critical community of concerned others (White and Levine 1986). Even Japanese mothers who work full time outside of their households view the role of preschools less as providing a substitute form of mothering than as offering something no mother can provide: a first experience of living out in the world.

Parents in contemporary Japan, living in inner-city high rises and in apartments in the newly created "bed towns" that ring the larger cities, look to preschools to give their children the chance to enjoy the kind of spontaneous interactions with other children that they recall experiencing as children growing up in families of four and five children surrounded by a friendly sea of cousins, family friends, and neighbors. In this rapidly changing world, the Japanese believe that it is in preschools with large ratios and large classes that children are most likely to get the chance to interact intensively with other children and to learn *shakaisei* (social consciousness) and *shūdan seikatsu* (group life) (Shigaki 1983; Taniuchi 1984).

But curiously, the system of large classes currently in use throughout Japan reflects Japanese borrowing from the West. The contemporary Japanese school system originated a little over a century ago in the early

Meiji era. It was based on Western educational models of the time and was revised, under American direction, during the Occupation. Japanese education, before the era of Western influence, emphasized individual tutorials, hands-on training, and learning through apprenticeship (Dore 1965; Rubinger 1982). The contemporary Japanese education system is traditionally Japanese less in the sense of being a legacy of the distant past than in the sense of promoting what the Japanese believe to be important traditional values. Large class size and large ratios have become increasingly important strategies for promoting traditional Japanese values and for combating what many Japanese believe to be the dangers of Western-style individualism.

Implications for the United States

Our discussions with parents and teachers in Japan suggest that in preschools (and perhaps at other levels of education as well) there may be a danger zone of ratios and class size running from approximately twelve to approximately twenty children per teacher per class. Inside this danger zone, children may tend to become frustrated and confused as they try to compete for their teacher's attention and approval. A teacher with such a class may be tempted to relate to the children on a one-to-one, intense basis but will find herself thwarted in her attempts by the sheer numbers of students in her care. In classes of this size, a student may be tempted to approach the teacher for some individual attention only to be interrupted by one of the other equally needy and now perhaps jealous students. The illusion that the teacher is available and in control may tend to preclude children evolving into a real group and discourage children from taking on roles of leadership and responsibility in the classroom. In classes with ratios greater than twenty to one, teachers and students are more likely to realize intuitively that mutually satisfying one-on-one interactions between teacher and student are unlikely to occur. They may tend to have more realistic expectations and to adjust their modes of interaction accordingly.

While most Americans believe large class size and high student/teacher ratios to be undesirable, where they are unavoidable, Americans might benefit from rethinking their pedagogical strategies more along Japanese lines. Rather than employing a watered-down, second-rate version of the American, individual-oriented, small-group teaching style, we might do well to look to Japanese large-group, preschool teaching techniques including (1) delegating authority to children, (2) intervening less quickly in children's fights and arguments, (3) having lower expectations for children's noise level and comportment, (4) using more musical cues and fewer verbal ones, (5) organizing more highly structured, large-group daily activities such as *taisō* (morning group exercise), (6) using a method of choral recitation for answering the teacher's questions rather than calling on individuals, and (7) making more use of peer-group approval and opprobrium to influence children's behavior.

This article is excerpted from Joseph J. Tobin, David Y. H. Wu, and Dana H. Davidson, "Class Size and Student/Teacher Ratios in the Japanese Preschool," *Comparative Education Review* 31 (1987): 533–49.

REFERENCES

Clark-Stuart, A., and C. Gruber. "Day Care Forms and Features." In *The Child and the Day Care Setting,* edited by R. Ainslie. New York: Praeger, 1984.

Dore, Ronald P. *Education in Tokugawa, Japan.* Berkeley: University of California Press, 1965.

Husein, T., ed. *International Study of Achievement in Mathematics: A Comparison of Twelve Countries.* New York: Wiley, 1967.

Iritani, T. *The Value of Children: A Cross-National Study, Japan.* Honolulu: East West Center, 1979.

Koyama, T. "Changing Family Structure in Japan." In *Japanese Culture: Its Development and Characteristics,* edited by R. Smith and R. Beardsley. Chicago: Aldine, 1962.

Lewis, Catherine. "Cooperation and Control in Japanese Nursery Schools." *Comparative Education Review* 28 (1984): 69–84.

Linhart, S. "Changing Family Structure and Problems of Older People in Japan: Present Trends and Future Prospects." In *Social Structures and Economic Dynamics in Japan Up to 1980* I, edited by G. Fodella and M. Gianna. Milan: Luigi Bocconi University, 1975.

Peak, Lois. "Training Learning Skills and Attitudes in Japanese Early Education Settings." In *Early Experience and the Development of Competence: New Directions for Child Development* 32, edited by W. Fowler. San Francisco: Jossey-Bass, 1986: 111–23.

Rubinger, Richard. *Private Academies of Tokugawa, Japan.* Princeton, NJ: Princeton University Press, 1982.

Shigaki, I. "Child Care Practices in Japan and the United States: How Do They Reflect Cultural Values in Young Children?" *Young Children* 38 (1983): 13–24.

Stigler, J. W., S. Y. Lee, G. W. Lucker, and H. W. Stevenson. "Curriculum and Achievement in Mathematics: A Study of Elementary School Children in Japan, Taiwan, and the United States." *Journal of Educational Psychology* 74 (1983): 315–22.

Taeber, T. *The Population of Japan.* Princeton, NJ: Princeton University Press, 1958.

Taniuchi, Lois. "Inter-Relationships between Home and Early Formal Learning Situations for Japanese Children." Paper presented at the meeting of the Comparative and International Education Society, New York, November 1984.

Vogel, Ezra. *Japan's New Middle Class*. Berkeley: University of California Press, 1971.

White, M., and R. Levine. "What Is an *Ii ko*?" In *Child Development in Japan*, edited by H. Stevenson, H. Azuma, and K. Hakuta. New York: Freeman, 1986.

The capacity of Japanese teachers to evoke the commitment of learners to hard work, practice, and attentive study results in educational environments which exude a dynamic spirit and uncommon enthusiasm that is distinctly Japanese. In the following article John Singleton describes the spirit of *gambaru*—the call to persist, hang on, do one's best, inspire others—and, in the process, reminds us that habits of the heart are as important as habits of the mind for the educational achievement of Japanese youngsters.

The Spirit of *Gambaru*

JOHN SINGLETON

T here are, in every society, unstated assumptions about people and how they learn, which act as a set of self-fulfilling prophecies that invisibly guide whatever educational processes may occur there. They act as a kind of unintentional hidden curriculum, or what an anthropologist might call a cultural theory of learning. It is these cultural assumptions about education as they operate in Japan, whether intentional or incidental, that I will describe here. These are, of course, the product of cross-cultural comparative observations and reflect the observer's cultural baggage as well as Japanese culture. What we see during a cross-cultural observation are the cultural differences. Where we think alike, nothing stands out. The one difference that has specifically impressed me is the Japanese emphasis on *gambaru* (to persist) in explaining and organizing education. This contrasts with the American emphasis on ability (that is, intelligence and talent) and is an underlying assumption of the Japanese cultural theory of learning.

The data here come from ethnographic observations of a Japanese junior high school and from observations, as a parent, of my own children's experiences in Japanese educational settings. Over the years there have been four major settings for parental observation. The first was our home in the Japanese countryside where our landlady became a grandmother to my infant son when my wife and I moved into her household in 1962. Next was the kindergartens where my two older sons learned to fold origami and participate enthusiastically in group-oriented cooperative activities. The third was a country elementary school, where my oldest son, a new first-grader, learned in less than six months to read and write in *kana* (Japanese syllabary) before he had instruction in English literacy. The last setting, more than twenty years later, was a rural potter's household where my second son, then twenty-six, lived in 1982–83 for more than a year as a traditional potter's apprentice (Singleton 1967; Singleton and Singelton 1984).

My formal ethnographic observations of Japanese education were made in a Japanese public junior high school in 1962–63. There I was able to watch the processes of school and community concern about educational advancement for a group of ninth-grade students as they prepared for their first major examination ordeal—the entrance exams for senior high school. Both teachers and parents helped me understand their problems and purposes as they made educational choices with, and for, the children.

Twenty years later, as director of a study-abroad program for thirty-three American university students, I was able to observe the educational and social worlds of a private Japanese university. While I thought of this experience as a chance to learn about Japanese higher education, the observations of my American students in their urban Japanese host families gave me key data for a more general understanding of Japanese education.

That was, for instance, my second experience with the Japanese *kyōiku mama* (education mama). A constant topic of conversation among the host-family "mothers" was the scores that their visiting "children" received on their most recent class quizzes. Most talkative were those whose guest students had received the highest grades. I should have expected this intense motherly interest and competition—but even I was surprised by the enthusiastic way in which the mothers joined in the school game of their temporarily adopted children.

While my school observations were separated by twenty years, my return trip convinced me that the major changes in Japanese schooling were more related to national wealth and new school buildings than to the cultural assumptions underlying what went on inside those buildings. As I became familiar with the private school system associated with my Japanese university, I was able to see that the continuity with my earlier public school observations was dramatic.

There is an outwardly gentle, but relentless, school career progression. It begins with the delightful, usually nonacademic, *yōchien* experience, where three-to-five-year-old children learn group routines for group activity. During the six-year elementary school experience, learning is fun, at least in the early years. In the junior high school, educational endeavor becomes real and earnest in preparation for senior high school entrance exams. Senior high school is usually the first separation into ability-graded career tracks. The university, home to a small, high-status elite, is where students can relax for the first time since they were in elementary school and put their energies into intensive student club activities—whose demands often take precedence over class attendance.

Underlying all understandings and anticipations of this schooling, the related tutoring, and even the learning of non-school-connected arts and skills is the principle of gambaru, a critical cultural assumption in contemporary Japanese learning theory. Literally, *gambaru* is a verb that means "to persist, hang on, or do one's best." In its imperative form (*gambare*), it is "used among members of a group to encourage each other in cooperative activities" (Wagatsuma 1983).

I first had to look up the term in my pocket dictionary when I was tagging along with the junior high school teachers on their annual visits with parents of the children in their ninth-grade homeroom classes. At each home conference, the teacher and one or both parents would confer about the child of the household. During the conference, the most important topic was usually the child's chances for admission to one of the seven or eight hierarchically graded and specialized public high schools within commuting distance of the junior high school district. There were often fine calculations of the chances for entrance to a particular academic level of high school. Most of the conferences concluded with a stock phrase from the teacher in response to the parents' concern about what might be done to help the child achieve the best possible entrance exam results: "*Mō sukoshi gambaha hō ga ī to omoimasu*" ("I think a little more persistence would be good"). Whether talking about the top student in the class or the bottom, the laziest or the most diligent, the answer never changed.

I then began to follow up on these students and talked with the teachers privately about the students' academic records and characteristics. The teachers had no problem reciting the students' school grades, scores on their last practice entrance exam, their study habits, and other details. When I asked about their IQs, even in rough terms, however, they inevitably referred me to the student files that were kept in the school office. They knew that the IQ scores were on file, but the scores themselves were not an item of teacher interest or concern. They would not assess children as underachievers or overachievers. Gambaru could be measured by test scores achieved. Comparison with IQ scores was irrelevant. Persistence is the secret; effort, not IQ, is the Japanese explanation for educational achievement.

The important curriculum in Japanese schools has nothing to do with the government-prescribed course of study, which is really only a means to other goals. The real content of any educational process is the cultural curriculum, that is, *seishin* (individual spirit and character development) and *shūdan ishiki* (group consciousness, belongingness) or *dantai ishiki* (organizational consciousness). This holds not only in the schools but in the society at large. It underlies the wide public and government support for school-based moral education and guides corporate training programs for new employees.

Junior and senior high schools are model experiences for such training. It is not the content of the entrance exams but the intense experience of exam preparation that is believed to strengthen an individual's character and moral fiber. In cooperative endeavor with one's peers and coaches (teachers, tutors, and parents), one prepares for the time of individual ordeal, but others can help only in preparation for the lonely trial. It cannot be taken collectively, though collective support and encouragement for the individual is assured, at least within the family.

To understand the nature of this moral training from a Western perspective, there is no better description than that given by the German philosopher Eugen Herrigel (1971). He describes his frustrations in attempting to learn Zen philosophy through training in the art of archery. He learns from the experience of unfathomable contradictions, conquering difficult tasks and developing selfless perfection in particular skills. The learning style is consistent with that encountered in preparation for entrance examinations.

Relentless tutoring in the answers to objective multiple-choice questions about esoteric facts is much of what goes on in the junior and senior high schools and associated tutoring. The students do manage to gain a broad understanding of mathematics, science, history, and even English grammar in the process. The self-discipline required is not unlike that of the Zen novice who must sit in uncomfortable positions for long hours of quiet meditation or the potter's apprentice who must spend many months, or even years, at the wheel making exact copies of a single basic and ordinary pot form. "Through intense application, strict obedience, and long apprenticeship, the pupil may one day hope to approach the level of competence that will wring a word of praise from the teacher" (Smith 1983).

Much like John Dewey, Japanese teachers see direct experience as the most powerful educational strategy. Carefully constructed experience is more powerful than lecture or explanation. One learns from experiencing hardships, conquering difficult tasks, and developing perfection in particular skills.

At the same time, the family, neighborhood, schools, corporations, and university student clubs (especially the sports clubs) convey the messages of shūdan ishiki. Exclusive group solidarity and commitment are part of the real (or hidden) curriculum of the educational process. The assumption is that commitment to exclusive groups is a necessary individual choice. Commitment, solidarity, achievement, egalitarianism—within the same age or status group—and the complementary hierarchy of *sempai-kōhai* relations (junior to senior obligations and privileges) are all important values related to one's group membership. Open, interpersonal competition within the group is seen as destructive of group harmony and, therefore, of individual learning.

> Modern Japanese institutions tend even today to be bound together by an intensity of commitment that is quite unfamiliar to their American counterparts. . . . Since the Japanese family is an institution that binds the individual for life, he is encouraged to view his relationship with other family members as one of continuing mutual support and participation in common goals. . . . The classroom situation parallels the family. Just as the child's relationships with his family are strong and permanent, so his relationships with classmates tend to be strong and permanent also. . . . The American classroom resembles a competitive arena, whereas the Japanese classroom resembles the training ground of a single team, learning how to play the game for [sic] life cooperatively (Kiefer 1970).

Kindergarten and elementary schoolteachers consciously teach group identity. Because school is a time for developing peer solidarity, automatic promotion is the norm. Failing or jumping grades is unthinkable. In-school ability grouping is avoided in almost every situation. Upper secondary schools, universities, and schools within a university are rigidly ability-graded (but by group rather than by individual rankings). Heterogeneous grouping for learning in large groups is practiced in most schooling. Large groups allow for peer cooperation in learning.

All groups provide numerous occasions for reinforcing individual identity with the group. Automatic promotion continues through schooling and even into corporate career life.

An organizational principle that supports this development of group identity is the institutional segregation of strict (*kibishī*) and indulgent (*amai*) discipline (*shitsuke*). Parents repeatedly encouraged teachers to be more kibishī in their relations with junior high school students but resisted any suggestion that they could be more kibishī with their own children. I once commented that a junior high school student whose uncle was a professional tutor had a special advantage in preparing for the high school entrance examinations. Her mother corrected me by saying, "But he's a member of the family." She implied that one who is a family member cannot be sufficiently kibishī to be an effective tutor.

When I inquired about the principle of sending one's child off to another household to learn the craft on which the family business was built, I would be told, "*Tanin no meshi o kū*" ("You [have to] eat someone else's rice"). You have to experience dependence on a stern disciplinarian to be able to develop the strength of character that is necessary to learn an adult skill, so families often send sons who will be inheriting a family business to another household for their apprenticeship in the family trade. In the same way, new bank employees are sometimes taken for a short period of military "boot camp" training at a Self-Defense Forces base camp (Rohlen 1984).

Discipline, when associated with the use of punishment for correction and training, is seen as a job for a person outside of the group within which good feelings must be maintained. The justification for some drinking parties and other social activities I observed in the junior high school was similarly tied to building group relations: "*Ii kankei o tamotsu tame ni*" ("We do it in order to promote good human feelings"). It is the idea that indulgence will reinforce human relationships within the group. How else could one maintain the unending commitment to one's family, group, or organization? Empathy and responsibility are the requirements for all group members (Glazer 1976).

The separation of entrance examinations from the schools in which children study promotes the same kind of separation between strictness and indulgence. The teachers can even be seen as indulgent coaches, separate from the strict examination system that distributes the real rewards and punishments: "By means of the entrance examination system, competition is taken out of the classroom into an impersonal setting in which contact and communication between competitors is minimized" (Kiefer 1970).

Inside the family, the kindergarten, and the elementary school there are many reinforcements for a "good-child" identity. Underlying this approach is the assumption that a child is basically good. A positive self-image is encouraged by parents, grandmothers, and kindergarten and elementary schoolteachers who would never accuse a child of willful mischief. The child just "doesn't understand" what is proper. Even when my boys were deliberately poking holes in the *shōji* (paper doors) of our house, "grandmother" would say "*Ii ko ne*" ("You're a good child, aren't you?") while I was saying sharply, "Stop that!" and thinking of them as willfully mischievous.

At the same time, children tend to enjoy their school experience though they too sometimes develop "school phobia" and are referred to psychiatrists or counselors to see if their "character" can be improved. If nothing else, the Japanese educational system in school and at home demonstrates the extent to which children can be pushed to learn those skills that the modern school can teach and to adapt to the arbitrary authoritarian structures of modern schooling.

It is in the assumptions about learning and about teaching strategies which lead to desired learning goals that we can begin to understand the rationale for organizing education in a Japanese way. American preoccupation with technical pedagogical differences—focusing, for example, on "time in school" and "time on task"—overlooks a simple cultural explanation of differences in our national systems. How we think about teaching and learning—our cultural theory of learning—makes an important difference in what can be accomplished in school or other educational institutions. The assumption that effort, not intelligence, is what leads to school success may be the most important contribution that comparative studies of Japanese education can make to American Schools.

This excerpt is taken from John Singleton, "*Gambaru:* A Japanese Cultural Theory of Learning," in *Japanese Schooling: Patterns of Socialization, Equality, and Political Control,* edited by J. J. Shields (University Park and London: The Pennsylvania State University Press, 1989), 1–8.

REFERENCES

Glazer, Nathan. "Social and Cultural Factors in Japanese Economic Growth." In *Asia's New Giant: How the Japanese Economy Works,* edited by Hugh Patrick and Henry Rosovsky. Washington, DC: The Brookings Institution, 1976.

Herrigel, Eugene. *Zen in the Art of Archery.* New York: Random House, Vintage Books, 1971.

Kiefer, Christie W. "The Psychological Interdependence of Family, School, and Bureaucracy in Japan." *American Anthropologist* 72 (1970): 66–75.

Rohlen, Thomas P. "*Seishin kyōiku* in a Japanese Bank." *Anthropology and Education Quarterly* 15 (1984): 17–28.

Singleton, John. *Nichu: A Japanese School: Case Studies in Education and Culture.* New York: Holt, Rinehart, and Winston, 1967.

Singleton, John, and Willi Singleton. "The Way of the Potter." In special issue of *Craft International* 32, edited by John Mock (January/March 1984): 14–17.

Smith, Robert J. *Japanese Society: Tradition, Self, and the Social Order.* Cambridge: Cambridge University Press, 1983.

Wagatsuma, Hiroshi. "*Gambaru.*" *Japan Encyclopedia.* Tokyo: Kodansha International Ltd., 1983.

In this elegant essay, Professor Nobuo Shimahara develops a way to explore relationships between education policy directives and educational practices. The excerpt included here does not do justice to the theoretical sophistication of the original article, but it does demonstrate important and sometimes unrecognized relationships between culture and teacher behavior in Japan.

Examination Rituals and Group Life

NOBUO SHIMAHARA

I n the postwar era, the Japanese college entrance examinations (CEE) waxed steadily in breadth and influence, finally assuming the proportions of a national obsession. Year by year, the lengthening shadow of the examinations fell upon larger segments of society and altered not only the orientation of secondary education but also the behavior of adolescents and their families. The purpose of this article is to inquire into the nature of the linkage between individual behaviors and CEE policies. To put it another way, why has the pressure to succeed in the CEE grown so oppressive, and why has it been allowed to continue?

College Entrance Examinations

Every year about 45 percent of Japan's high school graduates seek enrollment at 996 postsecondary institutions: 460 four-year colleges and 536 two-year colleges. The CEE are currently persistent sources of tension in Japanese life. Pressures for shaping the socialization of adolescents and the structure of secondary schools as they attempt to meet the requirements of the examinations have become a source of perpetual, culturally sanctioned anxiety for students, parents, and teachers. Vogel (1971), in his study of city life in Tokyo in the early 1960s, describes these pressures:

No single event, with the possible exception of marriage, determines the course of a young man's life as much as an entrance examination, and nothing, including marriage, requires as many years of planning and hard work. . . . These arduous preparations constitute a kind of rite de passage whereby a young man proves that he has the qualities of ability and endurance for becoming a salaried man (40).

The Influence of the CEE on Schooling

The CEE has a powerful effect upon secondary education. It imposes a particular framework on the socialization and schooling of adolescents, and these forces, in turn, help shape students' cognitive and motivational orientations to education. For example, a majority of students in the academic high schools tend to view schooling as truly relevant when it promotes preparation for the CEE and as only marginally useful when it does not contribute directly to university admission. Adolescents undergo a great deal of personal sacrifice and have little intrinsic motivation for learning because of the extrinsic pressures imposed upon them. It is within this framework that most academic high schools prepare students for the CEE. In the lower secondary schools, education has aimed increasingly at preparing for the high school entrance examinations.

At academic high schools, teaching methods and curricula are designed to meet the requirements for the CEE. Hence academic high schools have evolved into cram systems in one way or another. As Thomas Rohlen's (1983) study of high schools in Kobe and my own research (Shimahara 1979) have revealed, many schools adopt a system of accelerated, text-based teaching, where subject matter is covered by the end of the second year or early in the third year of high school and the time remaining is devoted to drilling for the CEE. Drill books, consisting of past examination questions, are often used in place of texts. In addition most students, particularly seniors, are required to take a number of exercise tests, including a half-dozen mock entrance examinations.

Three Cases

The following examples should help to identify the characteristics of the instrumental activities under discussion (Shimahara 1979).

Established in a suburban area just outside the city limits of Nagoya in 1968, Tojo High School has a reputation for being a rigorous, new prefectural school that must match the academic standards of traditional schools in the city. It is considered the model for many recently established public high schools in Aichi Prefecture, of which Nagoya is the capital, and in other prefectures as well.

Most Tojo students were in the fiftieth to sixtieth percentile of their lower secondary schools in Nagoya. Teachers at Tojo admit that many of the school's entering tenth-grade students lack the basic cognitive skills essential to grade-level learning and lack the habit of sustained study. Yet every year Tojo places 95 percent of its graduates in colleges, and one-third of them win admission to national universities, outdistancing other recently established high schools in this respect.

Tojo faculty attribute their success to the cumulative effect of a group-oriented program called *seikatsu shidō* (guidance for living) that, from the school's inception, has stressed such behavioral and attitudinal attributes as diligence, concentration, conformity to the group, perseverance, prompt response to external expectations, and acceptance of teachers as the unquestioned sources of academic and moral authority.

New students are exposed to group training from the first day of school. Under the supervision of teachers and senior students, the program involves rigorous physical training for half a day, which requires swift and precise coordinated movement and quick response to authority. Each individual is regarded as part of the group, and individual misbehavior reflects badly on the group. Physical training is used as the model for other activities, including athletic contests, club activities, and daily cleaning of the school. In all cases there is an emphasis on orderliness, promptness, and competence.

Sophomores undergo an intensive three-day initiation ritual called *gempukushiki*. Gempukushiki further communicates the teachers' expectations that students should behave properly. The teachers have observed that after the gempukushiki ritual, most students begin to display the behaviors and orientations desired by the faculty.

During the ritual, teachers and students (and a few parent volunteers) spend three days in a distant mountainous area, staying at a local inn at night. All sophomores are required to participate in varied activities, including group living, mountain climbing, building campfires, and visiting temples. Each activity starts early in the morning when teachers whistle to signal that students must get up. Students are required to line up immediately in specified areas. Teachers emphasize promptness and punctuality and punish those who are disorderly and disobedient. Although this program is an extension of physical training, it is more intensive and many students find it shocking.

The faculty apply the aforementioned principles of behavior and attitudes in the classroom to develop disciplined habits necessary for learning. In the senior year, before and after the regularly scheduled classes, students receive supplementary drilling for the CEE. During summer the school offers seniors a condensed cram session lasting four days and three nights. This is intended to test students' endurance and their ability to concentrate. Tojo's primary techniques for CEE preparation are constant drilling and repetitive review to reinforce student mastery of the subjects essential to the CEE.

In the senior year, most students withdraw from extracurricular activities and concentrate on CEE preparation. The daily schedule of an above-average student three months prior to the CEE reveals the intensity of his preparation. The student gets up at 6:30 A.M. and reaches school at 7:30. From 7:30 to 8:30 he receives supplementary drilling; he then goes to his regular classes, and these are followed by afternoon drilling from 3:40 P.M. to 5:00 P.M. He returns home by 6:00 P.M. and after supper studies until midnight.

Tests are given periodically at Tojo to evaluate the students' performance. In addition, most students take national mock entrance examinations six times in the senior year to improve skills in test taking and also to identify their regional and national rankings.

Let us turn to another school. Asahi Prefectural High School in Nagoya was established in the early Meiji period. In sharp contrast to Tojo, Asahi has been regarded as a traditional preparatory school. In the past it enrolled only the best of students drawn from nearly two hundred lower secondary schools in Aichi Prefecture. Public criticism of Asahi's elitism mounted toward the end of the 1960s, however, and resulted, in 1973, in a policy requiring Asahi and comparable public schools in the city to accept less-qualified applicants.

Despite the lowering of admissions standards, Asahi's internal policy has changed very little. Faculty gear the organization and pacing of instruction and drilling, not to the average pupil but to the superior students. For example, by the early part of the senior year students have covered 20 percent more material than is required by the Education Ministry's prescribed course of study. This enables faculty to devote most of the year to drilling for the CEE. This policy affects not only seniors but also juniors and sophomores. Students are driven to excel from their first year at the school, though many fail.

In contrast to Tojo, Asahi has a far more relaxed orientation toward authority and the manner in which individual students prepare for the CEE. Bright students are expected to challenge teachers. The school does not offer supplementary drilling and related programs, other than prolonged, intensive drilling during class. Students are expected to make their own plans for CEE preparation. Nearly 50 percent of them either participate in condensed *yobikō* college preparatory school programs in spring or summer or attend yobikō or *juku* (cram schools) year-round. More than one-third of the students become *rōnin*, institutionally unattached young people studying for exams.

Differences and similarities between Tojo and Asahi students are obvious. Though Tojo's students receive in-school drilling to prepare them for the examination, Asahi's receive such preparation in yobikō and juku as well as at the school. The relevance of the high school experience to the students is determined by their devotion to CEE preparation. Emphasis is universally placed upon the deliberate development of orientational and behavioral responses to the CEE requirements. The world in which high school students live requires them to sacrifice pleasure, spontaneity, and youthful sparkle for examination success. No senior students interviewed, at the above schools and at others, had opportunities to date or go to movies during their senior year. They have no time to spend on leisure activities. Despite their interest in such experiences and in the opposite sex, they sublimate those interests until they enter college.

What happens when academic high schools deemphasize preparation for the CEE? Some schools do so, but they are the exception. I studied one of them, Fuji High School, which is attached to a national university in Nagoya. It is considered to lack the requisite rigor and to be inferior to CEE-oriented schools in the city.

Fuji's practice creates an inevitable dilemma for most of its students. Though they can appreciate the relatively relaxed atmosphere in the school, they often worry about their disadvantage in preparing for the CEE and their low rankings in the frequent mock entrance examinations. Hence the majority of students at Fuji seek assistance for CEE preparation from private tutors, yobikō, and juku. Examination pressures force Fuji students to conform to the typical scheme of drilling and thus narrow motivational and cognitive orientation. Because their school does not provide instrumental linkages between CEE activities and their cultural goals, students seek to establish that linkage by calling on outside assistance.

Linkages

Two relevant cultural goals are transmitted by these examination-oriented activities. First, the most obvious and immediate goal is to help students gain admission to universities and earn the education and credentials that universities provide. Second, the sustained cultural goal of examination-oriented activities is to ready students to participate in Japan's competitive meritocracy (Rohlen 1986). Educational credentials are essential to gaining lucrative employment and determining individual mobility in a hierarchically structured workplace characterized by life-time employment and a rigid seniority system (Aso 1981). The coveted goal is to gain lifetime employment leading to status enhancement.

The ideal pattern of social mobility in Japan is advancement within a single organization rather than achieving increased status by moving from one organization to another. Vertical mobility requires that individuals gain employment in a desirable organization immediately after they graduate from a university and that they form a quick commitment to the expectations of the organization. Once graduates gain employment, their social status is judged by the social prestige of the companies for which they work (Nakane 1970, 104–20). The social prestige and rank of the university from which youths graduate tend to determine the employment opportunities open to them.

As Japanese sociologists point out, the general hiring practice of large firms is to give preference to the graduates of the highly selective universities (Amano 1986b, 25). Ushiogi (1986, 206) reports that as late as 1979, 28 percent of Japanese firms permitted graduates of selective institutions to take employment examinations, whereas only 36 percent accepted employment applications from less selective institutions. Although preferential hiring has been criticized as discriminatory, the practice remains relatively unchanged.

Hiring practices in Japan reinforce the nation's stress on school credentials. Diplomas from particular schools are highly valued by industrial firms. Therefore, winning admission to a prestigious university significantly affects a young person's future; only graduation from a prestigious university will ensure employment by a socially prestigious corporation.

Beyond this, examination scores also confer social status even though, as certain scholars have indicated, the effect of educational credentials on income distribution has lately been reduced (Aso 1981; Ushiogi 1986).

Policy Issues

Intense entrance examinations are not a recent phenomenon or unique to postindustrial Japan. They were introduced in the fourth quarter of the nineteenth century, when the Meiji education system was firmly established. They were introduced as an objective meritocratic method of selecting applicants for middle and higher schools.

Being admitted to high school is less frenetic today than it once was. Classroom advisors, eager to avoid fierce competition and the trauma of rejection, carefully monitor the process, counsel students, and encourage them to take mock entrance examinations not only to give them practice but also to give them an indication as to how well or how badly they will do on the real examinations. Advisors meticulously match students' qualifications with the various levels of academic rigor required by the high schools, thereby reducing the risk of failure and ensuring that most applicants are admitted to the schools of their choice. Nonetheless, the entrance examinations impress students and convince them that preparing for admission to highly ranked regional and national schools is a serious business (U.S. Department of Education 1987, 38). Consequently, the free-for-all competition at examination time has, in the postwar system, shifted to admission to universities.

We now return to the question: why have these examinations remained largely unchanged for so many decades? As we have already seen, they are not ends in themselves. They are instruments that serve cultural goals—obtaining credentials from selective universities and career enhancement—and those goals themselves perpetuate the intensely competitive process of admission to a university.

The movement away from a class-based system of ascribed status to a meritocratic system of achieved status has had some ironic results. The new meritocracy is powered by a school-based credentialing system that ascribes status to high-achieving students. It is assumed that school success is a powerful predictor of job performance, so the system allows no alternative routes into the job market. The highly influential evaluation of Japanese education by the Organization of Economic Cooperation and Development (OECD) in 1971 points to problems in this single-route system.

> There is a general belief that a student's performance in one crucial examination at about the age of eighteen is likely to determine the rest of his life. . . . The university entrance examination is the primary sorting device for careers in Japanese society. The result is not an aristocracy of birth, but a sort of degree-ocracy. The system is egalitarian and flexible compared to a hereditary class system, but rigid and arbitrary as compared to systems in which individual performance over a much wider span of time helps sort people into appropriate careers and offers an opportunity for the motivated individual to catch up educationally and even change occupational status as he develops his capacities. This pattern will not change greatly as long as the "lifetime employment pattern" lasts.

The OECD report further notes that the CEE represents "a distorted . . . oversimplified, social evaluation of ability."

The OECD report and the report of the Central Council of Education, also issued in 1971, influenced the reform movement of the 1980s. School reformers for the first time began to pay serious attention to the linkage between CEE-related instrumental activities and their cultural goals. The first report of the National Council on Education Reform (NCER) articulately addressed the cultural goals issue.

> The first direction is to create, as a long-term objective, a lifelong-learning society relevant to the twenty-first century. In a society with excessive emphasis on educational background, special importance is attached to "when and where did he learn?" in evaluating the merit of an individual, while in a lifelong-learning society emphasis is placed on "what and to what extent did he learn?" (1985, 47).

In short, NCER has heightened an awareness of the need for alternative methods of recruiting applicants for employment in government and private industry: "multidimensional and diversified" strategies to evaluate individual abilities throughout individual careers and strategies to improve what the Japanese often refer to as *gakureki shakai,* a social structure that places excessive emphasis on one's specific school background as a criterion for employment and promotion. The NCER recommendations are largely general and abstract (Shimahara 1986, 91–93). NCER has articulated the important linkage factors influencing CEE instrumental activities, but it is not yet certain that individual firms and government will implement the recommendations.

A Concluding Word

I have contended here that in order to understand the continued intensity of competition in the CEE, we must examine the linkage between instrumental activities and cultural goals. Although Japanese reformers have begun to look critically at that linkage, they have stopped short of proposing concrete strategies for changing the hierarchical characteristics of universities, the hierarchical character of school credentials, hiring practices in business, and business promotion policies. They have also failed to propose radical changes in the CEE system which would have been consistent with their stress on the multidimensional evaluation of individual abilities appropriate to a lifelong learning society. To change the CEE system, Japanese universities' "closedness" and self-serving orientation must also be radically altered, as pointed out recently by Michio Nagai (1987), a distinguished scholar and former education minister. Reformers have not challenged the universities, and the shortcomings of the reform proposals suggest how deeply the CEE practice is rooted in the Japanese social structure. That the reformers are now concentrating on linkage factors is encouraging from the policy standpoint, but they must appreciate how the entrance examinations and the goals and practices of society reinforce each other's continuity. To change one without the other is futile.

This piece is excerpted from Nobuo Shimahara, "The College Entrance Examination System and Policy Issues in Japan," *Journal of Qualitative Studies in Education* I (1988): 39–49.

REFERENCES

Amano, Ikuo. "Continuity and Changes in the Structure of Japanese Education." In *The Changes in the Japanese University: Comparative Perspective,* edited by W. K. Cummings, I. Amano, and K. Kitamura. New York: Praeger, 1979: 10–39.

———. *Education and Selection.* Tokyo: Dai-ichi Hoki Shuppan, 1982.

———. *Social History of Examinations.* Tokyo: Tokyo University Press, 1986a.

———. "Educational Crisis in Japan." In *Educational Policies in Crisis,* edited by W. K. Cummings, E. R. Beauchamp, S. Ichikawa, V. N. Kobayashi, and M. Ushiogi. New York: Praeger, 1986b.

Aso, Makoto. "The Structural Pathology of a Credential Society." In *The Transformation of Japan's Credentialing Society,* edited by H. Takeuchi and M. Aso. Tokyo: Yuhikaku, 1981.

Nagai, Michio. *Asahi Shimbun.* 23 June 1987.

Nakane, Chie. *Japanese Society.* Berkeley: University of California Press, 1970.

National Council on Education Reform (NCER). *Report.* In *Rinkyoshin to kyōikukaikaku-jiyuka kara koseishugi e* (From Liberalization [Deregulation] to Putting an Emphasis on Individuality [Personality]), edited by Gyōsei. Tokyo: Gyōsei, 1985.

Organization of Economic Cooperation and Development (OECD). *A Review of Education: Japan.* Paris: OECD, 1971.

Rohlen, Thomas P. *Japan's High Schools.* Berkeley: University of California Press, 1983.

———. "Japanese Education." *The American Scholar* 55 (1986): 29-43.

Shimahara, Nobuo. *Adaptation and Education in Japan.* New York: Praeger, 1979.

———. "Japanese Education Reform in the 1980s." *Issues in Education* 4 (1986): 85–100.

U. S. Department of Education. *Japanese Education Today: A Report from the U.S. Study of Education in Japan.* Washington, DC: U.S. Government Printing Office, 1987.

Ushiogi, M. "Transition from School to Work: The Japanese Case." In *Educational Policies in Crisis,* edited by W. R. Cummings, E. R. Beauchamp, S. Ichikawa, V. N. Kobayashi, and M. Ushiogi. New York: Praeger, 1986.

Vogel, Ezra. *Japan's New Middle Class.* Berkeley: University of California Press, 1971.

PART IV

EDUCATION POLICY AND THE DILEMMAS OF REFORM

The Japanese education system, like that of the United States, is beset with historic dilemmas that defy quick fixes. As Barbara Finkelstein's introduction and the readings in the next two sections reveal, the Japanese perceive and respond to a variety of intractable moral, political, economic, and educational problems that are not only invisible to most Western observers but reveal a much more complex educational reality than is commonly portrayed, even by the best of scholars (Cummings 1980; Passin 1965; Shimahara 1979; Cummings, et. al. 1986; United States Department of Education 1987; Shields 1989). The readings in this section aim to correct three reigning images of Japanese education. When taken together, along with the articles in part 5, we believe that they present a balanced view of educational accomplishments and dilemmas in Japan.

Introduction

Images of Japanese Education

BARBARA FINKELSTEIN

A first image of Japanese schooling that we hope to correct is of the schools as nurseries for economic development, underlying the "Japan as number one" theme. From this perspective, schools come into focus as places where highly respected teachers cultivate dedicated, hard-working, high-achieving learners who somehow carry the fruits of their formal schooling into the marketplace, becoming disciplined and competent workers—an industrial army bringing Japan into the forefront of powerful nations (Vogel 1979; White 1987).

A second popular and scholar-generated image is that of the Japanese school as an instrument of egalitarianism, teaching the same things to all children, avoiding competitive distinctions and labels, preparing equally all who choose to take entrance examinations to high schools and colleges, and otherwise creating a meritocratic system which provides all students with opportunities to compete for valued places in status-conferring high schools and universities (Cummings 1980).

The third image of Japanese education is of schools as psychological pressure cookers, as examination hells and incubators of emotional volatility, where status degradations, outbursts of feeling, and feats of physical and mental endurance are daily demands and where students suffer from intolerable social and psychological pressures. (A fourth image, that of the schools as harmonious and conflict-free, will be dealt with in part 5.)

Like most cultural stereotypes, these images are not completely false. One thinks of the goals and plans of Japanese educational and political leaders, the relative uniformity of the national curriculum, the high-pressure examinations, and the shared commitment to harmonious face-to-face relationships as examples of the three images. Like most cultural generalizations and stereotypes, however, these images tend to obscure as much as they reveal. The following readings reveal the oversimplifications. The first, excerpted from a U.S. Department of Education study titled *Japanese Education Today* (1987), incorporates these stereotypes in an overview of Japanese educational purposes and processes. The other readings destabilize these perceptions by revealing three relatively invisible problems with which the Japanese struggle: the problem posed by private schooling, by unruly youth, and by minority groups.

One reality obscured by the presentation of Japan and the Japanese educational system as an egalitarian, high-pressure, uniform, harmony-based meritocracy is the large, informal network of private schools, which reinforces and reflects a differentiation in the social structure which is not always visible to the outside observer.

Some of these private schools serve low-achieving students who cannot pass entrance examinations for public high schools. Other, so-called escalator schools provide automatic access to prestigious colleges and universities for families who can afford them. Still others—*juku, yobikō*, or testing company schools—are private, profit-making institutions which play a variety of roles in Japanese education. They prepare students to pass entrance examinations for elite high schools and colleges by providing a special track for ambitious parents and students. They serve as alternative educational systems for unaffiliated (*rōnin*) students. Further, they offer an alternative educational structure, which relieves pressure on the official school system, and they provide opportunities for students to learn traditional arts and crafts not taught in the regular schools (Dore 1975; Kitamura 1986; Tsuneyoshi 1990).

Since private schools perform so many social functions in Japan, it is hardly surprising to discover that Japanese observers are, as a group, deeply ambivalent about the schools' relative benefits and weaknesses. Professor Kazuyuki Kitamura, founder of the Institute for Research in Higher Education at the University of Hiroshima and now director of Research in Higher Education at the Multi-Media Institute in Tokyo, describes in his article what he calls the "dual structure" of Japanese education as both a strength and a weakness.

The reconciliation of commitments to equality and merit is the focus of the articles by Fujita and Tsuneyoshi, who, as they explore the evolution of contemporary problems in education, reveal the challenges which private schools pose for traditional Japanese education. Professor Fujita views the prosperity and popularity of jukus, yobikōs, and testing company schools as inimical to historic Japanese commitments to the public schools as a means of preserving and transmitting uniform intellectual fare and moral attitudes among the Japanese. In a different mode, Professor Tsuneyoshi compares concepts of equality in Japan and the United

States and suggests that competition between students in Japanese public schools is muted because of the existence of an unofficial school system where ability differences are acknowledged and organized and where distinctions among students are systematized.

In the view of other Japanese education observers, the popularity of the informal system threatens the traditional emphasis on equality and harmony. Professor Teruhisa Horio of the University of Tokyo, for example, regards the proliferation of informal educational networks as a chapter in the evolution of industrial capitalism, where the principle of unconstrained competition becomes dominant and where economic goals overwhelm the moral purposes of schooling. According to this viewpoint, the popularity of for-profit private schools originates in a disposition to elevate competition as a value and to call on the government "to license and officially supervise the cram industry" (Horio 1988; see also Professor Horio's general critique of Japanese education which appears in part 5 of this book).

Another group of observers of Japanese private schools, represented here by Mamoru Tsukada, derives its points of view from studying student attitudes. Unlike the critics of the private schools, these observers regard the schools as benevolent institutions, providing an alternative educational environment for children who feel like failures. One experienced principal has, with some consternation, discovered that children will frequently cut school to go to cram school and gain rather than lose academic ground in the process.

> Embarrassing as it is to report, there are cases of children who are chronically absent from school, and when we investigate, we find that they are going to the juku instead and actually doing better academically. Again, the reason the children themselves give is that they can form their own friendships there—that it's more fun. More than that, the teachers in the juku have a better rapport with these children: in the regular schools, the teacher will often write off the student who is not doing well, but the juku povides a more humane kind of environment; it's not, as we have generally been thinking, a hardship on the students (Kazuhiro 1982).

The multiplicity of viewpoints about the relative benefits, functions, and potentials of the private school system all suggest that the stereotypical images of Japanese education cited above are oversimplified, if not altogether incorrect. Japanese schools are not perfectly smooth-working engines of group harmony where highly motivated students and dedicated teachers work together to reach levels of educational achievement that exceed those of almost every other country in the world. Nor are Japanese children overdriven, educational achievers willing to do anything to get into prestigious schools.

American and Japanese scholars alike have made much of Japan's overheated examination competitions, where ambitious students in lower and upper secondary schools put childish pursuits aside and immerse themselves in tutorial pressure cookers in order to gain seats in coveted, prestige-conferring schools leading to good jobs in industry and government (Rohlen 1980). Called "an insanity" by some (Horio 1988, 301), a diploma disease by others (Dore 1975), "academic pedigreeism" by still others (OECD Report 1971), Japan's examination hell is said to cause an array of social and educational problems—an increase in the numbers of teenage suicides, instances of group violence, corporal punishment, and student rebellions—especially in the junior high schools (Horio 1988; Kazuhiro 1982; Amano 1986).

In fact, Japan's examination hell is a middle- and upper-class affliction and one that is visited on boys much more than on girls. No more than one-third of the students in precollegiate schools enter the fierce competition for coveted places in junior and senior high schools. In large cities, where the competition is most intense, only half of the students attend informal schools at all. It is thus by no means a universal experience of Japanese students.

The readings which follow provide a view of Japanese education which is more balanced than that of an unvaryingly egalitarian pressure cooker imposing uniformity on a generation of docile and malleable students.

REFERENCES

Amano, Ikuo. "The Dilemma of Japanese Education Today." *Japan Foundation Newsletter* 13, 5 (1986): 1–10.

Beauchamp, Edward. "Education and Democracy in Japan." In *Japanese Democracy,* edited by Ishida Tadashi and Ellis Krauss. Santa Barbara, CA: Center for the Study of Democratic Institutions: 1987.

Cummings, William K. *Education and Equality in Japan.* Princeton: Princeton University Press, 1980.

Cummings, William K., Edward R. Beauchamp, Shogo Ichikawa, Victor N. Kobayashi, and Morikazu Ushiogi, eds. *Educational Policies in Crisis: Japanese and American Perspectives.* New York: Praeger, 1986, 159–65.

Dore, Ronald R. *The Diploma Disease,* Berkeley and Los Angeles: University of California Press, 1975.

Fujita, Hidenori. "A Crisis of Legitimacy in Japanese Education: Meritocracy and Cohesiveness." *Research Bulletin of School of Education, Nagoya University.* 1985: 117–33.

Horio, Teruhisa. *Educational Thought and Ideology in Modern Japan: State Authority and Intellectual Freedom,* edited and translated by Steven Platzer. Tokyo: University of Tokyo Press, 1988: 3–7, 12–18.

Ichikawa, Shogo. "Japan." In *Educational Policy: An International Survey,* edited by J. R. Hugh. New York: St. Martins Press, 1984.

––––. "American Perceptions of Japanese Education." In *Educational Policies in Crisis: Japanese and American Perspectives,* edited by William K. Cummings, Edward R. Beauchamp, Shogo Ichikawa, Victor N. Kobayashi, a n d Morikazu Ushiogi. New York: Praeger, 1986: 245.

Kazuhiro, Mochizuki. "The Present Situation of Japan's Education: A Report from School." Orientation Seminars on Japan 1, 11: 17. Tokyo: The Japan Foundation Office of Overseas Studies Center, 1982.

Kitamura, Kazuyuki. "The Decline and Reform of Education in Japan." In *Educational Policies in Crisis: Japanese and American Perspectives,* edited by William K. Cummings, Edward R. Beauchamp, Shogo Ichikawa, Victor N. Kobayashi, and Morikazu Ushiogi. New York: Praeger, 1986, 159–65.

Mikio, Sumiya. "The Function and Social Structure of Japan: Schools and Japanese Society," *Journal of Social and Political Ideas in Japan* 5 (1980): 117–31.

OECD Examiners' Report. *Reviews of National Policies for Education: Japan.* Paris: OECD, 1971.

Passin, Herbert. *Society and Education in Japan.* New York: Teachers College Press, 1965.

Rohlen, Thomas P. "Is Japanese Education Becoming Less Egalitarian?" *Journal of Japanese Studies,* 3, (1977).

––––. "The Juku Phenomenon: An Exploratory Essay." *Journal of Japanese Studies* 6, no. 25 (1980): 233.

––––. "Conflict in Japanese Education." In *Conflict in Contemporary Japan,* edited by Ellis Krauss, Thomas Rohlen, and Patricia Steinhoff. Honolulu: University of Hawaii Press, 1984.

Shields, James J., ed. *Japanese Schooling: Patterns of Socialization, Equality, and Political Control.* University Park: The Pennsylvania State University Press, 1989.

Shimahara, Nobuo. *Adaptation and Education in Japan.* New York: Praeger, 1979.

Tsukada, Mamoru. "Institutionalised Supplementary Education in Japan: The *Yobikō* and *Rōnin* Student Adaptations." *Comparative Education Review* 24, 3 (1988): 286–301.

Tsuneyoshi, Ryoko Kato. "Meanings of Equality: Lessons from Japanese Debate." *Educational Forum* 54 (Winter 1990): 185–95.

U.S. Department of Education. *Japanese Education Today: A Report from the U.S. Study of Education in Japan.* Washington, DC: U.S. Government Printing Office, 1987.

Vogel, Ezra. *Japan As Number One.* Cambridge, MA: Harvard University Press, 1979.

White, Merry. *The Japanese Educational Challenge: A Commitment to Children.* New York: The Free Press, 1987.

Emphasizing the aims of education, this small overview, taken from *Japanese Education Today,* provides a synthesis of images and perceptions articulated by an array of scholars and policymakers in the U.S. Prepared by a study team organized by the U.S. Department of Education and carefully qualified, this kind of description nonetheless supports the view that Japanese education is relatively uniform, homogeneous, hierarchical, and group-oriented and thus reinforces prevailing stereotypes.

Japanese Education Today

UNITED STATES DEPARTMENT OF EDUCATION

J apanese education is a powerful instrument of cultural continuity and national policy. The explicit and implicit content of the school curriculum and the manner in which teaching and learning are accomplished impart the attitudes, knowledge, sensitivities, and skills expected of emerging citizens of Japanese society. These lessons are further reinforced in the context of family and society.

Linguistically, racially, and ethnically, Japan is a comparatively homogeneous nation with a strong sense of cultural identity and national unity. But Japanese society is not monolithic, and there is considerable individuality. There are finely calibrated distinctions in status based on age, gender, employment, and social and educational background.

Despite these differences, the Japanese prefer to define themselves on the basis of their commonly held beliefs and values. While popular culture and lifestyles have undergone some dramatic changes since World War II, there remains a high degree of public consensus regarding social values, appropriate standards of behavior, and the importance and goals of education.

The Goals of Education

The origins of the Japanese commitment to education lie in the Confucian and Buddhist heritage in which great respect is accorded learning and educational endeavor as the means to personal and societal improvement. Today, there is a clear consensus that education is essential for both individual and national development and that it requires active, sustained commitment of energy and resources at all levels of society. Parents and children take education seriously because success in school is a crucial determinant of economic and social status in adult life. Government policymakers and business leaders view the content and quality of public education as central to national cohesion, economic development, and effective international relations.

To the Japanese, education has always had important goals in addition to the acquisition of academic knowledge, intellectual growth, or vocational skills. Moral education and character development are also among the central concerns. There is a strong consensus that schools have the obligation and authority to impart fundamental Japanese values as the foundation of proper moral attitudes and personal habits.

Respect for society and the established order, the prizing of group goals above individual interests, diligence, self-criticism, and well-organized and disciplined study and work habits are all traits which are believed to be amenable to instruction. The child's learning experiences at each level from preschool through twelfth grade reinforce their acquisition. Japanese teachers believe that the proper development of these values, attitudes, and habits is fundamental to success in the classroom as well as in adult life.

Harmonious Relations and the Central Role of the Group

Japanese society places a high value on harmony in interpersonal relations and the ability to cooperate with others. The Japanese believe that being a member of a well-organized and tightly knit group that works hard toward common goals is a natural and pleasurable human experience. Schools reflect this cultural priority. Classroom activities are structured to encourage or require participation in group activities, to emphasize the responsibility of individual students to the class as a group and the school as a whole, and to develop group loyalty.

Particularly in elementary school, classes are organized into small groups, which are the basic units of instruction, discipline, and other activities. Teachers attempt to foster group cohesion and a strong group spirit by avoiding overt recognition of differences in individual ability and minimizing one-against-one competition. Daily life in a Japanese classroom requires considerable mutual assistance and adaptation of individual views and interests to group goals and standards of behavior. The heavy emphasis on group activities and social consensus results in considerable conformity in behavior. There is a strong tradition of viewing conformity and group orientation as demonstrations of moral character.

To most Westerners, a high degree of behavioral conformity is typically associated with top-down control. However, Japanese teachers are not typically authoritarian, nor is harshness a characteristic of classroom life in Japan. Instead, the cultural emphasis on harmony and hard work requires that each individual within the system be a willing contributor to the group effort. Group leadership, Japanese style, orchestrates the members' motivations and expectations so that order and discipline, both in the classroom and the larger society, are natural outgrowths of achieving a high degree of individual identification with group goals.

Hard Work, Diligence, and Perseverance

The Japanese believe that hard work, diligence, and perseverance yield success in education as well as in other aspects of life. A certain amount of difficulty and hardship is believed to strengthen students' character and their resolve to do their best in learning and other important endeavors.

The amount of time and effort spent in study is believed to be more important than intelligence in determining educational outcomes. Most Japanese parents and educators are unshakably optimistic that virtually all children have the potential to master the challenging academic curriculum, provided they work hard and long enough. Some teachers and students are less sanguine. The educational results achieved by most Japanese students in international comparisons provide considerable support for the beliefs and expectations of the majority, particularly in light of the fact that there is no credible evidence that Japanese children have a higher level of native intelligence than, for example, American children.

A recent comparative study by Robert Hess and others attest to the Japanese emphasis on effort.

> In Japan, poor performance in mathematics was attributed to lack of effort; in the United States explanations were more evenly divided among ability, effort, and training at school. Japanese mothers were less likely to blame training at school as a cause of low achievement in mathematics.... Their children generally shared this view of things (Hess et al. 1980).

Parents and teachers encourage regular study habits from the first grade on. A careful, reflective approach which achieves accuracy and precision rather than speed or intuitive insight is emphasized, particularly during the early years. Repetition and memorization continue to be important in the learning process, particularly in preparation for the arduous and important high school and college entrance examinations.

Motivation

The cultural emphasis on student effort and diligence is balanced by a recognition of the important responsibility borne by teachers, parents, and schools to awaken the desire to try. Japanese teachers do not believe that motivation is primarily a matter of luck, family background, or personality traits. They believe that the desire to learn—like character itself—is something which can be shaped by teachers and influenced through the school environment. Students are unceasingly taught and urged to "do their best," in groups and as individuals.

A major method of motivating students is the encouragement of group activities, which are believed to be more enjoyable for students than solitary endeavor. Motivation through group activity is accomplished by promoting a strong sense of shared identity and by allowing individuals opportunity to influence group goals and activities. Wearing school uniforms, rotating student monitors, and planning and staging class and school activities all contribute to the process.

Particularly at the secondary level, entrance examinations provide special motivation for study. Students know that their scores on high school and university entrance examinations will strongly influence their future life path. Parents reinforce this concept by urging their children to study hard, by providing a home environment conducive to study, and by financing extra lessons and tutorial assistance.

Legacy

Japanese history and cultural values permeate Japanese education. The heritage is reflected in the national consensus on the importance of education, its role in character development, and the willingness of both parents and children to sustain effort and to sacrifice year after year to achieve success in school. It helps form the invisible foundation of the contemporary educational system.

This reading is excerpted from U.S. Department of Education, *Japanese Education Today: Report from the U.S. Study of Education in Japan* (Washington, DC: U.S. Government Printing Office, 1987).

REFERENCES

Hess, Robert, et al. "Maternal Expectations for Early Mastery of Developmental Tasks in Japan and the U.S." *International Journal of Psychology* 15 (1980): 260.

In this comprehensive critique of arguments which blame problems of unmotivated students, school violence, juvenile delinquency, and examination pressures on postwar school reforms, industrial capitalism, severe entrance examinations, and "degreeocracy," Professor Hidenori Fujita of Tokyo University argues that Japan's educational problems are products of a historical legacy at least a century old. Among the more enduring features of the Japanese educational system are commitments to comprehensive school purposes, ritualism, principles of meritocracy and competition, and the maintenance of status hierarchies between, within, and among elementary, secondary, and higher education institutions. Through a reconstruction of social, pedagogical, and political traditions, Professor Fujita reveals the existence of historic commitments to schools as social sorting mechanisms rather than uniform instruments of egalitarian opportunity.

Education Policy Dilemmas as Historic Constructions

HIDENORI FUJITA

I n March 1983, police officers attended more than two thousand Japanese secondary school graduation ceremonies (approximately 13 percent of the total). Their presence was designed to prevent school violence on that most important of school events in Japan—graduation day. Among various pathological phenomena of school education in contemporary Japan, school violence is one of the most symbolic and serious. According to "A Summary Report on Juvenile Delinquency," written by the Police Board in 1983, 1,244 incidents of school violence were reported for the first half of the year 1983, 42 percent of which were perpetrated against teachers and, in many cases, involved collective rather than individual violence.

Some argue that current educational problems—the prevalence of competition in the schools, the emphasis on economic production in society (NHK Shuzaihan 1983), the pervasiveness of degreeocracy, and the severe entrance examination system (OECD 1971)—are the consequences of postwar school reforms. It seems to me, however, that the origin of the current crisis predates the postwar reforms and inheres in the principles and characteristics of Japanese education itself: ritualism, the commitment to schools as comprehensive agencies of socialization, the principle of meritocracy and competition, the hierarchical school structure and grading system, and prestige differentiation among schools within the same education level (upper secondary and tertiary levels). All of these emphases combined to create schools which functioned as sorting mechanisms in society. All originated during the first three decades of the Meiji era (1868-1912). I do not claim, of course, that these characteristics are unique to Japanese education.

Establishment of the Modern School System

After the Meiji restoration in 1867, a strong central government enacted various policies in order to establish a modern industrial nation state (Shimomura 1977; Aso 1982; Amano 1982). The government proclaimed a series of educational regulations and, over three decades, established a meritocratic system. The basic school system became hierarchical and multitracked, with the Imperial University of Tokyo at the top and numerous elementary schools at the bottom. In between were preparatory, middle, and higher schools for boys and high schools and vocational schools for girls. Examinations and grades became the principal means of evaluation and were institutionalized throughout the system. Even in elementary school, the order of seats or nameplates in the class was commonly set according to student standing on monthly examinations. End-of-term examinations were conducted in the presence of a superintendent and a village or town master, were open to the public, and served as occasions to award prizes to distinguished students. Interschool competitive examinations, where representative students gathered together and competed for the honor of their own schools, further reinforced the system. The lists of students and graduates of the Imperial University of Tokyo were ordered according to academic standing. Entrance examinations for middle and higher schools as well as imperial universities became competitive and selective. All of these measures served to motivate students and cultivate a meritocratic orientation. In the process, students were sorted into various educational and social tracks. This does not mean, however, that opportunities for higher academic standing and for higher levels of schooling were equal. Those with better family backgrounds had more opportunities to go on to middle school and beyond. Nevertheless, it seems that the new meritocratic system led parents of lower-and middle-class families to keep their children in schools.

Family, Community, and Polity

To establish new orders of family, society, economy, and polity, the government initiated many important reforms in the first three decades of the Meiji restoration (Kawashima 1957; Fukushima 1967; Amano 1982). It abolished the old class system of military, farmer, artisan, and merchant by issuing decrees which allowed the common people to have family names and make interclass marriages. It eliminated stipends for the old military class and effectively impoverished all of those who did not actually enter the military or marry into a noble family. It reformed the land tax, established conscription, and continued to impose heavy burdens on smaller farmers and peasants. Further, the government suppressed libertarian and civil rights movements as well as peasant uprisings, promulgated the Imperial Constitution, and carried out various measures to engage the government in economic planning, the expansion of government enterprises, promotion of private capital, and the establishment of priorities for production. Through all of these policies and measures, the government solidified its power.

The government was also eager to control the family, and through the creation of a census law in 1871 and a civil law in 1898, it invested the heads of families with patriarchal rights and duties such as approving marriages, defining the residence of family members, notifying the village or town master of changes in the status of family members, or being charged with a criminal offense if any or all of these duties were badly dispatched. Thus, the head of a family became an extension of the administrative machinery of the emperor.

Government control over families extended to social affairs as well, including informal sanctions against disreputable behavior, sneering, and gossiping. These intrusions, which reinforced government power, were especially disruptive in traditional Japanese communities, where neighborhood relationships were close. Nonetheless, most families in a community were knit together by the economic and social pressures of civil law, conscription, land tax and other regulations, and shared beliefs in Confucian moral codes. The further diffusion of Confucian morality was promoted by the Imperial Rescript on Education (1890), the introduction of an authoritarian textbook adoption system, and a strong emphasis on moral education in elementary school.

Through the creation of an administrative or regulatory chain from village or town master to the head of each family, the government imposed regulations, collected taxes, enforced the conscription laws, and in general exercised direct formal control over family life. Schooling, of course, was also controlled through similar lines of authority.

This brief overview of the early experiences of the Meiji era suggests how family, local community, polity, and school became integrated within the emperor system. Family and polity became joined—institutionally as a political arm of the hierarchical ruling machinery and psychologically by the imposition of an ideology joining the family and the emperor in emotional bonds with as much cohesive power as bonds connecting children, parents, and ancestry. The neighborhood community reinforced the Confucian norm and moral order and imposed informal social sanctions. School education became an institutional nexus among family, community, and polity, and in turn served to diffuse various formal doctrines, promoting diligence at work and in school, advocating the virtues of loyalty and filial piety, and strengthening the Confucian moral order and the emperor system.

School Rituals and School Community

School rituals reinforced the role of the school and fostered the development of emotional ties within the school community (Karasawa 1972; Aso 1982). Ceremonial rituals and gatherings abounded—at entrance and graduation times, opening and closing ceremonies, seasonal festivals, and commemorations. Athletic meets and interschool competitive examinations were also organized ceremonial occasions. As cultural anthropologists suggest, these ceremonies, when combined with entrance and term examinations, could function as rites of passage and contribute to making school the center of childhood. In school, his Imperial Majesty's portrait was displayed, the order of worship was prescribed, and the Imperial Rescript on Education (1890) was recited in unison. These educational processes promoted the transformation and integration of the traditional belief in a tutelary deity into a broader national belief system. School, of course, became a major agent for moral and religious socialization of children.

Events such as athletic meets, entrance and graduation ceremonies, and interschool competitive examinations constituted regional ceremonies in which many parents and community leaders participated. Elementary schools were supervised by the superintendent, generally a man of high repute in the community who functioned as an agent of the national school supervisory system.

School rituals, like the school curriculum, served to instill emotional discipline, industry, good manners, and orderly behavior, which were encouraged on all ceremonial occasions and were reinforced through repeated rehearsals. Moral precepts, like respect for age, were built into school routines. An educational trip became a "trinity march" during which students were expected to develop themselves in three areas: knowledge, self-discipline, and emotional bonding with each other and with teachers. Students in elementary schools all over Japan would be greeted each morning by the inspiring statue of Kinjiro Ninomiya, a child out of Japanese folklore who was depicted reading a book while carrying a load of firewood on his back. The statue symbolized the importance attached to the virtue of industry and the value of learning during this era.

It should come as no surprise that parents supported the schools because the school curriculum stressed moral education and promoted the prevailing moral order. And when schools provided the means of upward mobility and a better life, people had utilitarian reasons to send their children to school. In fact, the idea that school achievement and career advancement were closely linked became a commonly accepted notion in the wake of the Sino-Japanese and Russo-Japanese wars, when the occupational structure changed and manpower demands increased radically.

Overall Expansion of School Education

The expansion of Japanese education took place in three stages. The first, from 1895–1907, as we have seen, established the fundamental structure of the Japanese school system. During this time elementary schooling became universal, free, and compulsory for six years. Secondary education served a small elite. The second period, from 1915–1955, initiated an expansion of secondary education to serve a larger number of people, between 15-50 percent of the population. During a third reform period, from 1955 to the present, schooling became universally available, advancement beyond elementary school became a reality for more than 50 percent of the people, social grouping and educational opportunity were not so closely coupled, and school education became "a defensive expenditure necessary to protect one's economic and social status" (Thurow 1972).

Change in the Notion of Equal Educational Opportunity

The meaning of equality of educational opportunity has changed as schools have expanded. In 1872 equality meant equal access to elementary, rather than secondary, schooling. The Decree for Encouragement of Learning (1872) stated it precisely:

... from this time onward, everyone, irrespective of class origins such as nobility, military, farmer, artisan or merchant, and irrespective of one's sex, ought to learn, so that there should be no family without learning throughout the village and no person without learning in the family.... Although the higher learning is up to one's talent, parents should be to blame for the case that a child, irrespective of one's sex, does not engage in rudimentary learning.

In fact, in the period from 1872 to 1948, equal educational opportunity in terms of compulsory and free elementary schooling was realized. Secondary and tertiary schooling was accessible only to those young men who had talent and could afford it.

During the early twentieth century, as access to free elementary schooling became widespread, the notion of equal opportunity shifted to include secondary schooling. An array of demands from a variety of sources—government officials seeking moral regulation, economic needs requiring engineers and technical experts, middle-class families seeking opportunities for their children—led to an expansion of secondary education through the extension of various courses and curricula. The number of secondary schools increased by only 20 percent, however, and typically served a constituency primarily composed of upper- and middle-class families.

But the concept of opportunity which accompanied this modest expansion of the secondary schools did not emphasize universal access. Instead, opportunity was construed as the consolidation and expansion of three types of secondary schools: middle schools, which were most selective, academic, and prepared students for higher education; vocational schools, which expanded rapidly in the early twentieth century as industrialization and economic diversification progressed; and girls' high schools, the curriculum of which emphasized learning ladylike manners and being a good housewife.

The purpose was simply to increase the number of students and to provide more vocational training in order to respond to the growing manpower demands of the economy. All of these basic features continued in place throughout the prewar period.

Post-World War II Reforms

A drastic change took place after World War II, as educational reform proceeded under the Occupation policies of the supreme commander for the Allied Powers. An array of reforms transformed the old education system from one that was similar to that in European countries like Great Britain and Germany to one that was more like that of the United States.

Of particular importance was a shift in the definition of educational opportunity and two consequent reforms. One involved an expansion of free and compulsory secondary education to include the junior high school (until ninth grade) and, in the 1960s and 1970s, the senior high school as well. The other involved a shift toward an integrated, common curriculum designed to prepare independent citizens for a democratic society. In fact, the schools were transformed from a multitrack to a single-track system and most senior high schools became comprehensive and coeducational.

These two changes did not proceed without opposition. In response to increasing demands for industrial manpower in the 1960s, the number of specialized vocational courses and technical high schools expanded. On the issues of equal access to and availability of universal high school education, two opposing arguments became clear and resulted in a peculiar compromise known as the *gakkō-gun* system. Under gakkō-gun, a group of senior high schools selected and allocated students cooperatively. For their part, students selected a group of preferred schools but could not identify a single school as their top choice. The gakkō-gun system aims to mute the ill effects of prestige differences among the schools and the severity of entrance examinations among senior high schools. It has improved the situation, but it is far from a complete success.

The gakkō-gun system, as we have seen, results from a compromise between two major opposing opinions about the purposes of senior high school education: one emphasizes equality in high school education and, as a logical consequence, proposes the addition of a neighborhood high school to the elementary and lower secondary education system as it now exists; the other emphasizes the differences in students' ability and career perspectives and supports the differentiation of senior high schools in terms of selectivity and curriculum.

The Structure of Educational Opportunity

Within the gakkō-gun system, education attainments have differed among different groups in the population (Fujita 1978a). What causes the differences in achievement? To consider this question, it is important to understand that since World War II, selection factors have operated most critically at the ninth grade level when students prepare to enter hierarchically ranked senior high schools and where their choice of schools is governed almost wholly by scores on entrance examinations and on school achievement up to and through the ninth grade.

Statistics reveal great differences in scholastic achievement according to the father's education. The higher the father's education, the higher the scholastic achievements of his children (Ushiogi 1980). For example, most children ranking in the two highest achievement levels on the standard five-point scale had fathers who went to school beyond the compulsory level while fewer than one-third of children with fathers who completed school at the compulsory level (age fourteen) managed to do so. Not only are these data significant in themselves, they also suggest that the remarkable postwar expansion in secondary and higher education has made no difference in basic patterns of school achievement.

There are various explanations for the linkage between the father's education, family background, and different patterns of scholastic achievement. The explanations may be based on economics (a family's capacity to afford the direct and indirect costs of schooling), value differences, the severity of the entrance examination system, scholastic achievement, or academic ability. Differences may also be explained by the variations in material, motivational, linguistic, and other cultural conditions within families or communities. They may be explained structurally (by the cultural continuity and/or discontinuity between family and school) or institutionally (by biased attitudes of teachers toward children of different social strata). Some observers even attribute different academic achievement to genes (Fujita 1978a; Kawashima 1957).

None of these explanations, however, is definitive. Thus, it might be useful to explore the phenomenon of tracking and of educational opportunity as they are revealed in certain features of school education in contemporary Japan—high graduation rates, severe entrance examinations, prestige differentiation among schools, comprehensive purposes in elementary and secondary schools, and ritualism (Fujita 1978a, 1980).

High Graduation Rates

According to 1975 statistics, the graduation rate for senior high school was 97.1 percent in Japan, high as compared to 79.1 percent for senior high school in the U.S. in 1973, 62.9 percent for the lycée in France in 1973, 66.1 percent for the gymnasium in Germany in 1972, and 53.5 percent for the grammar school in Great Britain (Fujita 1978a). Similarly, the graduation rate for four-year undergraduate colleges is 87.9 percent, compared to 70.1 percent in the United States in 1964. These high graduation rates support to some extent the oft-heard layman's notion that in Japan's school system there is difficult entrance, easy promotion, and easy graduation (Fujita 1978b).

Entrance Examination and Prestige Differentiation

Today, as before, schools acquire status with reference to two factors, the difficulty of the entrance examination and the quality of career opportunities made available by the school.

The quality and severity of the examinations and the ranking of schools are objects of intense discussion among senior high school students and their parents. Similarly, rankings based on the results of facsimile (practice) examinations and on survey data about the results of regular entrance examinations emerge each year from publishers and *yobikō* (large preparatory schools).

Thus informed about the ranking of a school, students taking a facsimile examination can judge, by their own scores, which among several universities would be within their reach. In addition to these published rankings, many senior high schools have their own charts, providing data which inform students about their relative chances to enter one or another university. Schoolteachers, as well, advise students based on test score, the school chart, and the published ranking. It should be noted that the majority of universities, especially prestigious ones, select their entrants exclusively on the basis of the entrance examination.

A similar picture emerges at the high school level though the competition here is not nationwide but limited to each prefecture or each city. Under these circumstances, many junior and senior high schools arrange for senior students to take several of the facsimile examinations issued by testing companies, usually six to twelve times a year. After every facsimile examination, students are informed of their test scores in detail, subject by subject, and of their relative standing among students who took the same combination of subjects and who plan to apply for the same high school or university. In addition to these facsimile examinations, students take ordinal midterm and final examinations every trimester. Thus, as OECD examiners reported on Japanese education in 1971, "Students ... become more interested in examination techniques than in real learning and maturation" (OECD 1971). Unfortunately, teachers and parents often do too.

Concern about entrance examinations and school prestige ranking has been stimulated by the fact that the names of successful applicants to public senior high schools appear in a local newspaper in many prefectures on a specified day. During February and March, names of the successful applicants to universities also appear in local newspapers. This kind of reporting occurs even at the national level. Three major prestigious newspapers, each with a circulation of about six million, report the number of applicants and competition rates of several top universities, together with the number of successful applicants by prefecture, type of senior high school, and year of high school graduation. Weekly magazines, each with a circulation of one million or more, also report weekly in February and March on the details of the application situation and the results of entrance examinations, that is, the number of successful applicants to prestigious universities by prefecture and by senior high school.

Thus we see the persistence of prewar school characteristics even though the school system has changed fundamentally from the time when it was multitracked and organized ideologically around the emperor system.

Rōnin, Yobikō, and Juku

Yet another reflection of the relative stability of century-old educational characteristics is in the emergence of new categories of students (rōnin) and schools (yobikō and juku) (Fujita 1978b).

Rōnin refers to a student who has failed the entrance examination and is cramming to try again. According to 1981 statistics, the number of students admitted to universities in 1981 was about 413,000. (This does not include those admitted to two-year colleges and new, higher technical schools.) Of this number, 277,000 (66.9 percent) were new senior high school graduates. The remaining 134,000 thousand were rōnin. During the last three decades the proportion of rōnin entering college each year has been between 30 and 40 percent. About 40 percent of the entrants to Tokyo University and about 60 percent of those accepted for the Politics-Economics Department of Waseda University are rōnin.

In many large cities, especially in Tokyo, Nagoya, Kyoto, and Osaka, there are yobikō where rōnin prepare for entrance examinations with an especially tailored curriculum. A famous teacher in a yobikō—once a professor in a prestigious national university—said in a radio interview that students at preparatory schools are much more intent on learning than university students.

Another peculiar phenomenon is the existence of juku, a private study class or school in which elementary and secondary school children study under the supervision of one or several teachers in the afternoon or in the evening after formal school is over.

The large number of rōnin, yobikō, and juku suggests a widespread belief that entrance examinations measure a student's cognitive development level. Thus we see the persistence of a belief that selection by an entrance examination is meritocratic and fair—a belief that has remained constant since the early period of Japanese education.

Custodial Care and Moral Education

The statistics documenting high graduation rates suggest the belief that students should complete school successfully and that the school should bear the responsibility for students to graduate. Less obviously, perhaps, they also suggest that dropping out of school, especially from senior high school, tends to be a stigma.

These beliefs are reinforced by the structure and character of school activities and programs and are linked inextricably with the strong custodial and generally comprehensive role of school in Japan. For example, in most secondary schools, extracurricular activities such as athletics are popular, and many students remain for training at school until six or seven o'clock in the evening. Even on Sunday or during summer vacation, many students go to school for club activities, especially athletics. Thus, one of the major duties of secondary schoolteachers in Japan is to oversee and guide these various extracurricular activities. Through these activities, students are expected to learn the discipline of group life and the value of perseverance, to develop their physical strength, and to identify themselves with the school community. As is often said, extracurricular activities and summer-sponsored vacations keep students busy and serve to diminish delinquency.

It is also generally assumed that elementary and secondary schools should exercise supervisory power over students' behavior outside the school. Thus, almost all elementary and secondary schools prescribe the details of permissible behavior both in and out of school including the clothes students should wear and places they might go on their own or with their parents or other adults. Some secondary schools require students and parents to report to school authorities before they take a long trip during the summer or spring vacation. All of these examples suggest the broad custodial role of the school in Japan.

Parents also harbor broad expectations of the school (Fujita 1978b). According to survey data collected in 1977, parents expect school to teach children the following: discipline of group life (98.3 percent), cognitive training (90.5 percent), love of one's local place (75.3 percent), punctuality (75.0 percent), friendship, good peer relations (75.0 percent), and public morality (63.9 percent). These expectations suggest, in yet another way, how broad and comprehensive the role of the school is in Japan and how little has changed between the prewar and postwar periods. Like their century-old predecessors, elementary and secondary school students clean their classroom and school building every day by turns—an activity through which they are expected to develop the discipline of group life, a sense of responsibility, a sense of cleanliness, and public morality. Many of the ceremonial gatherings and events described earlier still persist in almost all elementary and secondary schools and continue to play an important role in Japanese education and highlight the relative importance of moral education. On the other hand, jukus, yobikōs, and testing companies are flourishing. It is ironic that people expect the school to be a total agency of socialization while undermining that role by leaving important aspects of education to these alternative institutions. This attitude, however, is not new in Japanese education. As the statue of Kinjiro Ninomiya suggests, being diligent has always meant to work hard, though this orientation has become more thoroughly institutionalized today.

A Crisis of Legitimacy in Public Education

What then is wrong with the Japanese educational system? There is reason to believe that Japanese schools are beset with problems. Among the more important are questions of student motivation. Since the 1970s economic growth has brought a fairly high standard of living, increased job opportunities, and low unemployment rates. According to several national surveys, between 80 and 90 percent of the people perceive themselves as belonging to the middle class. Under these circumstances, many students lose the incentive to study hard and get ahead, believing they have already achieved the good life.

Second, schools are unable to develop evaluation systems that would stimulate students to do more than pass tests. The commitment to the entrance examination system and to achievement has resulted in a failure to provide the kind of vision and hope regarding occupational and career possibilities that would sustain its legitimacy.

Third, because of the perceived unidimensional, meritocratic evaluation scale and because of the system's custodial orientation and ritualistic qualities, schools have occupied a central position in the life of Japanese children. Dropping out of school stigmatizes the child rather than the school.

Fourth, because of the density of the formal curriculum, the pressure of the entrance examinations, and poor teaching conditions (like large class size, e.g., forty students per teacher), a significant number of students do not understand what they are taught in class. Although it seems to be an exaggeration, educational critics often condemn the system as *shichi-go-san*. Shichi-go-san is the rhyme which means a gala day for children of three, five, and seven years of age and refers to the estimate that in elementary school 70 percent of the students understand the subjects, in junior high 50 percent, and in senior high 30 percent.

Fifth, school rituals tend to produce ritualism, formalism, and trivialism among teachers. For example, many secondary schools require school uniforms. Not uncommonly in the morning at the front gate of a school, a teacher is standing with a yardstick measuring the width of boys' trousers and the length of girls' skirts. Hairstyles are similarly monitored. Although these practices should not be criticized unduly, it is easy to argue that this kind of formalism and trivial behavior among teachers tends to bar the development of rapport between students and teachers and, hence, the development of a cohesive school community.

Sixth, since the 1970s, opposing views and attitudes about pedagogy, academic evaluation, discipline, and other aspects of schooling in Japan have become increasingly apparent. This is partly because the postwar generations have become teachers and tend to harbor different opinions and attitudes, partly because economic growth and urbanization have fostered more diversified lifestyles and engendered in parents a greater awareness of their own tastes than before, and partly because the school itself, in terms both of organization and curriculum, has become secularized. Hence, both teachers and parents feel freer to express their own opinions and tastes.

All of this indicates that a qualitative change has taken place in the linkages between school, family, and community and that the effectiveness of indoctrination at the heart of education in Japan has been undermined.

Seventh, until recently, public schools had been monolithic agents of cognitive training, and teachers had had a monopoly on knowledge, skills, and moral authority. However, as higher education has reached the masses and more and more parents feel as qualified as teachers to judge the educational process, the teachers' authority has weakened. Further, as yobikō and juku have become more important, the school's intellectual role has been diluted—thus the crisis of legitimacy in Japanese education today.

This article first appeared in 1985 and was originally presented at the annual conference of the Comparative and International Education Society held at Houston, Texas, in March 1984. Hidenori Fujita, "A Crisis of Legitimacy in Japanese Education: Meritocracy and Cohesiveness," *Bulletin of Research* (Nagoya University) 32 (1985): 117–33.

REFERENCES

Amano, Ikuo. *Kyōiku to senbatsu* (Education and Selection). Tokyo: Dai-ichi Hoki Shuppan, 1982.

Aso, Makoto. *Kindaika to kyōiku* (Modernization and Education) Tokyo: Dai-ichi Hoki Shuppan, 1982.

Fujita, Hidenori. "Education and Status Attainment in Modern Japan." Unpublished Ph.D. dissertation, 1978a.

————. "Gendaishakai ni okeru shitsuke to gakkō-kyōiku" (Discipline and School Education in Contemporary Japan). *Research Bulletin of School of Education, Nagoya University*. 25 (1978b): 167–79.

————. "Kōkō-kyōiku no genjō to shōrai" (The Present and Future of Secondary Education). In *Kōkō-kyōiku gimuka no kanosei ni- kansuru kisoteki-kenkyū* (Possibilities of Upper Secondary Education in Japan), edited by Morikazu Ushiogi. Toyota Foundation Research Report III-004 (1979): 9–50.

————. "The Structure of Opportunities for Status Attainment: The Role of Education and Social Tracking." A paper presented at the Japan-U.S. Conference on Social Stratification and Mobility held in Hawaii, January 1980.

————. "Kyōiku no kikai" (Opportunity of Education). In *Kyōiku- shakai-gaku* (Sociology of Education), edited by Yasumasa Tomoda. Tokyo: Ushindo (1982): 160–82.

————. "Gakkō to shakai" (School and Society). *Sōgō kyōiku-gijustu* (April 1981 and March 1982), two articles in a series.

Fukushima, Maso. *Nihon shihonshugi to "Ie" seido* (Japanese Capit alism and the "Family System"). Tokyo: Aigaku Shuppankai, 1967.

Karasawa, Tomitaro. *Zusetsu Meiji hyakunen kodomo no rekishi* (Explanatory Illustrations of a History of Children: One Hundred Years since the Meiji Restoration). Tokyo: Kodansha International Ltd., 1972.

Kawashima, Takeyoshi, *Ideology to shiteno kazoku-seido* (The Family System As an Ideology). Tokyo: Iwanami Shoten, 1957.

Kawashima, Takeyoshi, and Hidenori Fujita. "Gakkō no shakaiteki-kinō ni kansuru ichikōsatsu" (A Study of the Function of School). *Research Bulletin of School of Education, Nagoya University* 28 (1981): 119–33.

Ministry of Education, Japan. *Educational Standards in Japan, 1975*. Tokyo: Ministry of Education, 1976.

————. *Zenkoku gakushū-juku ni kansuru jittaichōsa*. Tokyo: Gyōsei, 1977.

————. "Gakkō kihonchōsa hōkokusho" (Annual Report of a Fundamental Survey on Schools). Tokyo: Ministry of Education, 1982.

NHK Shuzaihan (NHK news team). *Naigai kyōiku*. Tokyo: Jiji Tsujuin, March 15, 1977.

————. *Nihon no jōken 11: Kyōiku 2* (The State of Affairs in Japan 11: Education 2) (1983): 248–50.

Organization of Economic Cooperation and Development. *Reviews of National Policies for Education: Japan*. Paris: OECD, 1971.

Shimomura, Tetsuo. *Nihon no kindaiteki gimukyōiku seido no seiritsu to sekai kyōikushi kenkyūkai* (An Outline of the World's History of Education: A History of Compulsory Education). Tokyo: Kodansha International Ltd., 1977: 114–234.

Thurow, Lester C. "Education and Social Inequality." *The Public Interest* 28 (1972): 66–81.

Trow, Martin. "The Second Transformation of Secondary Education." *International Journal of Comparative Sociology* II (1961): 2. "The Democratization of Higher Education in America." *European Journal of Sociology* III (1972): 231–62.

Ushiogi, Morikazu, et al. "Chūgakkō-bunka no kōzōteki-bunseki (An Analysis of the Structure of Junior High School Culture). *Research Bulletin of School of Education, Nagoya University* 27 (1980): 171–216.

Professor Kazuyuki Kitamura, founder of the Institute for Research in Higher Education at the University of Hiroshima and currently professor at the Multi-Media Institute in Tokyo, has documented an increase in the number of academic achievement problems, episodes of violence in junior high schools, and high school dropouts. To explain them, he alludes to financial problems and a declining faith in Japanese formal education both at home and abroad, and he projects a future of declining college enrollments. In analyzing the debate now raging over the future of education in Japan, he has demolished the vision of the Japanese education system as unvaryingly uniform, static, fair, or even consistently effective.

In this excerpt, Professor Kitamura examines changes in the function of Japan's dual educational system, which, he argues, ". . . is no longer simply a subordinate system supporting the formal school system, but an increasingy important means for high school students to make their college choice and prepare for entrance examinations." The informal or private system allows the public schools to function according to traditional principles by providing an alternative for those students who are unable to achieve within the public schools. In doing so, however, they threaten the continuation of a commitment to principles of egalitarianism and uniformity within the society.

Japan's Dual Educational Structure

KAZUYUKI KITAMURA

I would argue that the weaknesses and strengths of Japanese formal education stem from its dual structure. On the one hand, there is the contrast between the limited public sector and the market-driven private sector. On the other hand, there is the perverse complementarity of the formal and the nonformal systems. These structures were fairly well balanced until the mid-1970s but since then have been gradually disrupted by both social changes and the advent of student consumerism.

The private sector, particularly in higher education, has been dominant, comprising nearly three-quarters of Japan's students and roughly the same percentage of its institutions. The cost of public higher education is lower than in private universities (on average, less than 30 percent of private universities' fees in 1983) and generally has better conditions as measured by teacher-student ratios, floor space per student, and books per student (Ichikawa 1984). As public higher education is open to only 25 percent of the student population, the majority of young people are forced to attend the more costly but generally educationally disadvantaged and crowded private universities.

The traditional policy of the Japanese central government was to concentrate educational resources in the public sector in order to preserve academic quality while leaving quantitative expansion to private institutions, which are more responsive to changing social demands. The rapid expansion of Japanese higher education without substantial investment from public funds has been due to this two-sector policy, which the central government maintained throughout Japan's one-hundred-year bid for modernization. Faced with the increasing imbalance of manpower needs in various fields, financial crises at private universities, and increased dissatisfaction of parents and students with the unequal academic conditions that existed between the private and public sectors, the government finally changed its policy of withholding support from the private sector. In 1970 it approved a new policy to provide direct financial assistance to private institutions, covering up to half of each institution's current expenses. This was perhaps the greatest reversal of educational policy in Japan's history.

Since then the traditional hierarchy of universities and colleges in Japan has been gradually changing. The monopoly of prestige that top national and local public universities long enjoyed no longer exists. For instance, as a result of the introduction in 1979 of a new examination system for admission to universities, college-bound students applying to public universities are now required to take a nationally uniform achievement test consisting of seven subjects as a primary screening and then another test for the university of their choice. It is a one-time opportunity, and students may apply to only one public university. These rigid requirements have precipitated a dramatic change in college choice among students. Most of the major private universities, which require tests in only a few subjects, have attracted increasing numbers of able applicants, whereas many of the major public universities (except for top institutions like the University of Tokyo) have suffered from a decrease in both number and quality of applicants. Because almost none of the private universities (composing more than 70 percent of all universities) participate in the nationally uniform test, the reform has not succeeded in improving the university entrance examination system as a whole.

Thus, the reform of the entrance examination system in the public sector has resulted only in pushing talented students away from the public system, just as the high school examination reform of the late 1960s, which was "a major drive to end the stratification of public high schools, only led to a strengthening of . . . private schools" (Rohlen 1983, 312). These two examples illustrate how close the interaction is between the public and private educational sectors and how the traditional hierarchy has been changing. The traditional balance between public and private institutions seems to have been lost with the advent of student consumerism. College choice is extremely responsive to changes in the educational world and the society at large. Such changes include not only the introduction of entrance examination systems but also shifts in employment market trends.

A second dimension of the dual structure of Japanese education is the increasing interdependence of formal and nonformal education. If we look at the educational system from the broadest perspective, the formal schools (those that form the backbone of the system) and the nonformal institutions (those catering to special educational needs) are so mutually dependent and supportive that without the links that connect them the educational objectives of Japanese society could not be realized.

The relation between the formal and nonformal educational systems is like that between figure and ground in painting. Each stage of formal schooling is closely connected with a supporting system that is continuously changing according to social demand. This supporting system is composed of private college preparatory and cram schools (*yobikō* and *juku*), proprietary technical and vocational schools, and various learning and training programs usually provided by corporations as part of on-the-job training.

The dominant values of the Japanese public primary school are egalitarianism and uniformity: pupils are not classified according to their academic ability because all pupils are supposed to keep up with the progress of the class. There they are taught by means of a nationally controlled, uniform curriculum. Despite its principles of egalitarianism and uniformity, however, the school inevitably must produce high achievers and low achievers. The school and its teachers are unable to counter these disparities because they are bound by the two mandatory principles. So troubled teachers assume the role of traffic police, directing high achievers who are dissatisfied with the progress of the school class to attend a preparatory school for elite students, where they can take more advanced classes, while sending prospective dropouts to another type of cram school offering remedial classes. Then, thanks to the existence of these two kinds of supporting institutions, the formal school itself can continue to function according to the principles of egalitarianism and uniformity.

According to a national survey conducted by Japan's Ministry of Education, Science, and Culture (1977), the number of primary and junior high school pupils attending juku was approximately 1.3 million (12 percent) and 1.8 million (38 percent), respectively. The number of such schools was estimated to be more than fifty thousand. A survey of Tokyo children conducted by the Tokyo Metropolitan Agency in 1977 revealed that 24.4 percent of primary school children and 55.9 percent of junior high school pupils went to juku two or three times a week for one to three hours per day.

One important reason why the new uniform entrance examination system has not been successful is that students and parents rely extensively on the major university preparatory schools (the so-called *juken sangyō,* or "examination industry") in developing their strategy for applying to and selecting universities. These schools have amassed huge data banks on the admissions requirements and standards of all universities and colleges. Upon receiving their test results, students look to the preparatory schools for identifying colleges appropriate to their academic abilities, and these suggestions almost ensure their admissions. Because admission requirements of private colleges vary greatly, unlike the rigid requirements of public universities, virtually any high school graduate can find a private school that will accept him or her. Even highly qualified students who aspire to Japan's most prestigious universities tend to prepare for entry to at least one other college where they have a high probability of being accepted, and that is almost invariably a private one. The choice of a public or private university is generally made in the last two years of high school, when academic preparation differs according to the type of institution an individual seeks to enter. With their ability to assess quite accurately students' chances for admission to certain universities, the nonformal institutions have in many cases a stronger influence over students' choices than do high school teachers, and even the teachers have found the information provided by this industry useful for advising students.

This nonformal educational system is no longer simply a subordinate system supporting the formal school system but an increasingly important means for high school students to make their college choice and to prepare for the entrance examinations. The nonformal sector plays such an important role in secondary education that the traditional balance between the formal and nonformal systems is teetering.

This reading is excerpted from Kazuyuki Kitamura, "Japan's Dual Educational Structure," in *Educational Policies in Crisis: Japanese and American Perspectives,* edited by William E. Cummings, et al. New York, Westport CT, London: Praeger, 1986: 135–69.

REFERENCES

Asahi Shimbun (Asahi News), Tokyo. "National Poll on Educational Problems" (in Japanese) June 6, 1984.

Ichikawa, Shogo. "Financing Higher Education in Japan." *Daigaku Ronshū—Research in Higher Education* 13 (1984): 19–38. Research Institute for Higher Education, Hiroshima University.

Japan, Ministry of Education, Science, and Culture (Monbusho). *Zenkoku no gakushūjuku gayoi no jittai* (Condition of Juku Attendance Throughout Japan). MEJ 6903. Tokyo: Gyōsei, 1977.

Rohlen, Thomas P. *Japan's High Schools.* Berkeley: University of California Press, 1983.

The contradictions between Japanese commitments to equality on the one hand and merit on the other are explored in Professor Ryoko Kato's analysis of official education reform efforts in Japan as contrasted with those of the United States. In addition to suggesting that Japanese and Americans harbor different concepts of equality and democracy, her analysis reveals tensions within and among competing factions of reformers in Japan, thus puncturing a common Western view that everyone agrees with everyone else in Japan. What is more, the article suggests that educational change occurs through a relatively turbulent process of political maneuvering which is as organized in the form of its public expression as it is revealing of deep divisions within Japanese society.

Reconciling Equality and Merit

RYOKO KATO TSUNEYOSHI

I n modern educational systems, culturally diverse nations like Japan and the United States face similar problems. One of the more intractable involves a reconciliation of commitments in education to equality on the one hand and quality on the other. What can be done to recognize differences in student ability and yet promote equality of educational opportunity and what criteria should educators and politicians invoke in the process?

Attempts to combine equal education with equal opportunity or to reconcile tensions between them is proceeding apace in both nations, where there have been heated arguments about reforming the existing educational system (Takahashi 1985). In Japan certain unfortunate phenomena—examination hell, increases in juvenile delinquency, school violence, and *ijime* (group teasing)—led the Japanese government to organize *Rinji Kyōiku Shingikai* (the Education Commission) in 1984 and to call upon it to guide a reform of education policy.

In its proposal submitted in 1985 the commission addressed, among other things, the issue of equality versus quality, better known in Japan as equality versus *nōryokushugi*, "abilityism." The commission itself was split over the issue.

In the U.S., concern about decreasing levels of academic excellence, high dropout rates, and the capacity of American schools to prepare the younger generation to compete in the world economic stage, has led to a government-sponsored report, *A Nation at Risk* (National Commission 1984), where concerns about achieving a balance between the demands of quality and the challenges of offering equal opportunity were also expressed.

It is no small irony that reformers in each country have looked to the other for guidance. Impressed by Japan's economic success and the high performance of schoolchildren on international examinations, Americans often study Japanese education in search of an alternative model. They note the high quality of primary and secondary education and the ability of the Japanese to obtain academic excellence with comparatively fewer teachers and lower costs. American writers suggest that Japanese schools have less violence and disorder, fewer dropouts, and seem to achieve egalitarian results—despite findings which show that Japan has become less egalitarian over the years (Cummings 1980; Reischauer 1977; Rohlen 1983).

The Japanese, likewise, have looked intermittently to the United States for educational alternatives. In Japanese eyes, America's positive qualities reside in the quality of creativity its educational system encourages, the leadership qualities it generates, and the democratic impulses it reflects. The Japanese commonly invoke the United States when they look for educational alternatives. Nevertheless, America's widely publicized educational problems together with Japan's increasing confidence have led many Japanese to doubt the wisdom of a major new infusion of American practices and philosophy.

Both countries seek to reconcile the quality/equality issue while reforming what are perceived as negative aspects of their systems. The adjustments which they make may have far-reaching consequences, not only for the much discussed international competitive edge each seeks in the world economy but also for the realization of social justice at home, which in the end may be the more important question.

Concepts of Equality in the United States and Japan

American educators commonly proceed on the assumption that there are inherited differences among children. The Japanese do not. American schools have programs for gifted children. Japanese schools do not. Students in the U.S. may skip grades. Japanese children can not. Americans rely on IQ tests to track children. The Japanese prefer tests of achievement. In the U.S. the concept of uniform treatment is rarely invoked.

In addition to assuming that there are innate differences among children, many Americans also assume that the concept of democracy is inseparable from that of socioeconomic equality. In contrast to Japan, American discussions of equality incorporate problems of race, class, gender, and ability. Indeed, the heterogeneous population of the U.S. has introduced another distinct dimension into the problem of equality in education—a concern with differences within and among groups. According to Caroline Persell (1977), the concept of equal educational treatment for each child was short-lived. With the rise of industrialism and mass education, it became a concept of "appropriate" education, fitting each child equally well for his or her lifework.

The belief in individual differences and inherited intelligence constitutes an important challenge to democracy in a nation with diverse racial and ethnic minorities, where concepts of equal educational opportunity are commonly tied to the right of individuals to achieve academic success and have access to various levels of the occupational ladder. It is in this context that attempts to explain the low academic achievement of certain minority groups evoke attention. For example, blacks are commonly viewed as culturally "disadvantaged," that is, ill prepared by the language patterns and cognitive styles of their families to succeed in school (Shade 1976). Placing the burden of response on schools rather than on families, this construction of academic failure calls for change based on a concept of individual rights—that each individual regardless of his or her socioeconomic background should be given an equal opportunity for success. Those who are poor, according to arguments in the U.S., are by virtue of their poverty and segregated places of residence denied equal opportunity to enter schools of their choice (Karier, Violas, and Spring 1973).

The heterogeneous population of the United States introduces different dimensions into the problem of quality. James Coleman et al. (1966) tackled the issue of equality by reporting that "schools make no difference" in educational achievement as measured by standard tests; it is the families that make the difference. In a book titled *Inequality* (1972), Christopher Jencks confirmed this proposition.

If schools do not make the difference, what does? Various explanations have emerged to explain how minorities are handicapped in the schooling process, ranging from how standardized tests are biased in favor of middle-class values to the notion that the culture of blacks is not geared for success in school.

No matter which explanation is considered valid, it is fair to say that the U.S. has a differentiated school system which proscribes unrestricted equality. For Americans, issues become questions of fairness: do education policies in the U. S. disadvantage children because of socioeconomic position, test-taking abilities, or innate qualities? Does the education system produce a handful of very proficient persons—an elite—while the rest lag behind? For Americans the issue is not whether differentiation should occur in education, but whether methods to distinguish classes of students are fair.

Concepts of Equality and Democracy Compared

In contrast to the emphasis on socioeconomic factors within American public discourse, the Japanese, though differing among one another about the meaning of equality and democracy in education, uniformly emphasize motivation, that is, the effort and aspirations of children and parents to explain school achievement.

They invoke a concept of democracy that redefines the meaning of individualism and individuality. Although individualism is at the heart of what is interpreted as American democracy, the term is carefully avoided when Japanese talk about democracy and education. For them, the term *individualism* implies self-centeredness, and they go to great efforts to devise terms that do not carry the negative ring of egoism. For example, words such as *kosei* (uniqueness), *shutaisei* (autonomy), and *jiritsu* (independence) imply respect for the personality rather than the rights of individuals and are summed up in a word used frequently in current Japanese educational debates, "personalityism."

In addition, the Japanese rarely invoke hereditary difference as a meaningful basis for sorting students even though they harbor two opposing concepts of equality in education. The first, articulated by the Teachers Union in deliberations of the Education Commission (Nikkyoso 1985), defines equality in education as unrestricted equality in which competitive evaluation and ability grouping is discouraged. The other, championed by the business community and the Ministry of Education among others, proceeds on an assumption that democratic values are realized when resources are allocated on the basis of student achievement on examinations.

No matter what their point of view, Japanese generally believe that high-achieving children are diligent and reliable while low-achieving children are not. That there may be differences in innate abilities is simply not considered—a not so surprising omission in a relatively homogeneous society where racial and ethnic differences are not so obvious and variations in achievement not so dramatic.

Models of Equality in Japanese Education

Although the Japanese share certain assumptions about the basis for school achievement, Japanese education nonetheless institutionalizes two contradictory concepts of equality. The first—the commitment to unrestricted equality and uniform treatment of students—is embodied in the school system; the second—the commitment to equality based on competitive test scores and subject matter mastery—is embodied in the examination system (Amano 1985; Mitsui 1973).

The school system model rests on an assumption that children should receive a standardized education, have standardized texts, and prepare for standardized examinations that differentiate strictly according to test scores. According to this point of view, a system that accords everyone a fair chance to compete for coveted places in relatively inexpensive national universities is fair. The school system model is praised for its egalitarian character, its commitment to unrestricted equal treatment, and its view that anybody can reach a certain level if only he or she tries hard enough (Cummings 1980). This form of thinking, championed by the Teachers Union, is antithetical to educational policies encouraging the identification of ability differences among children.

The examination model has recently gained advocates among parents, children, and certain factions within the Education Commission and the government. Contrary to the school system model, the examination model supports competition and differentiation among children. From the point of view of examination advocates, public distinctions between the successful and the unsuccessful and between the academic performances of students and schools is fair. So too, are ability tracks, a hierarchical education system, and principles of meritocracy.

The popularity of cram schools suggests widespread recognition, if not total acceptance, of the principles of competition, differentiated experience, and stiff examinations (Rohlen 1980; Yoshida 1978). *Juku* and *yobiko* are more accessible to relatively wealthy urban dwellers, serve more boys than girls, and have more junior and senior high than elementary school students (Japan Ministry of Education 1977). The 1985 slogan of Sundai Yobikō, one of the mass cram schools in the Tokyo district, symbolizes the principle of differentiation: "lessons according to ability."

Competition and Tradition

The examination model resonates with traditional Japanese values—effort, hard work, and mental fortitude—even more than the school model. An NHK survey (1984) suggests that elderly people value exam work as an opportunity for mental training. Even though there are indications that many members of the younger generation do not value diligence as highly, an array of surveys suggests that a substantial majority (61.1 percent) of high school students regarded "... hardship as precious, [and] exam work as good for mental fortitude" (NHK 1984, 109).

None of the surveys suggest that the Japanese generally consider innate differences as meaningful. Indeed, the possibility of differences in potentiality is ignored. Through an analysis of data gathered on the achievement of elementary and secondary school children, Masashi Fukaya (1983) concluded that children did well because they studied harder, not because they had different innate abilities. Parents also supported this view.

Within Japan, people have begun to attack schools for sticking so rigorously to the principle of unrestricted equal treatment (Mitsui 1973). It is this principle that has caused the proliferation of juku, argues one critic (Fukaya 1977). Others accuse the schools of pursuing "bad equality," a too uniform treatment of children, where the system is rigid, individual abilities and differences are ignored, and juku are needed to identify otherwise unattended ability differences among individuals. From across the sea, similar critiques of Japanese education are heard. Thomas Rohlen, in *Japan's High Schools* (1983), described Japanese high schools as efficient but uniform and controlled.

This line of criticism has also found expression in one faction of the Education Commission, the *jiyūkaronja* (liberationists), who have called for a loosening of uniform state control and for encouraging differentiation through the examination system. As Koyama, a member of the commission, wrote: "Equal opportunity that forgets appropriate treatment by ability degenerates into state control, bad equality [*aku byōdō*] and uniformity" (Koyama 1985a, 79). In this new age of creativity, asserts a commission proposal, Japanese education requires *koseishugi,* the establishment of "the nobility of the individual, respect for uniqueness, freedom, self-reliance, and self-responsibility." The jiyūkaronja, calling for the pursuit of happiness through education, aim to overwhelm what is believed to be uniformity, closed-mindedness, and anti-international character in postwar schooling.

In Defense of the School System Model

Opponents of the examination model on the commission, in the Ministry of Education, and in the Teachers Union support the school system model. They are anti-jiyūka and wary of introducing competition and other measures supported by the jiyukaron, who they consider individualistic. They call on the state to assure every child a basic education of equal quality. As one of them puts it, "Children are not guinea pigs and should not be the objects of experiments" (Arita 1985).

The Commission Report

The Report of the Education Commission promotes four important points of view: first, that postwar Japan has successfully modernized, achieved economic success, and experienced an upsurge of confidence and pride in Japanese tradition and society; second, that education should adjust to the needs of a larger society and world and respond to external criticism by encouraging creativity, cultivating future leaders, and becoming less rigid, less uniform, and more sensitive to the individual; third, that equality and uniformity are linked. Finally, their arguments reflect the view of the business world which calls for the application of "abilityism" in education—the promotion of fair competition, the recognition of ability differences and differential treatment of students, and the identification and promotion of special talent. The report, however, disavowed any intention to foster individualism. The commission proposal incorporates an underlying notion of ability differences and the examination model of education. It supports competition. It recognizes differences among children. It calls for the evaluation and differentiation of the children according to ability measures.

If the commission's proposals are adopted, a somewhat altered examination model would replace the more traditional school model, and Japanese and American schools would proceed on more convergent principles. Whether it is possible, as the commission wishes, to combine some features of the American and Japanese systems without doing basic violence to the strengths in Japanese education is problematic. It should be remembered that the principle of unrestricted equal treatment, which the commission condemns, also cultivates other values considered basic in Japan—the stress on socioeconomic equality and on such things as effort and hard work. To abandon uniform treatment is to put enormous pressure on these equally powerful traditional commitments.

The Teachers Union has called such views reactionary and reasserts its commitment to the principles of the Fundamental Education Law. The union calls for the abolition of competitive evaluations, for a semicompulsory high school completely accessible to all, and for other reforms such as smaller classes, "antiabilityism," and promotion of peace education. It espouses reform by the people and is against government reform imposed from above. It supports the egalitarian rather than the examination model of schooling in Japan.

The legitimization of the school system as egalitarian has, after all, rested on two assumptions: (1) that all children have similar potential and differentiate themselves according to effort and (2) that the system does not discriminate based on family background, place of residence, etc. If, however, examinations were to be differentiated, the curriculum destandardized, and individual differences recognized, and if tracking and ability grouping were to be introduced, then students from wealthier backgrounds might be unfairly advantaged, criteria for admissions might be unclear, and admissions decisions might be arbitrary. In a country where there is a relatively hierarchical distribution of universities, and where admission into prestigious universities promotes social mobility gained by effort, the proposal may face serious opposition.

The commission itself identified the tensions when it called for choice and ability grouping and at the same time disavowed a commitment to individuality: "Freedom does not mean neglect or confusion, irresponsibility, or anomie. Freedom is accompanied by important responsibilities ... to work for one's interest is to work for the interest of others, to know oneself is to know others, to respect oneself is to respect others and the opposite holds. They are opposite sides of the relationship." "We must love others as we love ourselves and work to better society for our own sake" (Matsushita 1985). Here, helping others is seen as helping oneself. This concept of democracy has within it an underlying cooperative, groupist tendency. It is not the same as the concept of democracy in the United States.

This excerpt is taken from Ryoko Kato Tsuneyoshi, "Meanings of Equality: Lessons from Japanese Debate," *Educational Forum* 54 (Winter 1990): 185–95.

NOTE. Since the time when Professor Tsuneyoshi completed this article, the final report of the Education Commission in Japan has been issued. The Commission has called for education policies that realize three purposes: internationalization, personalityism, and lifelong learning. The three concepts represent a compromise among the various points of view articulated in her article. As they are institutionalized, we will be able to observe how the Japanese effectively reconcile what Professor Tsuneyoshi describes as significant tensions.

REFERENCES

Amano, Ikuo. *Kyōiku kaikaku o kangaeru* (Thoughts Concerned with Education Reform). Tokyo: Todai Shuppankai, 1985: 17.

Arita, Kazuhisa. "'Gakkōkyōiku no jiyūka' ni tsuite" (National Council on Educational Reform). In *Rinkyōshin to kyōikukaikaku—jiyūka kara koseishugi e* (From Liberalization [Deregulation] to Putting an Emphasis on Individuality [Personality]), edited by Gyōsei. Tokyo: Gyōsei, 1985: 171–76.

————. "Kyōikukaikaku o hihansuru: Imada kojinshugi no teteisenu nihon shakai ni jiyūka wa shōso da" (Criticizing the Education Reform: Too Early to Introduce Liberalization into Japanese Society Where Individualism Has Not Completely Dominated). *Voice* (1985): 171–78, reprinted in *Gendai no esupuri* 216 (1985): 171–78.

Coleman, James, et al. *Equality of Educational Opportunity.* Washington, DC: U.S. Government Printing Office, 1966.

Cummings, William K. *Education and Equality in Japan.* Princeton: Princeton University Press, 1980.

Fujita, Hidenori. "Career Choices and Status Attainment of Young People." In *Seinenki no shinrosentaku: Kōgakureki jidai no jiritsu no jōken* (Conditions of Independence in the Society Where Persons Have High Educational Backgrounds), edited by Takeshi Yamamura and Ikuo Amano. Tokyo: Yuhikaku Sensho, 1980.

Fukaya, Masashi. "Shingakujuku to sono kinō: Shudan mensetsu o tegakari to shite" (Academic Elitism and School Culture). *Kyōiku shakaigaku kenkyū,* 32 (1977): 51–64.

————. "Gakureki shugi to gakkō bunka" (Credentialism and the Culture of the School). *Gendai no esupuri* 212 (1983): 116–32.

————. "Juku gayoi no genshō no haikei" (Background of the Phenomenon of Attending *Juku*). *Gendai no esupuri* 212 (1985): 5-25.

Japan Ministry of Education, Science and Culture (Monbusho). *Zenkoku no gakushū juku gayoi no jittai: Jidō seito no gakkōgai gakushūkatsudō ni kansuru jittai chōsa sokuhō* (Condition of *Juku* Attendance throughout Japan). MEJ 6903. Tokyo: Gyōsei, 1977: 5.

Jencks, Christopher. *Inequality: A Reassessment of the Effect of Family and Schooling in America.* New York: Basic Books, Inc., 1972.

Karier, Clarence J., Paul Violas, and Joel Spring. *Roots of Crisis: American Education in the Twentieth Century.* Chicago: Rand McNally & Company, 1973.

Kato, Hiroshi. "Kyōiku kōhai no kongen ni arumono" (Origins of Educational Decline). *Gendai no esupuri* 216 (1985): 133–45.

Katsuda, Kichitaro. "Kyōiku kōhai no kongen to kaikaku e no yosei: Kindaikagata kyōiku wa owatta" (Roots of the Ruin of Education: Ending of Modernization in Education). *Gendai no esupuri* 216 (1985): 100–11.

Kawai, Hayao. *Boseishakai Nihon no byōri* (Pathology in Maternal Japanese Society). Tokyo: Chuokoronsha, 1976: 52.

Keizai, Doyukai. "Kyōiku mondai linkai, tayōka e no chōsen" (Challenges toward Diversity). In *Rinkyōshin to kyōikukaikaku— jiyūka kara koseishugi e* (From Liberalization [Deregulation] to Putting an Emphasis on Individuality [Personality]), edited by Gyōsei. Tokyo: Gyōsei, 1985: 261–73.

Koyama, Kenichi. "Kakuitsusei ni shi o: Tōdai o shigaku ni seyo" (Uniformity Should Decline: Make Private Tōdai University). *Gendai no esupuri* 216 (1985a): 79–90.

————. "Monbusho kaikaku no hitsuyōsei ni kansuru kōsatsu: 'Han jiyūkaron' hihan" (Thoughts Concerning the Need for Reform of the Monbusho and a Critique of Anti-Liberalization). *Gendai no esupuri* 216 (1985b): 190–96.

Kyoto Zakai (Kyoto Conference). "Sekai o kangaeru gakkōkyōiku kaseika no tameno nanatsu no teigen" (Seven Agendas for School Reform). In *Rinkyōshin to kyōikukaikaku—jiyūka kara koseishugi e* (From Liberalization [Deregulation] to Putting an Emphasis on Individuality [Personality]), edited by Gyōsei. Tokyo: Gyōsei, 1985: 210–14.

Matsushita, Kōnosuke. "Otona no sekinin o hatasu: Kikan kyōiku ni tsuite" (Fulfilling Adult's Responsibility). *Gendai no esupuri* 216 (1985): 48–53.

Mitsui, Naritomo. "Gakushūjuku to gakkōkyōiku: Dochira ni gunbai ga agaru ka" (Academic *Juku* and Formal Schools of Education: Which Wins the Competition). *Jidōshinri* 324 (1973): 152–57.

Nakane, Chie. *Tate shakai no ningen kankei: Tanitsu shakai no riron* (Japanese Society). Tokyo: Kodansha Gendaishinsho, 1967.

National Commission on Excellence in Education. *A Nation at Risk: The Full Account*. Cambridge, MA: U.S.A. Research, 1984.

National Council on Education Reform. "Bunka to kyōiku ni kansuru kondai kai 'hōkoku' " (Report of the Study Group on Culture and Education). In *Rinkyōshin to kyōikukaikaku—jiyūka kara koseishugi e* (From Liberalization [Deregulation] to Putting an Emphasis on Individuality [Personality]), edited by Gyōsei. Tokyo: Gyōsei, 1985: 215–24.

NHK. *Yoronchōsa Shiryōshū* (Resource Report of a Public Opinion Poll). Tokyo: Nihonhōsō Shuppankyōkai, 1980: 881.

———. *Nihon no kodomotachi: Seikatsu to ishiki* (Children in Japan: Their Lives and Attitudes). Tokyo: Nihonhoso Shuppankyokai, 1980: 50.

———.*Chūgakusei kōkōsei no ishiki: Juken, kōnaibōryoku oyakokankei* (Attitudes of Junior and Senior High School Students: Entrance Examinations, School Vandalism and Parent-Child Relationships). Tokyo: Nihonhoso Shuppankyokai, 1984: 108.

Nikkyōso taikai sengen (Teachers Union Declaration at Annual Meeting). *Kyōiku Hyōron* (Journal of Education) 8 (1984): 34-35. "Rinkyōshin shingikeika no gaiyō sono 2 ni tsuite no kenkai" (Opinions about the Outline Report of the Deliberation Process in the National Council on Educational Reform). *Kikan kyōikuhō* 57 (Summer 1985): 176–77.

Nikkyōso dainijikyōiku seido kentō inkai (Teachers Union, Second Committee on Education). "Gendai nihon no kaikaku, yōshi" (Reform in Japan, Summary). In *Rinkyōshin to kyōikukaikaku—jiyūka kara koseishugi e* (From Liberalization [Deregulation] to Putting an Emphasis on Individuality [Personality]), edited by Gyōsei. Tokyo: Gyōsei, 1985: 286–92.

Nomura, Tetsuya. "Toshi kōkōsei no seikatsutaido to kachikan" (Lives and Values of Urban Senior High School Students). *Kyōiku shakaigaku kenkyū* 22 (1973): 70–88.

Persell, Caroline. *Education and Inequality: A Theoretical and Empirical Synthesis*. New York: The Free Press, 1977: 46.

Reischauer, Edwin O. *The Japanese*. Cambridge: Belknap Press of Harvard University Press, 1977: 147.

Rohlen, Thomas P. "The *Juku* Phenomena: An Exploratory Essay." *Journal of Japanese Studies* 6, no. 25 (1980): 207–42.

————. *Japan's High Schools*. Berkeley: University of California Press, 1983.

Shade, Barbara J. "Afro-American Cognitive Style: A Variable in Success?" *Review of Educational Research* 46 (Spring 1976): 185–213.

"Shingikeika no gaiyō sono 2" (Outline Report of the Deliberation Process). *In Rinkyōshin to kyōikukaikaku—jiyūka kara koseishugi e* (From Liberalization [Deregulation] to Putting an Emphasis on Individuality [Personality]), edited by Gyōsei. Tokyo: Gyōsei, 1985: 158–66.

Sōrifu Survey. *Seishōnen hakusho* (A White Paper on Children and Young People). Tokyo: Prime Minister's Office, 1982: 68.

Takahashi, Shiro. "Rinkyoshin" (Liberalization). *Gendai no esupuri* 216 (1985): 5–22.

Takeuchi, Kiyoshi. "Kōkō ni okeru gakkōkakusa bunka" (The Culture of Education in Senior High Schools). *Kyōiku shakaigaku kenkyu* 36 (1981): 137–44.

Ushiogi, Morikazu. *Gakureki shakai no Tenkan* (Development of Credential System). Tokyo: Tōdai Shuppankai, 1978.

Yamamura, Takeshi, and Ikuo Amano, eds. *Seinenki no shinrosentaku: Kōgakureki jidai no jiritsu no jōken* (Career Choices of Young People). Tokyo: Yuhikaku Sensho, 1980.

Yoshida, Noboru, et al. *Gendai seinen no ishiki to kōdō* (Attitudes and Activities of Contemporary Young People). Tokyo: Nihonhōsō Shuppankyōkai 1978: 123.

In this insightful and unusual examination of student responses to examination failures and the experience of being *rōnin* in Japanese society, Professor Mamoru Tsukada lays to rest some of the darker stereotypes about private schools as educational pressure cookers that have clouded the vision of American educational observers.

Student Perspectives on *Juku, Yobikō,* and the Examination System

MAMORU TSUKADA

The Japanese educational system is famous for its university entrance examination, the so-called "examination hell" (*shiken jigoku*). Is the examination a dreaded, evil force, worthy of its name? If so, who are its victims? My aim in this paper is not to defend the examination system, which many critics argue has undesirable effects on curriculum, on foreign language instruction, on family life, and on children's emotional, physical, and intellectual development. Rather, my aim is to explore the feelings of students who take the exams and specifically of students who fail the exams for the university of their choice.

In Japan, admission to postsecondary education is based almost solely on entrance examinations. Two private educational institutions, *juku* and *yobikō,* prepare students to take them. The yobikō is a full-time school for *rōnin*—high school graduates who fail entrance examinations and opt to study for an additional year or more to prepare for the next year's exam. They are attached to neither a high school nor a college. The yobikō became an important articulation between secondary and higher education in Japan after World War II with the rapid rise in the number of students applying to college and university. The percentage of college students with rōnin experience peaked at 39.5 percent in 1964 and has remained at about 30 percent since 1983. The percentage of yobikō alumni at Japan's most elite universities is considerably higher: in 1985, 53 percent of entering students at Tokyo University were rōnin. Approximately one-fourth of rōnin spend two or more years in yobikō before entering university.

Approximately two-thirds of Japanese students do not take any university entrance examinations and approximately one-half of Japanese high school graduates each year seek employment immediately after graduation. Another 15 percent enroll in *senmon gakkō* (trade and vocational schools). Of the 36 percent of Japanese high school graduates who choose to go on to college or university, approximately two-thirds either pass the entrance exam of the university of their choice or pass the exam of their second or third choice school and matriculate there. The remaining one-third of college-bound students refuse to have their aspirations "cooled-out" by their initial examination failure and choose instead to become full-time students in yobikō and to try their luck the next year.

This paper presents the personal reactions of rōnin to failure in the college entrance examination. These reactions were gathered in interviews with rōnin as part of fieldwork I conducted as an instructor of English in a large Hiroshima yobikō.

Rōnin invariably are described in sensational terms by the Japanese press: "Rōnin stabs his mother after getting angry at her words, 'Study hard!'"; "Female rōnin burns herself to death"; "Another rōnin suicide attributed to anxiety over entrance exams." Whenever newspapers report an incident involving a rōnin, they automatically attribute the cause to anxiety or stress related to examination hell.

Stories in the Japanese mass media imply a high correlation between rōnin status and suicide. But government statistics suggest otherwise: according to the Ministry of Health and Welfare, the number of suicides of persons aged between fifteen and nineteen was 2,217 in 1960, while the number of rōnin was about 83,000. In 1970 the number of rōnin was up to about 130,000 while the number of suicides in this age group was down dramatically to 757. In 1975, when the number of rōnin was up to 180,000, the number of suicides was 857. From year to year there is no correlation between adolescent suicide and the intensity of examination competition (Rohlen 1983). The social critics and the mass media cynically portray rōnin as suicide-prone victims of examination hell in order to fuel their critique of the Japanese educational system and to appeal to widespread popular educational dissatisfaction and anxiety.

Let's listen to the reactions of rōnin to their failure on the college entrance examination and their views on becoming rōnin. Rōnin status is anathema to high school students aspiring to enter prestigious universities. But how do these students respond to this stigmatized status once it becomes a reality?

Most rōnin as high school students had reason to fear or even expect that they would fail entrance examinations based on their scores in a series of mock exams. Major yobiko and publishers which specialize in entrance examination study guides hold mock college entrance examinations several times per year. About 200,000 students (rōnin as well as high school seniors) take these mock exams each year. On the basis of their mock exam performance students can predict their chances to pass the entrance examinations of various universities. Yet, despite this note of warning, most rōnin reported feeling shocked when they first heard their examination results. For example, one female rōnin wrote:

> I received a telegram from a university student I paid to notify me of my entrance examination result. It read, "There was a storm in Shinji Lake (meaning, you failed). We pray for your next challenge." I said to myself, "I was prepared for this...." But actually I could not help being shocked at my failure. I will never forget the indescribable feeling that I had when I realized I would have to become a rōnin. It was as if I had been hit by a hammer and my heart was nearly crushed. My heart was filled with confused feelings, including ruing not feeling well on the day I took the exam, regretting my inefficient way of studying, feeling I had been treated unfairly by fate, as well as feeling the humiliation of being a loser, and sorrow for my parents.... For the time being I was paralyzed (female, composition, October 1985).

Most rōnin in their hearts predicted their examination failure but unrealistically hoped that it would not happen to them. One male student who took the entrance examination of the University of Tokyo, the most prestigious national university in Japan, said:

> In front of the board which displayed the names of those who passed the entrance examination, I said to myself, "I guess I just couldn't quite pull it off." I felt neither regretful nor sad at this result. I just accepted it as a fact.... That day I made arrangements to enter a yobiko in Hiroshima. On the train to Hiroshima, I suddenly felt sad. Suddenly it hit me how different passing the exam is from failing. I was determined that I would not be defeated by the exam again (male, composition, August 1985).

Graduates of exam-oriented high schools which produce a high percentage of rōnin students each year are generally knowledgeable about the realities of the exam system and thus prepared for failure and are quick to become rōnin. One of them said:

> I was not very good at English so that even before I took the test, I had almost given up expecting to pass. I felt it was OK for me to become a rōnin

student because almost all of my classmates became rōnin. Of course, it would be better to enter the university without becoming rōnin, but it was OK for a year, but not more than that (male, interview, November 1985).

Thus, although most rōnin knew in advance that they were likely to fail the entrance examination based on their mock exam performance and academic counseling, they decided they would rather fail the entrance examination of the university of their choice than to compromise and take the entrance exams only for universities they had a realistic chance of entering.

After experiencing the first shock and disappointment of failure, students begin to prepare themselves for rōnin life by rationalizing their failure to themselves as well as to others. In order to hang on to the belief that they have the potential to enter a first-choice university, rōnin must find a plausible cause for their examination failure. Many attribute their failure to insufficient effort in their high school days:

If you didn't pass the exam simply because you didn't study well, you can easily recover from your shock of failure. If I had failed after studying hard, then I would be terribly shocked and depressed at that (Male A).

We really didn't study (nodding to Male A). We thought that it would be better to become rōnin rather than to enter a university which our scores in the National Common Examination should have enabled us to enter. We prepared for the High School Cultural Festival by staying at school each day until about seven in the evening. After the festival ended in the middle of October, the excitement of it stayed with us for over a month. We knew the entrance examinations were just around the corner, but we thought that we had much more time to study (three males, interview, September 1985).

Others attribute their failure to bad luck on the day when they took the examination. One rōnin said:

I failed to pass the entrance examination of the university because of my bad health condition when taking the exam. After I returned home, I had a severe fever and suffered from diarrhea.

Another referred to his psychological condition, saying:

I am weak on real examinations (but not on mock exams). I wanted to enter Kwansei Gakuin University so badly that I tensed up while taking its entrance exam. That's why I failed. In contrast, when I took the entrance examination for Kansai University, I felt totally relaxed since I didn't want to go there anyway, so of course I passed that test (male, interview, May 1985).

By retrospectively justifying their failure, rōnin reduce their anxiety about failing again. Interestingly, the rōnin I interviewed tended not to suggest that they failed because the examination was unfair, arbitrary, or random. Perhaps to question the legitimacy or predictability of the entrance examination process would be to undermine the core belief rōnin must hold on to that with hard work and determination they will succeed. Typically, it is only after they enter university that they begin to criticize the whole system.

This article was especially prepared for this volume. The research appears in its entirety in Mamoru Tsukada, "Institutionalized Supplementary Education in Japan: The *Yobikō* and *Rōnin* Student Adaptations," *Comparative Education Review* 24, 3 (1988): 286–301.

REFERENCES

Rohlen, Thomas P. *Japan's High Schools*. Berkeley: University of California Press, 1983.

PART V

INTERGROUP TENSIONS IN JAPANESE SCHOOL AND SOCIETY

Disagreements among education reformers about the best way to reconcile commitments to harmony and creativity, merit and equality, and public and private schooling are not the only expressions of tension among the Japanese. The readings in this section reveal three other intergroup tensions: (1) generational (between children and adults, teachers and students), (2) social (between a Japanese cultural majority and minority groups), and (3) cultural (between families who have been abroad and Japanese educators who are commonly intolerant of returnee children).

Conflict in Japanese Schools

BARBARA FINKELSTEIN

C ontrary to prevailing views of Japanese children as overdriven and highly disciplined, there is evidence suggesting that there are significant numbers who are less tractable, docile, and motivated than is usually assumed. In 1984 alone a government survey of bullying incidents documented 531 cases of assault and battery, blackmail, and other acts of violence perpetrated against teachers. Nearly 1,120 children were taken into protective custody. Seven elementary and junior high school students committed suicide and four children were murdered (Fujita 1985).

As careful observers of the Japanese education scene recognize, students are not simply victims of an overheated examination system. They are young people in revolt against the work habits, cultural preferences, ideological structures, and moral constraints on which the current education system has been built. As Professors Amano (1986) and Kitamura (1986) have suggested, they are part of a "baby boom" generation who have grown up to believe that educational achievement will reap social and economic rewards but face an economy which cannot absorb many of their number. More radical critics view unmotivated students as physical and mental dropouts who understand that educational achievement is a key to economic success and upward mobility but lack the financial wherewithal, worldly ambition, psychological disposition, hope-filled aspiration, and/or family advantages that would justify succumbing to the pressure to compete (Horio 1988).

Others are angry young people, the "bullies" to whom Yoshio Murakami refers in his article, "Bullies in the Classroom." Like angry young people in every culture, they strike out physically and emotionally against authority and against one another, eschew the work ethic, and otherwise refuse to compete. Less motivated, less achievement-oriented, less tractable, and less attached to big-time careers in industry and government, junior high school students offer a major challenge to the educational house the Japanese have built. They are in revolt against an educational system which promises opportunity but constrains it, requires dedication but does not necessarily reward it, demands human sensitivity but emphasizes an intellectual and technical curriculum. The educationally unmotivated young, newly labeled *shinjinrui* (new race), are, according to Japan's most acute observers, a principal object of the third educational reform currently under way in Japan.

The readings by Yasumasa Hirasawa and Yasuhiro Kobayashi, focusing on the education of minority groups and returnee children, refute the view that Japan is a homogeneous culture without racial, national, ethnic, or cultural variation. The existence of minority group problems is not advertised widely by the Japanese, who take pride in their egalitarian commitments and who value harmony and inclusiveness.

There are small but significant minorities in Japan—more than 600,000 Koreans, several thousand *gaijin* (foreigners) resident in Japan, nearly one million indigenous Ainu (a people, Caucasian in appearance, who arrived in the islands of Japan before the Japanese; thought by some to have come from Eastern Europe), Hibakusha (atomic bomb victims), children of mixed ancestry, Indochinese refugees, and exploited female laborers from Southeast Asia (see also Beauchamp 1987 and Tadashi and Krauss 1987). There are almost 10,000 so-called returnees, the children of Japanese families who have lived abroad a year or more.

The largest minority group, with an estimated population of more than one and a half million, are the *burakumin*, who have no distinct cultural or physical attributes separating them from the majority of Japanese. As described by Hirasawa (1983), they are linguistically, culturally, and racially identical with other Japanese, but they carry the burden of a historic legacy of outcast status. Living in nearly 6,452 segregated communities, they occupy a subordinate position, suffer from social disabilities, and share a common identity. Their total numbers would be much higher if those who had passed into majority neighborhoods were included (see also Shimahara 1984; Finkelstein 1987).

Problems of educational discrimination plague each of these minority groups differently. Returnees, for example, are typically children of elite families who have lived in other nations for several years and experience severe reentry problems when they return to Japanese schools. According to Professor Tetsuya Kobayashi (as quoted in the article by Yasuhiro Kobayashi that appears in this section), "Neither society nor school is expected to adjust itself to the new situations which have arisen from the influx of returning children. It is only the children who are expected to change." Koreans choosing to attend Korean schools are barred from taking entrance examinations for Japanese universities (Beauchamp 1987). Burakumin children commonly suffer status degradations heaped on them by insensitive educators.

The plight of minority groups offers a challenge to the Japanese sense of justice and commitment to compassion. It also disassembles another stereotype about Japanese education: the image of Japanese education policy as centralized and uniformly administered within clearly defined geographic units, that is, Japan's forty-five prefectures.

Actually, Japan is a country with pronounced local variation in education. Different treatment of minority groups within and among prefectures illustrates such variation. In Kobe, a city awash in historic relationships with foreigners and controlled by political progressives, the board of education has faced discrimination problems head on. It has published antidiscrimination materials for use in both junior and senior high schools in an attempt to deal with discriminatory attitudes toward burakumin and Koreans (Beauchamp 1987). In Osaka prefecture, where the Burakumin Liberation League is active and effective, the board of education supports the principles of *Dôwa Kyôiku* (integrated education), championing the rights of minorities, mandating the exposure and acknowledgement of discrimination, promoting the integration and acceptance of foreign nationals and handicapped children, recognizing women's rights and burakumin and Korean ethnicity, and preparing teachers to work sensitively with minorities (Hawkins 1983; Shimahara 1984; Finkelstein 1987). The board has identified and supported especially trained Dôwa educators, often burakumin and Koreans, to engage students in the preparation of community histories and community self-help activities. It has authorized the use of *Ningen*—supplementary moral education materials that champion human rights, recount burakumin history, and encourage principles of toleration and multicultural acceptance. It has designated certain public schools as "peace" and "liberation" schools.

In other prefectures on Shikoku and Honshu islands, where there are concentrations of minorities but less effective political pressure, the boards of education have felt free to ignore minority problems entirely. Similarly, as Kobayashi notes, responses to returnee children have varied. In large metropolitan regions, Tokyo-Kanagawa-Chiba and Osaka-Kobe, an array of educational arrangements exists for the children of returnees, including special classes, experimental schools, and university centers which gradually integrate children into the educational mainstream. A very few even make use of the returnees' international learning. More commonly, however, returning children enter "adjustment classes," have access to "adjustment education," and are commonly advised to forget what they have learned abroad. In 1983 the Ministry of Education designated eleven cities as Areas for Promoting Education for Returning Children, but their policies are anything but uniformly organized and applied.

As the readings here reveal, Japanese educational forms are diverse, serving different groups of children in different ways, providing opportunity for some and constraint for others. Indeed, the Japanese educational landscape is dotted with variation and steeped in change. As Professor Shogo Ichikawa puts it, ". . . even in Japan, a small country whose educational system is said to preserve uniformity . . . differences exist at each level of education and also among school districts and individual schools. . ." (Ichikawa 1984).

The book ends with a vigorous critique of Japanese education by Teruhisa Horio and a final commentary by Barbara Finkelstein, in which she attempts to pull together the themes embodied in the articles included.

REFERENCES

Amano, Ikuo. "The Dilemma of Japanese Education Today." *Educational Policies in Crisis,* edited by William K. Cummings, Edward R. Beauchamp, Shogo Ichikawa, Victor N. Kobayashi, and Morikazu Ushiogi. New York: Praeger, 1986.

Beauchamp, Edward. "Education and Democracy in Japan." In *Japanese Democracy,* edited by Ishida Tadashi and Ellis Krauss. Santa Barbara, CA: Center for the Study of Democratic Institutions, 1987.

Finkelstein, Barbara. "Double Binds: The Minority Child and the Group in Japan." College Park, MD: Center for the Study of Education Policy and Human Values, University of Maryland, 1987.

Fujita, Hidenori. "A Crisis of Legitimacy in Japanese Education: Meritocracy and Cohesiveness." *Research Bulletin of School of Education, Nagoya University* (1985): 117–33.

Hawkins, John N. "Educational Demands and Institutional Response: *Dōwa* Education in Japan." *Comparative Education Review* 27 (1983): 204–26.

Hirasawa, Yasumasa. "Japan." *Integrated Education* 120 (November-December 1983): 18–22.

Horio, Teruhisa. *Educational Thought and Ideology in Modern Japan: State Authority and Intellectual Freedom,* edited and translated by Steven Platzer. Tokyo: University of Tokyo Press, 1988.

Ichikawa, Shogo. "Japan." In *Educational Policy: An International Survey,* edited by J. R. Hough. New York: St. Martins Press, 1984.

————. "American Perceptions of Japanese Education." In *Educational Policies in Crisis,* edited by William K. Cummings, Edward R. Beauchamp, Shogo Ichikawa, Victor N. Kobayashi, and Morikazu Ushiogi. New York: Praeger, 1986.

Japanese Ministry of Foreign Affairs. Office for Regional Improvement, Management and Coordination Agency. *Dowa Problem: Present Situation and Government Measures,* 1984.

Kazuhiro, Mochizuki. "The Present Situation of Japan's Education: A Report from School." *Orientation Seminars on Japan* 1, 11. Tokyo: The Japan Foundation Office of Overseas Studies Center, 1982.

Kitamura, Kazuyuki. "The Decline and Reform of Education in Japan." In *Educational Policies in Crisis: Japanese and American Perspectives,* edited by William K. Cummings, Edward R. Beauchamp, Shogo Ichikawa, Victor N. Kobayashi, and Morikazu Ushiogi. New York: Praeger, 1986.

Kobayashi, Tetsuya. "Educational Problems for Returning Children in Japan." Kyoto: Kyoto University, 1987.

Mikio, Sumiya. "The Function and Social Structure of Japan: Schools and Japanese Society." *Journal of Social and Political Ideas in Japan* 5 (1980): 117–31.

Murakami, Yoshio. "Bullies in the Classroom." *Japan Quarterly* 32 (October–December 1985): 407–11.

Organization of Economic Cooperation and Development (OECD) Examiners' Report. *Reviews of National Policies for Education: Japan.* Paris: OECD, 1971.

Rohlen, Thomas P. "Is Japanese Education Becoming Less Egalitarian?" *Journal of Japanese Studies* 3 (1977).

Shimahara, Nobuo. "Toward the Equality of a Japanese Minority: The Case of Burakumin." *Comparative Education* 20 (1984): 339–53.

Tadashi, I. and Ellis Krass. *Japanese Democracy.* Santa Barbara, CA: Center for the Study of Democratic Institutions, 1987.

Tsuneyoshi, Ryoko Kato. "Meanings of Equality: Lessons from Japanese Debate." *Educational Forum* 54 (Winter 1990): 185–95.

In this article, Yoshio Murakami protests the quantity and quality of group teasing in the schools. He suggests that the problem is long-standing, adult-caused, teacher-sustained—the product of an unhealthy "mind your own business" attitude. He also documents the presence of corporal punishment and severe tensions among and between students and teachers in schools.

Bullies in the Classroom

YOSHIO MURAKAMI

B ullying among children is nothing new. Over sixty years ago Japan's beloved author of juvenile literature, Miyazawa Kenji, movingly depicted bullying in a passage of his *Ginga Tetsudô no Yoru* (Night of the Milky Way Railroad). The young protagonist of this work, Giovanni, who lives with his invalid mother, looks forward to the day when his father will return from his fishing job in distant northern waters with a sea-otter jacket he has promised his son.

A vicious rumor, however, has been circulating among Giovanni's classmates that the boy's father has actually been put in prison. The ringleader, Zanelli, takes every opportunity to taunt Giovanni: "Giovanni, your sea-otter jacket's on its way." Only words, but they send a chill through the young boy's heart.

One day after school Giovanni runs into a group of classmates, Zanelli among them, on his way home. Zanelli starts the chant, and the others take it up. "Giovanni, your sea-otter jacket's on its way." Redfaced with shame, Giovanni starts to walk past the boys when he spots his friend Campanella among the bullies. Campanella stands there mutely with a wan smile, as if to say, "Try not to be angry."

As the story unfolds, Giovanni joins his friend Campanella on a dreamlike trip on the Milky Way Railroad.

In whatever age or society, rare is the child who does not possess a streak of cruelty, and in almost every group of children you will find the bully and the bully's victim. What has made bullying such a big social problem in the last five years or so is that, once it gets started, it knows no stopping point and can easily escalate into suicide or murder. What was abnormal has become normal, like a festering sore which will not heal.

In November 1984 a first-year high school student in Osaka was murdered by two of his classmates. The gruesome way the boy was murdered was bad enough, but what shocked the adult world even more was the revelation that the murder had been triggered by the victim's tormenting of the two boys who murdered him. The objects of constant harassment, the boys had ended up taking revenge on their tormenter. The details of this case are worth going into for what they reveal about the bullying problem.

Kamazawa Yoshiaki, sixteen, was the son of a sushi shop operator in Osaka and attended a private high school in the city. His body was found on the afternoon of November 2 in a river in the Tenma area. His head had been struck dozens of times with a hammer and his eyes had been gouged out. Police suspicions focused almost immediately on two of Yoshiaki's classmates, both fifteen. After preliminary questioning, they were arrested on November 11 on suspicion of murder.

The suspects were members of a group of which Yoshiaki had been the leader. Yoshiaki, a stocky boy, had belonged to the school's judo club and was considered one of the club's most promising new members when he joined. The suspects belonged to the gymnastics club. It was a mutual interest in sports that brought the three together, and at first they evidently got on quite well.

The boys' high school puts a great deal of emphasis on sports and is particularly strong in judo. Yoshiaki was told that if he worked hard at his judo, he was sure to make the regular team by his third year. When he realized what a long haul he had ahead of him, he became discouraged, and in the summer of 1984 he dropped out of the club.

It was just about that time that Yoshiaki began tormenting the other two boys. He would order them to wallop this or that classmate, and if they didn't, he would beat or kick them. "What number do you like?" he would ask, and then strike them that number of times. Or he would get on his motorbike and order them to follow him on bicycles. If they didn't keep up, he would beat them again.

According to the boys' confession, the last straw came when Yoshiaki told them they had to perform an indecent act with an adult toy in their classroom in front of classmates. If we let him get away with this, they reasoned, what will he make us do next?

But even so, what a brutal method of murder! The two took Yoshiaki to a park one night, took turns striking him with a hammer, then, using the claw end, gouged out his eyes. Was it fear that Yoshiaki might come back to life that made them give themselves so relentlessly to the task? When they were done battering him, they dragged the body fifty meters to the river and threw it in. That is how terrified the two were of the boy.

The boys say that on a number of occasions they told teachers and friends about what Yoshiaki was doing to them and sought help. The school maintains that it knew nothing about what was going on. Indeed, one of the most disturbing things about this case and others like it is the pat, bureaucratic response on the part of the school. "We weren't aware of a thing. We're as shocked as anyone. We'll investigate and make sure this kind of thing doesn't happen again." Were the teachers really as ignorant of the situation as they claim?

When I asked if I could interview a few people at the school, a teacher replied in an eerily matter-of-fact way, "We have a lot of wild kids here, and we don't want you setting them off; there's no telling what they might do. And don't interview any teachers; there's no telling what they might do either." In the subtle but very real atmosphere of violence at this school, both teachers and students have become insensitive to it. They offer threats instead of concern.

Both the victim and the two murderers in this case come from homes where both parents are present and in their prime, homes with no discernible family problems. In recent years there has been a sharp increase in cases of children from such normal homes suddenly engaging in extreme, abnormal behavior.

Yoshiaki's case has a number of things to teach us. If we review what has been reported on it, the following points emerge. First, a person who was constantly harassed at a certain point abruptly became the harasser; the roles of victim and assailant were reversed. Second, although physical violence was used—beating up, etc.—it was mental or psychological violence (being told they had to perform an indecent act in front of a group of people) that directly triggered the crime. Third, the crime was extremely brutal in nature. Fourth, fellow students acted as if they did not know what was going on. No peacemaker or friend emerged to put a stop to the bullying. Fifth, although help was sought from the school, it was evidently not forthcoming. Finally, an atmosphere of violence prevailed at the school so that even the teachers' behavior was hostile. The characteristics of this case are common to other cases as well.

Victims Have No Friends

Take the case of the second-year junior high school boy in Tokyo's Adachi Ward who hanged himself in January 1979. Before taking his life, the boy wrote a message in the class diary, a portion of which we will quote here.

I decided to kill myself because day after day I go to school and only bad things happen. Nothing good ever happens to me. If the kids in my class could be in my shoes, they would understand how I feel. If only they knew how I feel every day. Even in my dreams there are nothing but bad things. The only one I can talk to is the hamster, but the hamster can't speak back. Maybe I'm just not suited to this world. Maybe July 7, 1964—my being born—was a mistake. I can't stop the tears now. There was one, only one, thing that I wanted while I was alive—a friend I could talk to, really talk to, from the heart. Just one friend like that, only one, was all I wanted.

The boy was a sensitive child and not strong physically, and for this he was made the object of almost daily bullying at school. One cannot help but be deeply dismayed at the rapid spread of an inhuman atmosphere among children these days. When vulnerability is detected in another child, the tendency seems to be to push on the weak points until the individual is crushed.

Let me give another specific example. The setting this time is a small town in the bleak Hokuriku district on the Japan Sea side of Honshu. In February 1984 a second-year student at the junior high school in the town was taken by a number of classmates into the athletic equipment room and there beaten up. When he got home, his face bruised and swollen, his shocked father pressed him for an explanation. The boy reluctantly revealed that this was but the latest episode in six months of almost daily bullying.

They would wait for him on the way home from school. They would emerge suddenly from the shadows, block any escape route, then take him down an alley where they would start hitting him. Although the students were allowed to sit anywhere at lunchtime, no one would ever sit near him. When he went to the toilet, somebody would spread the word. His classmates would gather in the lavatory and stand on each other's shoulders to peek in on him. He would return to the classroom only to find his desk and chair had been dragged out in the hall. Trying to keep back the tears, he would take the desk back to its place, not a soul offering to help.

The students were not the only ones who gave the boy a hard time. There seems to have been a feeling of strong dislike for him among the teachers as well. One of the teachers powdered his head with chalk dust from the blackboard eraser. Another teacher would catch him up on the slightest mistake and hit him with a bamboo sword.

What had the boy done to deserve this concerted harassment, harassment that even included the violence of his teachers? At this school the boys were supposed to have crew cuts, but this young boy had somewhat longer hair. "At least, that's the only thing I can possibly think of," his father says.

> My son did something different, so he was persecuted. The length of your hair, the color of the clothes you wear—things like that are not supposed to be left up to the individual. When everybody's got to have a crew cut, everybody's got to wear the same color, the feeling builds up against anyone who is different: "We can't let that guy get away with that!" It's a very frightening thing. Well, I asked my son how he felt about it, we talked it over with the teacher, and he decided to let his hair grow.

The day after his son was beaten up, the father went to the principal, told him what had happened, and asked his help. Though he did not say so in so many words, the principal made it clear to the father that the boy was in the wrong for having broken the rules. As far as the father is concerned, this just goes to show what kind of school it is.

> To put it briefly, this is a violent school. You have the gym teacher pacing the floor with a bamboo sword in his hand. The student slips up and he's going to get a wallop. Inspections are held to check clothes, hair, what the kids have got in their desks. If your hair is the least bit long, the teacher gets after you with scissors and hair clippers. It's the atmosphere of coercion and violence in this school that gave rise to my son's being beaten up. And can you blame the kids for thinking like that? They figure if it's all right for the teachers to hit people, it's all right for them to do the same. Are they wrong?

The father is appealing to the teachers and to other parents to work to change the school. But there is no indication that either teachers or parents intend to do a thing. The boy in Tokyo who liked hamsters was bullied because he was weak. The boy in Hokuriku who stood out because of his long hair was the object of violence because he was different. We see here a buildup in the schools of unhealthy energy directed at isolating certain individuals—with the tacit approval or even complicity of responsible adults.

There are a few statistics that will be enlightening at this point. In April, the National Police Agency issued its first "Survey of Bullying Incidents," which covers the year 1984. The incidence of bullying cases has only recently warranted the collection of separate statistics. The survey reports that the police investigated 531 cases of assault and battery, other violence, blackmail, and acts of juvenile delinquency that were the result of *ijime* (bullying) and took 1,920 boys and girls into protective custody. Seven elementary and junior high school students committed suicide, apparently as a result of bullying, and four children were murdered or were the victims of attempted murder in retaliation for bullying. Of these cases, 80 percent involved junior high school students and one-third of those taken into protective custody were girls.

The violence inflicted was in many cases quite serious. In one case, a child was paralyzed from the waist down and in another a student was left with a serious speech impairment. But not only physical violence was involved—that is, beating up or pushing the victim around. Verbal abuse was very common, and most cases involved ostracism of the victim by fellow students. A set of statistics from the Tokyo Metropolitan Board of Education sheds light on the extent of such noncriminal bullying as well.

Of the 1,789 public schools in Tokyo, 76.9 percent reported cases of bullying between April 1984 and March 1985. Here is the breakdown: elementary schools (grades 1 to 6), 5,450 cases; junior high schools (grades 7 to 9), 3,519 cases; and high schools (grades 10 to 12), 515 cases. The last three years of school seem to be relatively free of bullying.

Of the bullying activities, 70 percent could be categorized as psychological bullying. This includes making threats, calling names, leaving classmates out of games and other activities, and ostracizing them completely. Some typical bullying taunts are *baikin* (germ), *shi ne* (drop dead), and *kusai* (you stink). The recipients of such abuse are usually the weak children and the goody-goodies. While the strong always prey on the weak and bullying may be fun, the popularity of such psychological bullying might be explained by its invisibility. Those in authority are more likely to detect torn clothing and black eyes than a damaged ego.

Although the main concern here is violence committed by children, it should be noted that there has been a recent spate of cases in which students have been killed or have committed suicide as a result of corporal punishment inflicted by teachers. On May 9, 1985, a high school boy from Gifu Prefecture on a class trip to the international science exhibition at Tsukuba City died after his teacher severely punished him. He had violated a school rule by taking his hair dryer on the trip. In another case seven weeks earlier, a high school girl, also from Gifu Prefecture, hanged herself after enduring corporal punishment by the teacher in charge of the track and field club. "I'm sick and tired of being hit, and I'm sick and tired of crying," she wrote before she killed herself. A junior high school girl from Nagano Prefecture who had continually clashed with a teacher left this note before putting an end to her life. "I hate school. Everybody tries to cut you down. But I hate the teacher most of all because she gets you when you're down and then tramples all over you." In cases like this, is corporal punishment by teachers really all that different from bullying by fellow students?

One feature appears to be prominent in virtually all bullying cases: classmates and playmates close their eyes to the victimization of one of their fellows. They pretend indifference unless they are victims of the injustice of violence themselves. Bullying escalates to extremes because children, not having been taught about the dignity of life, close their eyes to others' misfortunes.

The interactions of children reflect society as a whole. If adults say, "It has nothing to do with me," children echo the sentiment. Only recently have adults begun to open their eyes. Now that an affluent society has been achieved, some adults are opening their eyes to the victims and unfortunate ones around them, confident that their problems can be solved. But we have not made the progress that we think we have. Most of us still think, "It has nothing to do with me." But it is our problem. All of us must learn to care for others.

While the Giovanni of Miyazawa Kenji's fable had to endure the bullying of Zanelli, he had the saving friendship of Campanella. There are many, many Zanellis among today's children but, alas, very few Campanellas. Will the day ever come when the countless Giovannis in Japan have the friends they need? Will they ever come into possession of the much-longed-for sea-otter jacket?

This article first appeared in the *Japan Quarterly*. Yoshio Murakami, "Bullies in the Classroom," *Japan Quarterly* 32 (October–December 1985): 407–11.

Yasumasa Hirasawa outlines the educational achievement of minority groups in Japan and, in the process, reveals the existence of invisible education policies which are discriminatory and conflict-generating. He documents an array of unexposed status degradations being heaped on minority children in schools. He alludes to discrimination in the conduct of certain teachers and in the content of textbooks and describes the consciousness-raising activities of certain advocate groups. He documents the magnitude and selectivity of school achievement problems for certain classes of children, thereby revealing some fundamental limitations on Japanese commitments to equality and harmony.

The Education of Minority Group Children in Japan

YASUMASA HIRASAWA

In a report called "Educational Standards of Our Nation" (1981), the Ministry of Education drew the following conclusions in its assessments of postwar education in Japan. First, the report asserted that Japanese education achieved a remarkable quantitative growth in the postwar decades and exceeded most nations of the world in the rate and distribution of enrollment in schools and colleges. Second, it suggested that education needed to be broadened in scope to include the enrichment of lifelong education and diversified educational opportunities and alternatives at all levels of education.

While almost uncritically praising the achievements in education, the report was silent about the inaccessibility of high school and college for certain groups of young people. It noted no disparities in educational attainment among prefectures and different social classes, increases in cases of school violence, massive teachers' protests, or opposition to government policies to increase centralized control over education practice. Nor did it note the unequal status of the education of minorities.

The view of Japanese education as effective, equal, and problem-free has been prevalent outside Japan as well. Human capital theorists often cite the case of rapid economic development of Japan after World War II as linked to the steady expansion of educational opportunities and as proof of the validity of their theories. For example, Glazer (1982) pointed to Japanese education as a model where successful government interventions led to "greater ambitions" in Japanese schools. Reischauer (1977) and Vogel (1979) referred to Japanese education as a key element in Japan's "miraculous" economic, political, and social development. Cummings (1980, 1982) has repeatedly argued that the postwar educational system has helped to equalize income distribution and promote equality and democratic orientations in the society.

These arguments looked selectively at certain aspects of success and failed to examine the views of many Japanese observers who are less satisfied with the state of educational opportunities. The major purpose of this report, therefore, is to present the other side of the success stories, thereby inviting more balanced inquiries into Japanese education.

As the pace of economic growth has slowed since the early 1970s and the growth of education has reached a peak, discussions within Japan have focused more on problems than on brilliant achievements. Early in the 1980s, *Asahi Shimbun* (March 29, 1982), a major daily newspaper, reported that 10 percent of Japan's junior high school authorities had requested police protection for teachers on graduation days. A recent police survey reported that the number of assaults on teachers had increased almost fivefold from 1978 to 1982 and that they were perpetrated by younger offenders than in the past. Furthermore, a junior high teacher in Tokyo stabbed a delinquent student in class earlier this year, an incident which captured wide media attention. It should be noted the children of the middle classes have produced about 90 percent of the incidents. Apparently, they are reflecting a general dissatisfaction with life and with the qualities of the Japanese school system that have produced the so-called miracle—its competitive, hierarchical, bureaucratically controlled, centrally planned national development and allocation of human resources policies. In the face of these circumstances, the prime minister has given the issue of school violence top priority in his public statements and parliamentary addresses while criticizing and blaming the practices of the Japan Teachers Union as "subversive," "ideological," and "stimulating delinquent acts and behaviors." There is, as yet, little agreement between the government and teachers over strategies to cope with the problem.

Another critical issue in 1982 involved a controversy over textbook revisions. School textbooks are written and published by private publishing houses but must be authorized by the Ministry of Education before being approved for classroom use. For the past twenty-seven years, the textbook authorization system has faced continuing protests and demands for its abolition. In July 1982, both authors and publishers of high school history textbooks were told to revise wording or delete certain passages about Japanese military invasions of China, Korea, and other countries in Southeast Asia during World War II. The following are some of the examples:

1. Japan's military actions in China have been changed from "invasions" to the more neutral "advances."
2. The number of victims of the Japanese army in the massacre known as the 1937 Rape of Nanking, estimated at 200,000, has been deleted. The atrocity has been attributed to provocation by Chinese resistance fighters.
3. The March 1919 Korean movement for independence from Japanese colonial control has been termed "rioting."
4. The forcing of Koreans to take Japanese names, prohibiting the use of Korean, and requiring, after 1940, that only Japanese be spoken in Korea are described as "making Japanese the common language."

The Japan Teachers Union, progressive scholars, a large number of citizens, and major opposition parties began to protest revisions. Not until the governments and media of the People's Republic of China, Korea, and other neighboring countries lodged protests, however, did the Japanese government respond. On August 26, 1982, top government officials, including the prime minister, publicly issued an official statement promising to correct the disputed revisions by 1985. This calmed the neighbors but left them wary.

An exhibition called *Shinryaku* (invasion) was held in Osaka and attracted 18,000 people. The exhibition attempted to convey the historical facts to the next generation, to sustain historical memory, to prevent future occurrences, and to protest the textbook revisions. It traveled throughout Japan from September to the end of 1982, featuring over two hundred large panel photographs of such atrocities as the Rape of Nanking, the invasion of Korea, public beheadings of Chinese citizens, the Japanese army massacre of Okinawans, and other brutalities.

Yet another issue arose in 1982 in the wake of budget cuts for education and social welfare. In the context of the so-called *gyōkaku* (administrative reform) calling for reductions in government spending, the education budget had been marked as the first to be reduced. Among the measures to be taken were several that disadvantaged the poor and minorities: (1) to charge interest in the repayment of scholarships that had been interest-free; (2) to have elementary school textbooks purchased by students, although they had been free since 1962; (3) to reduce or cut financial support to private schools within five years; and (4) to reduce fiscal support for school lunches.

Education of Minorities

The *burakumin,* generally referred to as descendants of outcasts in the Edo caste system (early seventeenth century to the Emancipation Edict of 1871), are the biggest minority group in Japan, with an estimated population of three million living in nearly six thousand communities scattered all over Japan, mainly in western regions. Discrimination against them is still prevalent, particularly with regard to employment and marriage.

An organized liberation movement calling for equal rights, equal treatment, and equal opportunities began in 1922 with the founding of *Suiheisha* (Leveler's Association). The year 1982 marked its sixtieth anniversary. The *Buraku* Liberation League, the successor of Suiheisha, has thirty-four prefectural headquarters and nearly two hundred thousand burakumin members.

The national government, under pressure from the liberation movement, officially admitted the persistence of severe discrimination against the burakumin in 1965 when it issued a special government report on integration. *Dōwa* (integration) measures were aimed at improving environmental conditions of burakus (communities with burakumin inhabitants) in order to mute the prejudice-producing effects of physical shabbiness. Although the physical conditions of the communities improved, the quality of intergroup relationships, the rates of employment and educational attainment, and political/professional representation in the society did not advance much.

In 1982, thirty-three years after the Dōwa Acts were initiated, the integration of the burakumin was set back when the Special Measures Law for Integration expired and was replaced by the Improvement Measures Law, which was to be in effect for only five more years. The Dōwa budget was reduced and the range of measures narrowed. The Buraku Liberation Movement was challenged by conservative Liberal Democratic party (LDP) members and their supporters.

Reflecting the conservative trend in the political climate and a reduction in economic growth, discriminatory incidents continued to occur in 1982. For example, Ku Tashiro, Justice Bureau Director of the central government, made the following remark at a research symposium on the effective execution of official duties in May 1982. "The rather unsavory parallel has been drawn, we dare say, that public servants are as much a fact of life as the *tokushu* buraku (special hamlet of the burakumin).

But public servants are, after all, just human beings." This statement is problematic on at least three levels. First, this top government official had not learned how derogatory the use of the term *tokushu buraku* was, even seventeen years after the government's 1965 report on the burakumin status; second, he contrasted public servants with tokushu buraku as if the burakumin were nonhuman; and third, most of the audience, made up of high-ranking local government officials, did not point out the nature of this discriminatory analogy. This incident symbolized the half-hearted aspect of integration efforts and reflected the still widespread prejudice against the burakumin population.

Yet another example of unconscious discrimination is evident in this incident. A Tokyo University professor of sociology denied the existence of discrimination against the burakumin in a research symposium held in Germany. As a consequence, two Austrian trade papers carried articles libeling the burakumin about their position on the liberalization of leather-products trade.

Preceding this incident, a leading Buddhist had protested the inclusion of statements about the status of Japan's burakumin in the resolution of the World Conference of Religionists for Peace held in Princeton, New Jersey, in 1979. In his call for censorship, he argued that avowals about burakumin status in Japan constituted a "shame" and called attention to a problem that did not exist.

These cases reveal several dark realities about the endurance of discrimination: first, that efforts by Japanese scholars and government officials to correctly inform foreign people about the burakumin problem have not been adequate; second, that the foreign press can perpetuate bigotry unless correct information is conveyed to them. As a result of mounting protests against these incidents, the Foreign Ministry established a special division dealing with overseas enlightenment activities.

Beyond the problem of the media, an increase in unemployment rates fueled feelings of frustration, and bigotry-laden graffiti and other expressions of hostility against the burakumin reemerged in 1982. For instance, "Kill the burakumin" was sprayed on a school wall in Osaka; "Shut burakumin up in an asylum and turn on the poison gas" appeared at Tokyo University. Letters saying things like "You are maggots of the society" were sent to members of the Buraku Liberation League.

On the other hand, the status and condition of the burakumin were being clarified by an array of newspaper articles, conferences, and systematic advocacy efforts. *Le Monde,* the leading French newspaper, covered the burakumin problem and the liberation movement in two separate articles. The First International Conference against Discrimination was successfully held in December 1982 with participants from the U.S. (members of the National Association for the Advancement of Colored

People), France, Germany, Britain, India, and a number of United Nations agencies. It was cosponsored by the Ministry of Foreign Affairs, the municipal governments of Tokyo and Osaka, and diverse civil rights organizations including the Buraku Liberation League. The participants discussed the particularities and commonalities among respective forms of discrimination in the world.

More progress is revealed in the emergence of a broad coalition which prevented the LDP from eliminating all integration measures and negotiated the Area Improvement Measures Law, a compromise bill which, if inadequate, nonetheless was a positive step.

In education, however, scant progress has been made. Special scholarships for burakumin high school and college students were changed from "grant" to "loan" as the Special Measures Law was replaced by the new law. The grant scholarships, specifically designated for the purpose of raising educational attainment among burakumin youth, were instrumental in expanding the enrollment of burakumin students in high schools and colleges and reducing the disparity in enrollment between burakumin and non-burakumin. The elimination of scholarships imposed enormous financial burdens on the burakumin, whose educational attainment is still far below the national average.

A large-scale survey of more than 80,000 burakumin, conducted between December 1982 and February 1983, documented the levels of educational attainment among the burakumin and found the following:

1. The percentage of burakumin not enrolled in schools of some kind was nearly twenty-five times as large as the prefectural and national average, including middle-aged and elderly persons for whom illiteracy was still a serious problem. Literacy classes were regularly held in burakumin communities in Osaka and other prefectures. In Osaka alone, 1,500 burakumin attend these classes.
2. The huge discrepancies in the percentage of graduates from secondary and postsecondary schools between burakumin and nonburakumin implied a disproportionately large distribution of burakumin in jobs as unskilled laborers, or in a semiemployed or unemployed status. Given the fact that graduation from senior high school has been a minimal requirement for employment at big corporations and local and national government offices for the past decade or so, the burakumin share is apt to be very small.

Not unexpectedly, burakumin are underrepresented in the high-prestige professions—doctors, lawyers, scholars, and educators. Since there have been no affirmative action or preferential admissions policies for burakumin and other minorities in professional schools, such discrepancies persist.

On the more positive side, one can point to instances where an array of advocates effectively illuminated problems and projected solutions. Among those that occurred in a single year (1982) were the National Research Study Meeting on Buraku Liberation (12,000 participants); the National Meeting on Liberation Preschool/Early Childhood Education (3,500 participants); the thirty-fifth annual Convention of the National Integrated Education Research Council (20,000 participants). All engaged in consciousness-raising and agenda-forming activities. Common concerns in these meetings were (1) the replacement of the Special Measures Law for Integration with the Improvement Measures Law, which was followed by a decrease of governmental commitments, (2) the poor quality of living conditions within burakumin households, and (3) the higher levels of tension between burakumin and nonburakumin. Taken together, these efforts represent a significant commitment to strengthen education for the oppressed.

For Korean minorities in Japan (more than 600,000 in number), postwar education policy has been oppressive and assimilatory also. Koreans were forcibly brought to Japan as low-wage earners following the 1910 Japanese occupation of Korea. They were required to speak the Japanese language and take Japanese names. Nonetheless, nearly 6,000 Korean schools with over 50,000 students emerged in Japan in the wake of Korean independence. But in 1948, these ethnic sponsorships were declared illegal by the Ministry of Education and the General Headquarters of the Occupation army, and Korean schools lost formal school status and financial support. Graduates were prohibited from taking entrance examinations to national and public colleges. Moreover, in all but a few municipalities, Koreans were barred from becoming public schoolteachers.

In 1982, the third annual Meeting on Educational Research for Koreans in Japan was attended by 595 teachers and scholars involved in efforts to develop ethnic awareness and bilingualism among Korean children. The meeting had three agenda items: (1) the construction of curriculum materials that could correct biased views on Korea and Koreans, (2) the cultivation of strategies to develop ethnic awareness among Korean children going to Japanese schools and to help improve their educational attainment, and (3) to mount a protest against the directive of the Ministry of Education barring employment of Korean teachers (*Asahi Shimbun,* October 2, 1982).

In the light of the assimilatory educational policy in the postwar decades, a gathering of this sort was significant. Not only did it elaborate an important agenda but it linked its goals and purposes to the movement of the burakumin.

This excerpt is taken from Yasumasa Hirasawa, "Japan," *Integrated Education* (now published as *Equity and Excellence*) 120 (November-December 1983): 18–22.

REFERENCES

Asahi Shimbun (Asahi News). Tokyo: Asahi Shimbunsha (Asahi News Press), 1982.

Buraku Kaihō Dōmei (Buraku Liberation). *Buraku no kodomo no kyōiku jittai* (Educational Standards of the *Burakumin* Children). Osaka: Buraku Kaihō Dōmei, 1978.

Buraku Kaihō Kenkyū-sho (Buraku Liberation Research Institute). "Osaka buraku jittai chōsa hōkoku" (A Report from the Buraku Survey in Osaka). *Buraku kaihō kenkyū* (Bulletin of Buraku Liberation) 33 (March 1983): 1–55. *Kaihō Shimbun* (Liberation News Press), 1982.

Cummings, William K. *Education and Equality in Japan.* Princeton: Princeton University Press, 1980.

———. "The Egalitarian Transformation of Postwar Japanese Education." *Comparative Education Review* 26 (February 1982): 16–32.

Glazer, Nathan. "Responses." *Harvard Educational Review* 52 (November 1982): 460–61.

Ministry of Education (Monbusho). *Waga kuni no kyōiku suijun* (Educational Standards of Our Nation). Tokyo: Monbusho, 1981.

Reischauer, Edwin O. *The Japanese.* Cambridge: Harvard University Press,1977.

Vogel, Ezra F. *Japan As Number One: Lessons for America.* Cambridge, MA: Harvard University Press, 1979.

In this article, Yasuhiro Kobayashi examines the problems of "returnees," children who have spent a year or more abroad. They are, when they return, out of the educational mainstream. Often harassed by teachers and students alike in regular public schools, their families form a relatively discontented minority seeking more diversity and flexibility in the school system. Though their gains have been modest, some schools and school districts have created special programs for them and have thus created more diversity in educational opportunity.

Japanese Schools Can't Cope with Cosmopolitan Kids

YASUHIRO KOBAYASHI

Japanese children who spend a few years in the United States or other foreign countries face a difficult reentry into their own society. On returning to Japan, they do not fit into the school system, nor is the school system comfortable with them.

According to Ministry of Education statistics issued in May 1986, almost 40,000 school-age boys and girls are living overseas, more than 16,000 in the U.S. alone. Every year 10,000 leave Japan, and about the same number return.

Businesses are increasingly sending personnel abroad to staff international operations, and usually the families go along. Not many years ago, only the largest corporations allowed dependents to accompany an employee, but now even fairly small companies do. The assignments are often for three or four years.

One angry mother has written a best-selling book about the parochial attitudes she found in the schools when her family returned to Japan after six years in New York. In *Under One Blue Sky*, Chikako Osawa relates the experience of her son, Tatsuya, in the sixth grade of a local public school.

Just as the boy seemed to be adjusting to his new environment, classmates began harassing him. His belongings were hidden, and pencil shavings were slipped into his lunch. Classmates roughed him up, jeering that "Americans belong in America." An anonymous note told him to "drop dead."

As if peer persecution were not bad enough, Tatsuya's teachers began to chide him for his un-Japanese mannerisms. The stress caused an ulcer, and the boy had to transfer to an international school.

Midori Namiki, senior counselor at the International Student Education Center, says:

> The education system has made a modest attempt to accommodate returning children. Eighty schools and thirteen school districts have been designated for special programs such as extra instruction in the Japanese language. More than a hundred universities have set up special admission quotas for such students. But the attitudes of other kids and educators haven't changed at all.

Namiki relates her astonishment on finding that English classes at a junior high school with many students who had lived abroad were no more advanced than at ordinary schools. The teacher confessed that he had reduced the time allotted to conversation in class. The returnees did not dare speak English well for fear of being bullied.

Tetsuya Kobayashi, a professor of comparative education at Kyoto University, says, "The Japanese educational system was designed for people who were expected to spend their entire lives in this country. Conformity to the norm is the implicit premise. Returnees are treated as problem children because they don't fit in. All the emphasis is on getting them to adapt. But some educators are finally beginning to suspect that maybe the fault lies with the schools, not these children."

A 1986 report, "Education for Internationalization," advocates a more open-minded approach. The authors blame the adjustment problems of returnees on educators' reluctance to acknowledge that every individual develops differently.

The study says: "A pedagogical approach that attempts to force every child into a narrow mold of 'Japaneseness' is incompatible with a cosmopolitan society whose salient feature is acceptance of cultural diversity."

One of the authors, Koji Kato of the National Institute for Educational Research, admits that this is still a minority viewpoint. He hopes that eventually the educational establishment can be weaned away from its preoccupation with "Japanizing" returning youngsters. Kato says, "Our aim is to adapt the schools to different kinds of children instead of making these kids adjust to the schools."

Kato and his family have lived overseas, so he knows the problems of returnees firsthand. Like author Osawa, he says the experience opened his eyes to the ethnocentrism of Japanese society.

Kato knows reforms will not be easy. "After all, we are trying to change people's basic assumptions. We want teachers and administrators to accept diversity rather than impose uniformity."

This article first appeared in the mass circulation newspaper *Asahi Shimbun.* Yasuhiro Kobayashi, "Japanese Schools Can't Cope with Cosmopolitan Kids," translated by the Asia Foundation Translation Service Center, 1987.

In a radical critique of the Japanese educational system, Professor Teruhisa Horio documents the existence of historic antagonisms between the prerogatives of central authority and those of the people. Focusing on the pervasiveness of conflict rather than harmony, he describes increases in classroom violence, bullying and discrimination, the decline in legitimate forms of teacher authority, and the emergence of an insensitive young elite, which he describes as being engaged morally and politically in assaults on human rights. He suggests that educational problems originate in antagonisms between a small elite who look on education as a form of social, political, and intellectual control and the many who define it in relationship to human feeling, nature's wonders, moral sensibility, and social awareness. In this essay, he calls for a radical overhaul of the Japanese educational system and emphasizes a need for decentralization, local control, academic freedom, children's rights, and a dismantling of the apparatus of authority currently sustaining Japanese education, which contributes to its moral and political impoverishment.

A Japanese Critique of Japanese Education

TERUHISA HORIO

The Crisis in Japanese Education Today

In recent years education has increasingly come to be thought of as one of our most basic human rights. Indeed, it is the right by virtue of which all other modern rights ultimately derive their substance and meaning. The ascendance of this way of thinking can be tied to a growing recognition of the fact that education plays a pivotal role in the process by which children mature as reasoning beings and develop into responsible members of society. This enlightened approach has generally come to be accepted by educators throughout the world and is clearly visible in Japan's postwar constitution as well as in our Fundamental Law of Education, adopted in 1947.

Notwithstanding the fact that our school system is legally rooted in these ideals, however, the reality of present-day Japanese education is such that these values have been subverted. As the freedom of our schools is continuously eroded by the ever-increasing interference of the state's administrative machinery, as educational values fall under the domination of an ideology dominated by the one-dimensional glorification of *nōryokushugi* (academic competence), and as schools come to be seen merely as arenas for the most vicious forms of competition related to social selection and advancement, it is becoming ever more impossible to take seriously the idea that education is the sine qua non of human rights. Thus, for example, when social studies teachers ask pupils to think of education as one of their inalienable human rights, it is hardly surprising that the latter should beg to be spared from having to shoulder the weight of a right that is so odious.

The Idea of Education As a Right

The notion that education is an irreplaceable human right is a recent arrival on the stage of man's intellectual history. It first appeared as an essential element of the modern bourgeois revolutions that transformed European social life from the end of the eighteenth century. Emerging from such fertile soil, this idea subsequently developed as a vital link in the discourse on the character of man's naturally given spiritual freedoms and was closely associated with the claim that the only just form of government is one based on the principle of popular sovereignty.

The notion that all people are endowed by nature with basic educational rights took root and matured in the field of modern pedagogic thought along with the discovery of the myriad possibilities for growth that reside in all human beings as they move from childhood to adolescence and on to adulthood. In the wake of these liberating discoveries, educators began to reorganize their institutions and instructional practices so as to give concrete form to what they understood to be the unique educational rights of the young.

The joining together of these two distinct but intimately related lines of thought has led to the idea that human beings are endowed from birth with inalienable educational rights. With time, these rights have come to be viewed as an essential part of the modern child's inherent right to grow up and develop into a fully formed human being.

It was this kind of thinking that lay at the root of the attempt to remake Japanese education in the years following the end of the Pacific War (World War II). But it has not been easy for us to implant these ideas in Japanese society. As many of the totalitarian aspects of prewar educational thought were revived and reworked within the context of the modern welfare state, the prospects for a genuine educational renaissance in Japan have gradually been eroded, and the proud hopes of those who wanted to transform Japan into a democratic society have been confounded again and again.

The Locus of Educational Authority

The crises enveloping education in Japan today can be traced back to the deep antagonisms between those who insist that educational authority must reside in the hands of the state and those who want to affirm the autonomy of the people's educational rights. Narrowly conceived, the problem of educational authority is related to the issue of to whom educational rights and competencies properly belong—parents, teachers, or the state; broadly conceived, it relates to the rights and duties of children, parents, and teachers in relation to the authority vested in the state and all other publicly constituted bodies. In short, this distinction leads us to reconsider the nature of the responsibilities involved in education and the way the boundaries between the responsible parties should be drawn and defended.

The fundamental difference I want to call attention to here can be formulated in an unresolved antagonism between those who advocate the people's educational authority (*kokumin no kyōikuken*) and those who believe that the organization and management of learning in Japan must be conceived as an exercise of the state's educational authority (*kokka no kyōikuken*). The basic difference between the two becomes readily apparent when one asks how each camp views the meaning of the child's right to learn, in particular, and the citizen's right to learn in general. The underlying theoretical differences between the two opposing approaches become all the more obvious when one asks how each regards the closely related problems of who should properly guarantee the existence of these rights and how this can best be accomplished.

There is a great deal of discussion in Japan these days about the need to drastically reform our educational system from the university right down to the nursery school. But since I am convinced that any proposal for reform is ultimately doomed to failure unless it is based on respect for each and every citizen's right to learn, I believe that all talk about improving our schools should proceed from this point. Furthermore, I want to argue that any educational transformation which is going to impart real substance to our constitutionally guaranteed right to learn must conceive this not merely as a passive right to receive an education but as an active right to learn. In other words, our current efforts to reform education in Japan must be tied to a view of democratization which is not construed as something people passively receive from the state, but rather as something actively demanded and achieved through unwavering effort.

To complete the reorganization of Japanese social life that began after the war, when the people were finally recognized as the masters of their government, their work, their ideas, and their own destinies, it is absolutely necessary to expand our thinking about the broader problems of human rights in general. The idea that these rights must be guaranteed in all phases of our daily lives offers us a valuable perspective from which to begin making greater efforts to more fully realize the promises unleashed by the legal reorganization of postwar Japan into a society founded on the principles of respect for the inviolable rights of individuals.

Japan's Educational Problems

I now want to call attention to some of the most distressing aspects of the crisis plaguing education in Japan today. My aim here is to demonstrate that when education is perceived as a basic human right, the many problems underlying our present-day educational difficulties appear deeply and intimately related to one another, even if they do not appear so when viewed from the conflicting standpoints of those—students, parents, and teachers—who are affected by them.

Judging from what one reads practically every day in the newspapers, Japanese children are now living in absolutely horrendous conditions. On a single recent day, for example, there were a number of particularly disturbing stories about lower secondary school students. In one of these reports we hear of a group of students who violently murdered a vagabond in Yokohama; in another we learn of two students in Osaka who violated a female teacher in the school's health office; and in still another we are introduced to a gang of wild students in Machida City who, after threatening other students with violence, stabbed one of them without even giving it a second thought. Recent police statistics indicate that the number of such cases is continually increasing. Add to this the persistence of suicide attempts and violent behavior at home and we can rightly infer that the problems which are causing such abhorrent behavior are only getting worse.

These behaviors result from the increasing pressures generated by our overheated school entrance examination system. They reflect nationwide trends in which delinquent forms of behavior can be seen breaking out at ever lower ages among our young men and in unprecedented numbers among young women as well. The growth in these forms of delinquency underscores both the severity of the problems being dropped in the laps of lower and upper secondary school teachers and the worsening sense of despair and helplessness felt by more and more parents.

Here we can also catch a glimpse of the circumstances in which (1) classroom violence is becoming an everyday occurrence, (2) teachers are losing the capacity to respond to conditions that are quite frankly growing out of control, (3) increased bullying is driving weaker students into deep fear and—in extreme, but widely reported, cases—suicide, and (4) ethnic discrimination is becoming more and more pronounced.

Ironically, however, according to Hozumi Takanobu's recent work, *Tsumiki Kuzushi* (Broken Toy Blocks) 1982, behind these socially unacceptable forms of behavior is the desperate desire of lonely young people, pushed into cutthroat competition with one another through the intensification of examination pressures, to have friends and form groups they can identify with. This has taught us that it is necessary to look behind the delinquent behavior of our misguided adolescents in order to see the distorted expressions of their desire to live socially satisfying lives. Takanobu has shown us, in other words, how important it is to recognize that within an overwhelmingly negative social environment, even patently antisocial forms of behavior may very well have a great deal of positive meaning and significance.

But there are also major distortions which result from the ways those on the "elite course" are being educated. Encouraged from early childhood to think of themselves as the victors in a race to succeed in school entrance examinations, more and more of these future leaders of society are developing thoroughly arrogant and coldhearted personalities. Moreover, these students, who are supposed to be the most intelligent young people being turned out by our society, are so thoroughly sold on themselves that they have little if any sense that we are facing very real and very serious problems. Having no critical consciousness, their very attitude belies the claims made about their supposed intelligence. In a speech he delivered at the time of his retirement from the Faculty of Economics at the University of Tokyo, the distinguished scholar Ouchi Tsutomu declared:

> Today's students have no historical consciousness and are thoroughly deficient when it comes to thinking critically about problems other than those they have been tutored to respond to on entrance examinations. I seriously wonder whether there is any future for scholarship in Japan.

The number of teachers who have lost the capacity to understand the feelings of their students is steadily growing, and this is as true of veteran teachers as it is of new and inexperienced ones. The following passage from a recent work by a lower secondary schoolteacher named Sayama Kisaku is convincing testimony:

Teachers no longer have any idea about how to make sense of the junior high school students who sit in front of me in the classroom. . . . Compared with the conditions prevailing thirty years ago, it is certainly true that Japan has become a very rich country, but if this is really so, then why is it that teaching and educating children has become such bitter and disheartening work?

Or consider the words of Uno Hajime, a high school principal with more than thirty years of experience as a teacher:

What has been accomplished through the reform of our educational system? If our students could have developed in the ways we hoped and worked for, Japan would not be in the mess it is in today. The current state of our education makes me feel more than a little sad; I no longer have any confidence about the way we are raising our young.

The despair and irritation of experienced and skillful teachers like Messrs. Sayama and Uno leave us wondering about the successes which our Ministry of Education bureaucrats are so eager to claim at every turn.

Indeed, as Mr. Uno noted, the conditions in which our children and adolescents are coming of age have steadily worsened since the 1960s. It is not surprising that the crime statistics being reported for the 1980s show a sharp increase in the number of juveniles being arrested.

These conditions are also reflected in the strains distorting the physical and mental development of our youth from infancy through adolescence. Obvious signs of the former were extensively reported in the 1960s and 1970s; large numbers of children had distorted posture and weakened vision as well as a marked proclivity towards broken bones and decreased muscle power. In the latter case we can cite an ever-growing number of anxiety-ridden children who have lost the flexibility, stamina, and emotional ease generally associated with youth. These strains have been accompanied by diminished sociability on the one hand and an increasing tendency to use hackneyed language on the other. Children flock together but rarely form groups in the true sense of the term.

But more deplorable is the fact that our children are growing up without developing (1) any profound feelings for nature, (2) any penetrating abilities to grasp the historically determined structure of society and to think about how its rules of organization might be improved, or (3) any deep sense of purpose and direction. In short, the growth of our youth into fully developed human beings is being seriously compromised from infancy through adolescence; and the vitality of our human relationships, whether in the home, in the school, or in society in general, is being thoroughly and dangerously eroded.

In spite of our recent prosperity, the competition to enter prestigious schools is becoming more and more intense, so much so that parents now feel pressured to enroll their three- and four-year-old children in famous nursery schools, believing that this will enable them to get a head start in the race to success in our society's system of *gakureki shakai* (stratification by school background). As the pressures increase to get children on the academic escalator leading to social success, we find growing numbers of young people having no time or place to play or friends to play with. Under the pressure of their parents' expectations and forced into endless studies intended to ensure later success in our society's entrance examination madness, our children are being robbed of their childhood.

These abuses of the child's rights to freely grow and learn result from the ideology of overmanagement which dominates contemporary Japanese society. Whether it be their hairstyle, the length of their skirts, the color of their socks, or the width of their bookbags, all aspects of our children's lives are being managed through the highly detailed rules enacted by and enforced in the nation's schools. Not only do teachers wait at the school gate to check the students' appearance when they enter the school grounds, even when children go out on their own after school hours they are required to wear their school uniforms and hats. It is particularly alarming that schools are increasingly administering physical punishment to those students who violate the school's arbitrarily determined rules of order. What kind of society are we living in that permits such flagrant infringements upon the freedom of individual expression?

It is not only students who are being made to feel the weight of this arbitrarily imposed authority. Young teachers are almost universally instructed in how to maintain this educational philosophy by their superiors within the administrative structure of the school; their failure to do so is met by severe disciplinary measures.

Particularly vexing from the standpoint of those concerned with stemming the erosion of human rights in our schools are the growing and related problems of *taibatsu* (corporal punishment) and *ijime* (bullying). School officials condone and even encourage the administration of corporal punishment to students who violate the rules of behavior arbitrarily determined by school officials themselves. Students who are singled out for these extreme forms of discipline in turn pick on and abuse weaker students. Ultimately, what makes this possible is the irresponsible attitude of parents who expect teachers to provide the discipline which they themselves fail to impart to their children. Indeed, it can be argued that bullying is not simply an educational problem but one that runs throughout Japanese society, so much so that it constitutes a major principle of social control. In this sense the abuses of human rights seen in the world of education can be thought of as an essential part of the structure of human rights abuses in general. Moreover, this is not limited to the domestic sphere. In the words of one Philippine researcher living in Japan: "Can't Japan's approach to its relations with the nations of Southeast Asia be seen as a form of bullying?"

In addition to the highly visible infringements of fundamental human rights discussed above, it is also important to call attention to those violations of the child's right to learn which are not nearly so obvious. These can be detected, for example, in the textbook screening system by means of which only those teaching materials officially approved by the Ministry of Education are allowed into the nation's schools. While current screening practices are not as blatantly repressive as was the case with the prewar system in which all heterodox ideas were subjected to unyielding censorship, the system now in use in many ways represents a more insidious (not to mention dangerous) violation of basic human rights. Even though the Ministry of Education has tried to represent this system as a neutral attempt to eliminate politically biased opinions, or as a scientifically objective effort to correct mistaken information, it, in fact, constitutes nothing less than an attempt to keep out of our schools all ideas which do not fit in with the state's view of the kinds of knowledge which are both appropriate and desirable to administer to Japanese youth.

Not only does this system breach the educational rights of the child; it also violates the intellectual and academic freedom of teachers and textbook authors as well by trying to channel their thinking into the same fixed framework.

Japanese education is at present riddled with many serious problems. Those who view these problems as if they are of merely momentary importance will never be able to grasp their depths or to make significant strides toward their resolution. The belief that all classroom problems can be entirely taken care of in the classroom, or that the responsibility for all our educational problems can be laid entirely at the doorsteps of our teachers, is an overly simplistic view of education which is extremely counterproductive and harmful. In other words, it is necessary to think about the problems involved in the organization and running of our schools in relation to the cultural consciousness of the society which supports those schools, and the problems implicit in the structure of our society. The conditions casting dark clouds over our nation's educational life—the conditions in which the work of our schools has been subordinated to the exam preparation industry, in which schools now function as the site of the struggle over social selection, and in which these days it is frequently said "As long as they know how to do well on exams, who cares whether or not they are educated?"—directly reflect the values which are impoverishing the intellectual life of our people.

This essay is excerpted from Teruhisa Horio, "Education Policy and Human Rights: A Case Study in Failure," in *Educational Thought and Ideology in Modern Japan: State Authority and Intellectual Freedom,* edited and translated by Steven Platzer (Tokyo: University of Tokyo Press, 1988).

Conclusions

Barbara Finkelstein

The intense interest in educational alternatives, the near universal concern with student motivation and student-teacher relationships, and the existence of serious minority group and returnee problems all suggest that portrayals of Japanese education as uniform, meritocratic, egalitarian, conflict-free, and centrally defined and controlled are oversimplified, if not altogether incorrect.

The essays in this book expose moral assumptions of everyday life at home and school in the relationships between mothers and children, teachers and students; in the forms of classroom culture and education policy; and in the multiplicity of views about educational realities. They reveal, in our view, a more complex and interesting Japan than we have traditionally seen.

The articles in this book also suggest that in Japan, as in the United States, the greatest cultural and educational strengths constitute its greatest weaknesses as well. Commitments to group harmony—so powerful in their capacity to cultivate respectful and generative human relationships—also contain the seeds of bullying, exclusivity, group intolerance, and ultranationalism. The commitment to harmony in face-to-face settings has also, as we have seen, reinforced the ferocity and power of external examinations and the relentless power of educational credentialism. The connections among and between human beings are strong, and human bonding is valued rather than feared. But the bonds that nurture belonging are the same bonds that engage the Japanese in an array of oppressive and sometimes intrusive interpersonal and public involvements within companies, families, governments, schools, and between men and women—and the Japanese are themselves fully aware of this.

The Japanese have an uncommon sensitivity to how individuals learn as well as how they connect with one another. The rough-and-tumble quality of Japanese preschools, the delicacy with which teachers encourage students to learn from one another, and the unwillingness of teachers to lead discussions reflect a respect for the learning powers of individual students and a high tolerance for unevaluated or even invisible outcomes. So too does the patience and care with which the typical Japanese teacher transforms teaching into a form of apprenticeship—requiring students to practice until perfect; to learn by stages and imitation; to value technique, craft, and precision. These twin commitments—to the pace of the learner and the value of imitation—make, conversely, for a certain indisposition to value discussion and interplay of ideas among and between learners and between teachers and students.

Yet another typically unnoticed strength of Japanese culture lies in an almost unqualified tolerance for intense subjectivity and an unfettered elaboration of individual imagination. These qualities are evidenced by the unwillingness of Japanese teachers, especially those in preschools and elementary schools, to prescribe children's responses to stories and/or activities and by the public availability of pornographic materials. Both, however, remain private among individual Japanese, and are invisible to anyone unfamiliar with the forms that Japanese individuality can take. The subjectification of the imagination means that individual creativity is, by definition, stripped of public expression. Thus protected, the individual can imagine anything privately, hide within a group, or even follow a leader with whom he or she deeply disagrees. Thus, the individual can find integrity in and through the group, and the imagination can flower almost completely uncensored and publicly unexpressed.

Japan is, as we have seen, a complex culture and one from which we in the West have much to learn. To borrow the title of Robert Rosenstone's recent book, Japan can function as "the mirror in the shrine." The material included here is intended to provide a small step on a long journey towards the demystification of Japanese culture and education. We hope it has accomplished that purpose.

GLOSSARY

aku byōdō   bad form of equality
amae   presuming on the benevolence of others
amai   indulgent
baikin   germ
banzai   cheers, hurrahs
danchi   an apartment-housing complex
dantai ishiki   group consciousness
dōryō   colleagues
Dōwa   integration
Dōwa Kyōiku   education for integration
gaijin   foreigner
gakkō-gun   group of schools
gakureki shakai   stratification by school background
gambaru   to persist, do one's best
gambare   persist!(imperative)
genkan   combination threshold and entrance hall
genki   vigor
gempukushiki   three-day initiation ritual
giri   obligations
gyōkaku   administrative reform (*gyōkaku* is an abbreviation for *gyōsei kaikaku*)
hansei   self-examination, introspection, evaluation
haragei   "belly art"
henna gaijin   strange foreigner

hoikuen   day-care center
honne   inner feeling
ie   family, home, household; lineal family system
ijime   group teasing; bullying
iki   classy, dandy
ishin denshin   telepathy, empathy
jiritsu   independence
jiyūkaronja   liberationists
jōzu   skillful
juken sangyō   examination industry
juku   cram school; class or school for elementary and secondary students in the afternoons or evenings; school in which to learn traditional arts and crafts, etc.
kamishibai   paper theater
kana   Japanese syllabary
kejime   distinctions
ketsuenshi-teki   racial historical
kibishī   strict
kōhai   junior
kokka no kyōikuken   advocates of the state's educational authority
kokoro   heart, mind
kokumin no kyōikuken   advocates of the people's educational authority
kosei   uniqueness of personality, individuality
koseishugi   a position that places an emphasis on originality and one's individual character
kusai   unpleasant; "you stink"
kyōiku mama   education mama
meishi   name cards
minarai kikan   period of apprenticeship, probation period
minzoku   race; ethnic group
mono no aware   pathos of things
Nihon minzoku   Japanese people
Nihonjin   Japanese
Ningen   "Human," a title for supplementary moral educational material that champions human rights, recounts burakumin history, and encourages principles of toleration and multicultural acceptance
ninjō   human feelings
nisei   second generation of Americans of Japanese ancestry
nōryokushugi   academic competence
o-bentō   packed lunch
omoiyari   empathy
omote   front, surface
on   kindness, a favor

onegai shimasu   "Please . . ."
ōyake   public
rōnin   literally "masterless samurai"; a high school graduate waiting for another chance to be enrolled in a college
sabi   antique and graceful
san   honorific to follow a person's name
sansei   third generation born in the United States
sayōnara   goodbye; farewell
seikatsu shidō   guidance for living
seishin   individual spirit and character development
seken   the ever-watching, supportive, and critical community of concerned others
semmon gakkō   trade and vocational schools
sempai   senior
sempai-kōhai   junior to senior obligations and privileges
sensei   honorific for teacher
shakaisei   social consciousness
shi ne   "Drop dead"
shichi-go-san   usually refers to a gala day for children aged three, five, and seven
shiken jigoku   examination hell
shiken jikoku   examination time
shinjinrui   new race
shitsuke   discipline
shōji   paper doors
shufu   housewife
shutaisei   autonomy
shūdan ishiki   group consciousness, belongingness
shūdan seikatsu   group life
soto   outside, public
taibatsu   corporal punishment
taisō   morning group exercise
tamashī   a soul, a spirit
tate shakai   vertical society
tatemae   external appearance of things, a principle, a policy
tenuki o-bentō   sloppily prepared lunch
tōban   monitors
uchi   house; home; private; inside; sometimes "I"
ura   back, rear
wabi   lonely, quiet
watakushi   "I" (see "uchi")
yobikō   large, privately operated college preparatory schools
yōchien   preschool, kindergarten